Gerald B. McCready is vice-president of administration of CAC,
a major national sport-governing body; the regional vice-president
of the Association of Marketing Educators; president of Business
Science Associates; and marketing program director of the
Professional Development Institute. He has written two university-level
texts in the field of marketing and has published numerous articles
in professional business journals.

Marketing Tactics Master Guide
FOR SMALL BUSINESS

Gerald B. McCready

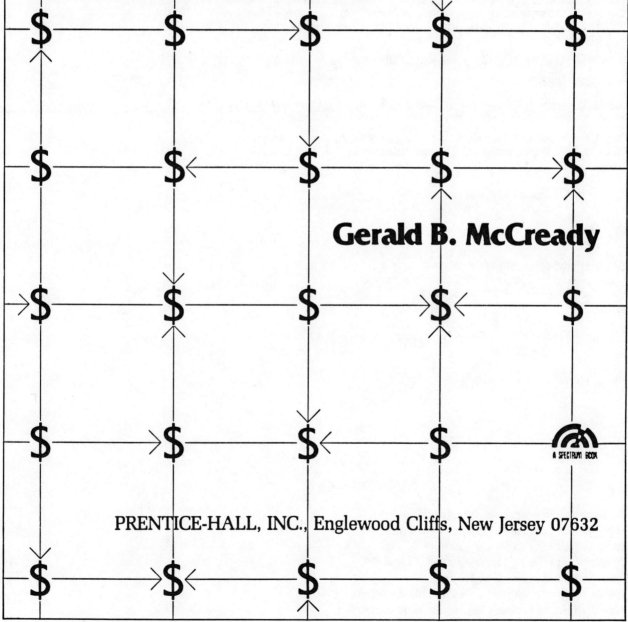

PRENTICE-HALL, INC., Englewood Cliffs, New Jersey 07632

A SPECTRUM BOOK

Library of Congress Cataloging in Publication Data

McCready, Gerald B.
    Marketing tactics master guide for small business.

    "A Spectrum Book."
    Includes bibliographies and index.
    1. Marketing—Handbooks, manuals, etc.   2. Small
business—Management—Handbooks, manuals, etc.   I. Title.
HF5415.M379   658.8   81–13952
                            AACR2

ISBN 0-13-558148-6

ISBN 0-13-558130-3 {PBK.}

This Spectrum Book is available to businesses and organizations at a special discount when ordered in large quantities. For information, contact Prentice-Hall, Inc., General Book Marketing, Special Sales Division, Englewood Cliffs, N. J. 07632.

Page 1, quote by Albert Jay Nock, reprinted by permission of Regnery Gateway, Inc., Book Publishers, Chicago, Illinois.

10 9 8 7 6 5 4 3 2 1

Printed in the United States of America

Editorial production/supervision
    and interior design by *Heath Lynn Silberfeld*
Manufacturing buyer: *Barbara A. Frick*

Prentice-Hall International, Inc., *London*
Prentice-Hall of Australia Pty. Limited, *Sydney*
Prentice-Hall of Canada, Ltd., *Toronto*
Prentice-Hall of India Private Limited, *New Delhi*
Prentice-Hall of Japan, Inc., *Tokyo*
Prentice-Hall of Southeast Asia Pte. Ltd., *Singapore*
Whitehall Books Limited, *Wellington, New Zealand*

To Queen, Dunc, Jane, and Stan

Contents

List of Exhibits

Maximizing Distribution Advantage: Tactic 4

Pricing Goods and Services to Sell: Tactic 5

Advertising for Results: Tactic 6

Preface

The primary objective of this book is to help readers become strong marketers and thereby to increase their money-making ability. Emphasis is placed on methods to improve the individual's marketing effectiveness. The book combines practical business advice and proven marketing concepts. The contents are directed toward small-business entrepreneurs, middle management, and marketing personnel who want to improve their chances of business success. All readers will find the book a handy reference guide and a source of exciting business ideas. Established career executives, as well as aspiring entrepreneurs, will derive substantial value from the book.

No special educational background is necessary. The contents are presented in seven easy-to-read chapters (The Seven Tactics for Marketing Success!), which will help readers achieve their business or personal objectives, make more money, and become better managers. Readers will note that the overall focus of the book is toward the achievement of effective results. Considerable emphasis is placed on the importance of clear goal setting, exacting marketing research, effective communication, and continuous performance evaluation. The need for teamwork and the development of responsive, participative management in the business enterprise are also stressed.

Many individuals have proven invaluable in their assistance and guidance during the preparation of this manuscript. Sincere appreciation is expressed to my good friends and colleagues, Bill Cowan, Dick Tindal, and Ian Wilson for their valuable intellectual stimulation and inspirational support. A number of typists and assistants have contributed many hours of work on the text; I am indebted to Susan Douglas, Louise Greaves, Linda Burgess, Denise Curry, Jill Courneya, Mary MacNeill, Patricia Gordon, Lynne Craven, Gemma Sepe, and Nancy Beauchesne for their help. A great debt is owed to many business and professional people who were generous with their time and knowledge. Their contributions are evident throughout the text. And last, much credit must be given to my family for their continued patience and support of my writing endeavors.

GERALD B. MCCREADY

Marketing Tactics Master Guide
FOR SMALL BUSINESS

Introduction

The Marketing Process

The opportunity to make money is enhanced a thousandfold for the person who has a fundamental appreciation of marketing. That's what this book is all about. This chapter contains a brief outline of the development of marketing, followed by an introduction to the Marketing Tactics model upon which the balance of the book is based.

Marketing can be described simply as any planned process that assists buyers and sellers in receiving mutual satisfaction as a result of some transaction. The marketing concept places the *customer at the nucleus*, around which the firm's activities revolve. Every company decision must be considered in light of its effect on the customer. Any potential course of action that is favorable to the seller, but undesirable to the customer, is rejected by management operating under the marketing concept. The ultimate marketing concern is the conveyance of some perceived benefit to an identified prospect.

As a discipline, marketing draws upon a host of other fields of study: mathematics, economics, accounting, psychology, and others. In recent years there has also been a growing application of computer technology and the behavioral sciences to marketing, and it is safe to assume that this contribution will continue as marketing professionals seek *more certain paths to profits*. The greatest change in marketing will undoubtedly result from the reconciliation of social problems and increased government regulations.

Yet marketing, in its most fundamental form, has been with us for thousands of years. Some people improperly interpret the term "marketing" merely as selling. In fact, selling is only one small facet of the marketing process. No less an authority than Peter Drucker has indicated that the ultimate aim of marketing should be to make selling unnecessary. Many other facets of business fall under the umbrella of marketing: Advertising, pricing, product development, and distribution are only a few of the components of a marketing program requiring attention by business people. As you shall see, these factors and more make up what is known as a planned marketing program, the central theme of this book.

Marketing activities represent a dominant force in both the consumer and industrial sectors of business. *Consumer marketing* is a branch of marketing that seeks to develop and promote products that

1

satisfy some individual buyer's needs or wants. *Industrial marketing* is a branch of marketing that supports consumer product development with commercial materials, technology, and business operating goods.

The two divisions of marketing have been formally recognized only during the past twenty years, even though both evolved from the centuries-old transfer of ownership of goods. In a *market*, commonly defined as the place where buyers and sellers meet, goods or services are offered for sale, and the transfer of ownership takes place if an agreement is reached. Each party, vendor, and purchaser thereby profits in some way. A perfect marketing arrangement is one in which both buyer and seller have been able to maximize their satisfaction.

A "market" can also be defined as the collective demand by a group of potential buyers for a certain product or service. Until recently, the quantity of goods demanded by a rapidly growing and increasingly sophisticated world population seemed unlimited. So throughout economic history, emphasis has been focused on manufacturing productivity, and there was little need for marketing as we know it today. Many languages, Russian and French being the most notable, do not have an equivalent word for marketing. A key factor in marketing success is therefore the ability of potential sellers to make contact with potential buyers.

Too often, this process is taken for granted, but the truly effective marketer is one who anticipates profit opportunities and who initiates action programs to ensure the enterprise's success. Business activities of the Western world under a free market system have produced high incomes, as well as an array of superior products for satisfying the most discerning shopper's needs and want. A competitive market system has encouraged industry to adopt a high degree of flexibility and innovation. Resources are largely allocated by the *natural forces* of supply and demand rather than by dictum from a central bureau.

In the free market economy, business people should focus their attention on, and take direction from this natural process in the marketplace. Sometimes, this seemingly simple principle is overlooked. Indeed, even dedicated career professionals who are responsible for specialized management functions in large, established corporations find that they have an ongoing need to reexamine their activities in relation to the demands of an ever changing marketplace. Marketing technology has advanced rapidly in recent years, and the discovery and mastery of new profit opportunities require an increasingly skillful and sophisticated marketing effort in order to assure success.

Although most readers are well aware of the well-publicized marketing successes of industry leaders in their field—such as Xerox, Kellogg's, Coca Cola, IBM, and MacDonald's Family Restaurants—profit-making business organizations are not alone in requiring an understanding of the marketing concept. There is considerable evidence that nonbusiness organizations can also benefit from this concept. Organizations such as colleges, unions, hospitals, churches, sports clubs, and community service groups must all rely upon marketing their services for continued growth and, in some cases, for survival.

Individuals who have the urge to join the entrepreneurial set are usually among the first to recognize the moneymaking potential of effective marketing programs. As the faithful will attest, to become a truly marketing-oriented person, the first step is a genuine acceptance of this principle: that most enterprises exist to generate some form of gain by *satisfying customers' wants and needs*. The adoption of this simple concept commonly results in three distinct changes in a person's overall business philosophy:

- *Behavioral change:* The person's attitude becomes far more sensitive to clients' and the market's needs; decision making based upon real customer needs becomes the priority.
- *Technological change:* The person more readily accepts a wide range of new business tools, including more precise marketing research, forecasting, pricing, product development, and promotion methods.
- *Perceptual change:* The person's vision expands from an inward focus to an extracompany view, one that permits looking upon the entire world as a marketplace of opportunity.

The marketing department of any business, large or small, faces a considerable challenge in analyzing market needs and in developing products superior in quality and price to those of competitors in the field. Only by demonstrating expertise in the development of effective marketing programs can this challenge be answered. Any organization that adopts the marketing concept as its basic operating philosophy will seek to direct its entire operations towards customers or end markets, as well as towards the satisfaction of their specific needs. This means that a company should not perceive itself merely as a supplier of standard electrical parts, for instance, but rather as an innovative supplier responding to the changing needs of the electrical, automotive, and telecommunications industries. As the management of a company becomes more *deeply committed* to the marketing concept, the changes within the organization become more and more dramatic.

The change that causes the greatest unrest within a nonmarketing organization is usually the introduction of proper marketing research. The development of an information system based upon client research shifts the emphasis within the company from a production-centered orientation towards greater customer sensitivity. Then formal marketing research eventually results in an increased concentration of effort toward satisfying identified customer needs, which in turn reinforces a firm's transition to marketing.

Disunity within the firm must be avoided in the development of a marketing organization. The introduction and legitimization of new marketing functions aimed at improved customer communications sometimes tends to alienate nonmarketing personnel within the firm who continue to view their activities purely as maintaining the status quo. A tradition-bound manufacturing or research-and-development department, for example, commonly feels the greatest impact of an increased flow of *market-derived forces* (client needs). Such a company whose operations are fragmentary will encounter considerable difficulty in attaining its marketing goals. Marketing-centered people must often embark on a highly diplomatic and low-key educational program within their own organization in order to win support for innovative ideas. Management seminars, local college courses, circulation of marketing literature, and occasional talks by outside consultants have been found to be most effective in this regard. The marketing concept is most easily introduced to a service business because of a more inherent, personal identification with client needs.

On the other hand, companies deeply immersed in manufacturing face the greater challenge (and need) for a "rediscovery" of the marketplace. Central in the achievement of an effective marketing organization is the development of an *appropriate marketing mix*, that is, the best combination of product, promotion, price and place factors.

The most appropriate mix is the one that best satisfies that particular market. As examples:

- A firm that overdevelops or underdevelops its product may alienate sales potential because the item does not satisfy the real needs.

- Too little or improper advertising may fail to stimulate buyer action, whereas too much advertising may attract business that cannot be satisified.
- A company that emphasizes a low selling price may imply low quality to the marketplace.
- Organizations must also take care to offer their product or service in the most accessible locations at the most convenient times for their customers.

Regardless of the "mix," a *planned marketing program*, based upon sound research, can benefit

EXHIBIT I–1
THE SEVEN TACTICS FOR MARKETING PROFITS: A MODEL FOR SUCCESS

	Major Focus	*What Must Be Done*
TACTIC 1	Researching Market Opportunities	Permit direction from the marketplace to shape all facets of the organization's operations.
TACTIC 2	Understanding Buyer Behavior	Attempt to develop complete knowledge of how and why various customers exercise different purchasing preferences.
TACTIC 3	Providing Appropriate Products and Services	Only offer those goods and services that have maximum appeal and benefits for major market segments.
TACTIC 4	Maximizing Distribution Advantage	Make customer purchases of the organization's products or services the most convenient and effortless experience possible.
TACTIC 5	Pricing Goods and Services to Sell	Adopt flexible pricing strategies and policies that provide optimum incentive for additional and repeated patronage.
TACTIC 6	Advertising for Results	Ensure that customers and sales prospects are kept aware of the unique benefits to be derived from use of the organization's products or services.
TACTIC 7	Building an Effective Sales Organization	Cultivate an appropriate organizational structure and market posture that will ensure the highest levels of client service and satisfaction.

any organization, whether profit-oriented or not. For example, a college, church, or sports organization that is experiencing declining enrollment, patronage, or membership must choose between two very different courses of action. One option involves a *regressive, cost-saving approach*, accomplished through reductions in staff, services, and promotion. Another choice is to increase the capacity of the organization and to maximize profits through an expanded *market development* approach. Herein lies one of the central issues confronting management. The cost-conscious route to profits is most often associated with a so-called myopic, production-oriented mentality, whereas the marketing concept proposes a more positive solution of *enhanced sales potential* through improved marketplace communication. Regardless of which is employed, the foundation of any marketing decision is strongly influenced by a company's steadfast determination to *achieve customer satisfaction* at all costs. The Tactical Model for Marketing Profits we are about to introduce is based on this fundamental tenet.

The Tactical Model
for Marketing Profits

Regardless of the type of enterprise in which you are involved, this well-proven, step-by-step program can be used to virtually assure marketing success. Developed by the author, it provides you with a simple, straightforward guide to improving existing sales,

new product successes, and customer satisfaction levels. The outcomes of effective marketing are enhanced profits, greater market share, and unwaivering customer loyalty. Each reader should evaluate his or her current or planned business operations according to each of the seven operational areas of effectiveness outlined in the model (Exhibit I-1). Use the model as a checklist to measure the well-being of your venture periodically, or each time you are thinking of expanding the scope of products or services offered.

The balance of this book is based on the seven components of the Marketing Tactics model. Note that the model identifies only the major areas of effectiveness and what must be accomplished in each. The specific methods, the "how's" of each tactic, are spelled out in succeeding chapters. The order of the major components of the model are those of the author's choosing, but they do not necessarily reflect a sequence that must be followed to the letter. Some of you may currently be operating a successful business enterprise and may be well advanced in your marketing program development. If such is the case, you may have already mastered a number of the components of the Marketing Tactics model and may wish to concentrate your attention on selected areas. Other readers will undoubtedly be at the starting gate, preparing to investigate a new venture and anxious for some practical guidance. For such people, the book will be a valuable asset in structuring their business plans in accordance with effective marketing practice. We know you will gain substantial value from the materials presented.

Researching Market Opportunities

TACTIC 1

It is a capital mistake to theorize before one has data.

SIR ARTHUR CONAN DOYLE
1859–1930
The Adventures of Sherlock Holmes

Before any organization makes a decision to expand services, to make new products, to acquire another operation, or even to change the color, style, or nature of existing products, some form of market research is required. In keeping with the marketing concept, your organization should always look to the marketplace for direction. Accordingly, market studies are concerned with increasing your understanding of the marketplace in which you are involved. You should use the results to shape management decision making, business objectives, and marketing plans.

A marketing study is developed through *the systematic collection and recording of data* pertinent to some marketing problem. When the research process is done on a continuous basis, it is often referred to as an "MIS" or "marketing information system." Marketing research studies may concentrate on competitive advertising programs, price policies, market size, or distribution methods, to name only a few areas. Marketing opportunities, rather than production resources, should be the essential determinant of business action. So the objective of any marketing research study is usually either *to resolve a particular problem* or *to gather market information on a* *continuous basis*, to aid management in the ongoing decision-making process.

DEFINING RESEARCH PROBLEMS

Most marketing research studies are designed, however, to gather information concerning new market opportunities; so much of our discussion will be oriented in this direction.

Identifying the Market

The first step in such a study is the identification either of the markets that the organization wishes to serve or, in the case of existing sales, of the markets already served. One product may have application in more than one market, and a given market may be able to use more than one type of the company's products. Marketing research (MR) involving specialized industrial goods, which are sold directly to selective markets, is much simpler to perform than studies involving consumer goods, which are moved to end-users through diverse intermediate channels of distribution. In the first case, commercial product purchasers such as construction companies and shoe manufacturers, for example, are easily identi-fied and have *clearly defined* buying needs. In the consumer sector, the producer must gather informa-tion on the wants and needs both of the distribution channel member and of the end-user customers.

MR Study Themes

To complete a given marketing research study, you may require an emphasis on the *measurement, ex-planation, description,* or *projection* of available information. The major groupings under which most MR studies can be categorized, along with a number of typical study themes commonly undertaken by business organizations, are as follows:

- *Situation analysis:* the assessment of industry trends; economic and technological forecasting; attitudinal and lifestyle change projections; as-sessment of productive capacities, political cli-mate, and social stability.
- *Market measurement:* identification of market characteristics; evaluation of potential market opportunities; assessment of client attitudes and behaviors; monitoring competitive business ac-tivity; predicting market growth patterns; mea-suring organization performance.
- *Response strategies:* development of optimum product characteristics; selection of most effec-tive distribution systems; design of most influ-ential promotions; implementation of appropri-ate price schedules; researching complementary goods.
- *Evaluation processes:* selection of suitable busi-ness locations; measuring sales performance; choosing between marketing projects; assessing barriers to trade; analyzing alternative methods of expansion; evaluating mergers and acquisitions.

Anyone can employ the step-by-step preparation method in this section. In a small business, for example, the owner–manager may be responsible not only for developing sales forecasts, allocating sales territories, or analyzing sales trends, but also for researching profitable new opportunities for the company. Organizations that maintain an estab-lished marketing research department are well ac-quainted with information-gathering methods. A firm embarking on its first formal marketing research effort may wish to enlist help from an external source, such as a private marketing consultant or researcher from a local college.

Whoever is responsible for the development and implementation of an MR study must simply apply the criteria of *objectivity, reliability, impartiality,* and *suitability.* That person also normally follows a well accepted format of activities, as follows:

1. *Clearly define the real problem.* All sorts of superficial symptoms usually cloud the central issue. To say that "insufficient orders" is the *cause* of declining sales is naive. The real cause is more likely to be a highly effective promotion by a competitor.
2. *Conduct a preliminary and brief investiga-tion,* to assure that there is ample justification to warrant a large-scale study of the problem. Sometimes a few telephone calls may be all that is needed. Evaluate the situation before jumping into a major research effort.
3. *Decide what information is needed,* and de-velop clearly written statements reflecting these needs. Too much information only con-fuses an issue; insufficient information frus-trates the achievement of accurate results.
4. *Evaluate available resources,* to determine the amount of time, energy, and people that can be made available to attack the research issue. Insufficient resource allocation is often a cause of study results with a low degree of reliability.
5. *Plan the research method.* A wide variety of research techniques—including mail surveys, personal interviews, client diary-keeping, ob-servation, and statistical analysis—are avail-able to the marketing researcher. The nature of the particular marketing problem determines the best combination.
6. *Gather all relevant information* that has ap-plication to solving the problem. Be sure that all data is cataloged according to source, date of receipt, reliability, and so on. This step can be taken by mailed questionnaires, personal interviews, or the review of published literature.
7. *Process all information* according to some meaningful and logical order. Apply the infor-mation directly to the central problem. In what way is this particular finding significant to the problem? To what degree does this information satisfy the issue?
8. *Develop alternative courses of action.* Rarely does any single problem have only one solu-tion. More often than not, a number of options will satisfy part or all of the issue.

9. *Evaluate the various payoffs* that might accrue as a result of different paths of action. Some decisions might result in lower costs, others in increased revenues, while still others may provide for improved market stability.

10. *Make a strong recommendation* as a result of your deliberations. Sometimes such a decision is a "go/no-go" elective, while other times a pathway through the middle ground can be successfully negotiated, to provide the organization with a most profitable outcome.

Achieving Reliability

Marketing researchers must establish realistic parameters to govern the standards of reliability that they desire from research studies. For each study, common sense and economic rationality must be exercised in arriving at the required reliability factor. The costs of increasing the reliability of information from a given research survey are often disproportionate to the importance placed upon such an exercise. Not all research findings have a high priority. An 80-percent reliability factor in one situation may be more than adequate, whereas a 90-percent factor may be wholly inadequate in another.

Diversification

The traditional line of thought that companies should stay in their original type of business is less relevant in today's rapidly changing business environment than in days past. The marketing firm can often find good opportunities in unrelated fields, as long as it has sufficient funds and qualified management, and as long as it conducts adequate research of the new venture.

Many large organizations enjoy a market environment conducive to expansion, but, as a result of *market insensitivity*, they fail to capitalize on profit opportunities available through diversification. Other companies often improve their chances for success in diversification by acquiring other established firms rather than by attempting a riskier grassroots start-up.

Smaller companies desiring to expand into unrelated fields should first examine the option of *vertical integration*—that is, producing a product that they also consume or controlling a channel of distribution that they can utilize for the movement of their products. For example, some dairies make their own cartons or plastic containers, and they also sell these packaging products to other dairies. Publishers can own their own lithography, marketing research, and advertising organizations. Fabric producers might produce decorative pillows, furniture, or clothing.

A variety of key factors must be carefully researched and analyzed prior to any such corporate expansion, diversification, or acquisition decision. First and foremost, the organization must do some soul-searching: Is the growth alternative being considered *really* the path or direction that the firm wishes to commit itself to over the coming years? Does this growth project *complement* the central nature of the firm's business? If not, what specific *strategic advantages* (or disadvantages) might accrue as a result of the firm moving in this direction? The important point is that profits alone should not be the major justification for the organization's expansion decision. The degree of risk involved, the prospects for a stable order volume, the absence of severe price competition, and the opportunity for market leadership are all valid decision criteria in the growth equation.

SELECTING THE BEST RESEARCH METHODS

Once a specific research problem has been identified, the next question is, What are the most effective research methods to obtain the necessary information? As many readers know, almost all forms of research studies use some aspects of both *primary* (personal investigation) and *secondary* information gathering (review of published data). The question also involves economics. For example, a full-scale field investigation involving dozens of researchers performing personal interviews for days on end may represent a huge waste of resources—if a number of directories, published articles, or statistical reviews would have provided most of the required information. (See Exhibit 1–1.)

Professional marketing research people rely upon their familiarity with a number of basic resource materials including: census data, municipal records, voter registration rolls, professional and business directories, trade association statistics, and available mailing lists, to name only a few. Most readers of this book, however, will be most interested in the *basic methods* of research that they might use to help solve their particular business problems. Effectiveness in the selection of appropriate research methods is commonly seen to be a function of satisfying the following types of criteria:

• Does the method provide enough reliable data

for the organization to make a decision in which it has a high degree of confidence?

- Does the method reflect the effective use of organizational resources, in terms of cost expenditure, time utilization, administrative capability, and ease of implementation?
- Does the method enable the organization to maintain the desired level of confidentiality, a positive public image, and a high degree of research objectivity?

EXHIBIT 1–1
EFFECTIVE TIPS FOR DOING RESEARCH AT LOW COST

1. Establish a contest requiring entrants to answer a few simple questions about the quality of your products or services. The entry form is dropped into a convenient deposit box at the exit door of your store or service department with the drawing at month end.

2. Piggyback a questionnaire about the quality of your product or services onto a company catalog or sales brochure. Be sure also to ask what other items the customer would like to see the organization offering. Such a system functions as an ongoing program of organization evaluation.

3. Every organization receives the occasional complaint from a disgruntled customer. Instead of treating such situations casually, many organizations now adopt a management-by-exception philosophy and give grievances a high priority. Management follow-up with an in-depth interview often results in the revelation of unsuspected problems.

4. Develop a standard set of questions regarding the quality of your organization's product and services suitable for administration by telephone. Have a secretary or part-time employee set aside a half-day a month in which twenty to thirty customers are called. Such a program often reminds customers to place an order. Many clients feel flattered that their opinions are sought.

5. Some organizations have succeeded by including research questionnaires in various products' packages. In this way they attempt to determine how a buyer heard about an item, why it was purchased from the firm, and so on. The only difficulty with this approach is that it focuses on customers and neglects research about the potential of sales to those who have not bought.

Sometimes a research study is of such a comprehensive nature, that a number of research methods are required. Such studies may have extensive budget allocations and a broad mandate to ensure that "no stone is left unturned" in the search for a solution to the issue at hand. A large-scale study of this nature might be typified by a single product firm, such as a producer of razor blades who is considering the possible introduction of a brand new shaving concept that would effectively obsolete their current product offering. Smaller business firms and non-profit organizations are less likely to use multiple research methods. More often than not, a single method such as a *telephone survey* suffices to generate the needed information to solve a specific problem. One simple technique all researchers should observe, is to gather the names and addresses of as many people as possible who might shed light on the problem. Exhibit 1–2 illustrates a typical partial list. Sometimes a marketer obtains excellent results from bringing together a *focus group* of people who can shed light on the researcher's problem.

EXHIBIT 1–2
EXAMPLE OF A KEY CONTACT AND RESOURCE LIST

Problem: To obtain complete information on the start-up and operation of a sports shoe shop.

Pony Shoes, Inc.
251 Park Avenue South
New York, New York 10010

Fastrak Footwear, Inc.
2400 Greenleaf Avenue
Elk Grove, Illinois 60007

National Jogging Association
919 18th Street, N.W.
Suite 830
Washington, D.C. 20006

Brooks Shoes Mfg., Inc.
Hanover, Pennsylvania 17331

Saucony Shoes, Inc.
12 Peach Street
Kutztown, Pennsylvania 19530

Puma Rubber
P. O. Box 1420
8522 Herzogenaurach
West Germany

Bata Shoe Company
59 Wyndford Drive
Toronto, Ontario
Canada

Famolare Shoes
4 East 5th Street
New York, New York 10022

Asics Sports, Inc.
2052 Alton Avenue
Irvine, California 92714

Osaga, Inc.
2468 West 11th Avenue
Eugene, Oregon 97402

Etonic, Inc.
Charles Eaton Co.
Brockton, Massachusetts 02403

Bancroft Sporting Goods
Tretorn and Hunt Shoes Division
Bancroft Street
Woonsocket, Rhode Island 02895

Nike Shoes
8285 S.E. Nimbus Avenue
Suite 115
Beaverton, Oregon 97005

Converse Rubber Co., Inc.
55 Fordham Road
Willmington, Massachusetts 01887

Bauer-Grebb Shoes
51 Ardelt Avenue
Kitchener, Ontario
Canada, N2G 4H4

Adidas
% Libco, Inc.
1 Silver Court
Springfield, New Jersey 07081

New Balance Shoes, Inc.
38 Everett Street
Boston, Massachusetts 02134

One question researchers should ask themselves is whether the particular method of research being considered is the best one for reaching the intended respondents? For example, if you are trying to obtain the opinions of busy business executives, you may find research through personal interviews to be most difficult to arrange. Persuasive telephone calls to the executive's secretary to arrange a short telephone interview usually works better. A personalized letter to the executive with a simple mailback questionnaire might be the very best approach. On the other hand, experience has shown that homemakers seem flattered to have their opinions sought on a personal doorstep interview format, but they respond poorly to telephone and mail solicitation methods. Every research method has both advantages and disadvantages of which the researcher must be fully aware. Let's examine three of these:

1. Personal interviews
2. Telephone research
3. Postal surveys

Personal Interviews. Interviews provide the re searcher with the benefit of seeing and hearing interviewees respond. The frowns and voice tone changes that accompany a given response and that can be noted during the interview may represent valuable information to the research investigator. This personal attention provided by the physical presence of the interviewer may have the effect of making respondents more willing to cooperate in giving details on the reasons behind their choices or feelings on some matter. On the negative side, personal interviewing is not only expensive and time-consuming process, but it is regarded by many as a gross violation of personal privacy.

Great care must be given to the selection of research personnel who are to be conducting personal interviews. Homemakers hired on a part-time basis to interview other homemakers have a good record of success, whereas older men hired to perform the same task are unlikely to be well accepted. By the same token, homemakers hired on a part-time basis for research will not be received well by business executives with whom they have little rapport. The use of college students to conduct primary research is most appropriate in shopping mall public opinion surveys, in traffic studies, or in research into topics of social concern, environmental issues, and the like.

Aside from selecting housewives or students, take considerable care in choosing individuals who will be carrying out personal interviews. Select only those who speak clearly, who have good manners, who are able to project a neat, clean appearance, and who have some reasonable understanding of the demands of research objectivity.

For each research project developed by an organization, a few hours must be set aside to provide the field investigators with a *proper orientation* and *trial interview* prior to the start of the study. If your organization can afford it, hire outsiders as poll takers to minimize bias. As a guideline, retail studies should be based upon 100 surveys per store at six to ten surveys per hour. Exhibit 1–3 outlines guidelines for personal interviews in marketing research, and it should be used as a preparation checklist.

Telephone Research. Often seen to have most of the advantages of interviews in person, the telephone method has as its major benefit a reduced cost factor. Many more people can be contacted in a shorter period of time.

EXHIBIT 1–3
GUIDELINES FOR CONDUCTING PERSONAL
INTERVIEWS IN MARKETING RESEARCH

What to Do

1. Clearly identify, among those you wish to make contact with, who represents the best potential for providing the required information? College students, production managers, career women, and so on.

2. Carefully develop a randomly selected survey sample of interviewees that is sufficient in size and representative enough of the total market in terms of social and demographic characteristics.

3. Whenever possible, arrange for a personal interview, establishing beforehand adequate time in a quiet setting.

4. Be organized. Arrange your questionnaires, report forms, pens, and other required materials together in an easy-to-use package.

5. Establish a friendly, open rapport with the interviewee before formal questioning by starting interview with some casual chitchat.

6. Be sure to provide the respondent with some basic background on the purpose of your study, how they were chosen, and the importance of their answers.

7. All interviewers being used should undergo training to ensure that they use the same words, voice tone, level of voice volume, and inflection.

8. In order to overcome vague respondent answers to questions, interviewers should know how to use probing skills to uncover hard reliable data.

9. Establish standard methods of accurately recording, tabulating, and interpreting response information to assure accuracy and objectivity.

10. Design a proper exit procedure from interviews such that the interviewee feels the process was worthwhile and appreciated.

What to Watch For

1. Interviewers who have not received proper training may not be able to cope with uncooperative interviewees or to overcome vague answers to questions.

2. Randomly selected interviews at people's homes may be disproportionately weighted in favor of the married, poor, aged, disabled, or ill because they are at home more than most.

3. In survey work, the number of not-at-homes selected increases in summer months, in highly urban areas, in later days of the week, in childless households, and in well-to-do neighborhoods.

4. Interview questions should be specific and quantifiable wherever possible. Rather than asking an interviewee, "Have you been pleased with the trouble-free performance of your dryer?"—improved wording would be, "How many months of use has your dryer given you since you last had it repaired?"

5. Do not employ interviewers who have little in common with respondents, or response quality will suffer. The closer the match between interviewer and interviewee in terms of ethnic background, sex, age, education, and interests, the better will be the quality of survey results.

6. Most respondents have a natural tendency to "polish" their answers by distorting them toward the most favorable (socially acceptable) side. For example, researchers should expect that people will respond with larger-than-actual insurance coverage information, less-than-actual personal loan amounts, and greater-than-actual contributions to charities.

But some serious drawbacks are associated with telephone surveys. Respondents may terminate the interview midway through by simply hanging up the receiver. Also, the respondent usually feels less of a requirement to answer sensitive questions or to respond honestly. Great care must be taken, when developing a telephone survey, to ensure that the respondent group is truly representative of the larger population that you are seeking opinion from. Not all residential telephone subscribers own homes, have children, or are even at home during the day. In a given community, a substantial proportion may be male, unmarried, senior aged, unemployed, and living in a single rented room. Sometimes voter registration lists and city directories are valuable in discriminating between various target groups from which samples are to be drawn.

Developing a rehearsed (but credible) script to be used for each call is also important. Many telephone surveys have proven invalid because of inconsistencies in the verbal presentation made by the interviewer. Telephone researchers must be put through a training program that ensures a smooth-flowing, natural-sounding presentation. Generally accepted introductions are usually worded something like this.

> "Good morning. Is this Mrs. Jackson speaking?" [Receiving a "yes," the interviewer carries on. If not, they may or may not need to ask for her to come to the telephone, depending on the respondent required in the research design.] "Mrs. Jackson, this is Mary Brown of Accurate Home Surveys calling. We are doing research for a major food company, and I would appreciate your help in answering a few short questions about your shopping. It will only take two or three mintues." [Pause and wait for response—usually affirmative.]

The researcher must keep accurate records of each call on standard research forms that are provided.

Some of the most successful telephone research programs are those in which the researchers have been groomed to be somewhat naive and folksy in their approaches rather than superprofessional.

Many small consumer product firms have developed a well trained and reliable team of local homemakers who enjoy performing the telephone research role one or two days each month to earn some extra money and keep active in business.

Postal Surveys. As the most prevalent form of research by business and government, the postal survey involves the mailing of a printed questionnaire with an accompanying letter of explanation to a personally identified individual. The greatest single advantage of the postal survey is the economy of scale; a large number of potential respondents can be contacted at low cost. The mailed survey has another advantage over personal and telephone interviews in that they enable respondents to complete the research document in privacy and in their own time. Best results are obtained by the inclusion of a self-addressed, stamped envelope (SASE), along with some small token of appreciation such as a special discount coupon.

Well-designed mailed surveys usually obtain a 10- through 30-percent response rate as a general rule of thumb, but small, personal surveys to select audiences may generate much better rates. Surveys that are general in nature, that deal with a trivial issue, and that are mailed to anonymous recipients, usually result in *low response* rates.

Sometimes researchers code questionnaires according to membership in certain target groups, such as retailers, manufacturers, service organizations, and so on. Coding enables researchers to analyze the results of a study not only in their aggregate, but also according to the leanings of the study's constituent respondent groups. One form of coding is to make slight changes in the return address printed on the self-addressed, return envelope. In this way, mailed responses received in a given study can be grouped according to some common denominator—sex, occupation, geography, type of business, and so on.

DESIGNING RESEARCH QUESTIONNAIRES

Experience has shown that the greatest amount of objective information can be obtained from the well designed printed research questionnaire form. So the development of an appropriate design for a research questionnaire should be attempted with great care. Too often you are confronted with a request to complete a research form that is incomplete, poorly constructed, and full of grammatical and spelling errors. Such forms usually end up in a wastebasket, or they are given only superficial treatment by the respondent.

The Importance of Clarity

The first step in development of the questionnaire must be to state its purpose or central objective—what are you trying to accomplish? One of the greatest concerns of marketing people, of course, is to determine if a sufficiently large market exists to support a new business enterprise or expansion. But research studies can also involve various aspects of pricing, product features, competition, advertising, business location, and so on. A few typical questions might be to determine the following:

- What type of people are being attracted to a particular store or department
- The local people's attitudes toward a proposed new shopping center
- People's preferences toward certain new items being planned.

EXHIBIT 1–4
CHARACTERISTICS OF A GOOD MARKET RESEARCH QUESTIONNAIRE

1. The questionnaire maintains focus on achieving the predetermined objective.

2. Every question has a specific and significant purpose.

3. The wording and format of each question contains no elements that are unclear, misleading, or ambiguous.

4. Each question can be answered with a simple pen mark or a few written symbols for ease of completion by the respondent.

5. All questions have been carefully screened and pretested to eliminate inherent bias and maintain objectivity.

6. Respondent-qualifying questions (relating to the person's age, sex, income, and the like) have been kept to the absolute minimum.

7. Questions have been arranged such that broad general topics are queried first and specific details are left to last.

8. Questionnaire design is constructed in such a way to permit the easy and accurate tabulation and interpretation of results.

9. Mail questionnaires are accompanied by a clear letter of explanation, a self-addressed, stamped envelope, and some simple token of appreciation if such is appropriate.

10. The appearance of the questionnaire document has been carefully examined for legibility, ease of use, and professional image.

Perhaps the most critical advice for the novice researcher is to keep the research effort simple and to-the-point. Do not incorporate questions that do not specifically address themselves to the *central objective* of the study. *Do* attempt to obtain clear yes/no, none/many, black/white type of response data. To construct questionnaires of this type, most people find they must go through a considerable trial-and-error process. The wording used in each question must be examined time and time again to find any faults, vagueness of interpretation, and possible bias that might be inferred.

EXHIBIT 1–5
COMMONLY USED MARKETING RESEARCH FORMATS

Multiple Choice

Please circle one of the cities listed below that would be your *first choice* for a vacation:

1. San Francisco
2. New York
3. Toronto
4. Atlanta

This question format is best used when the researcher is seeking a clear discrimination between a number of alternatives.

Scaled Response

Please place an X on the line below at the point that best indicates your *overall* level of satisfaction with this book.

(0)	(1)	(2)	(3)	(4)	(5)	(6)	(7)

Very   Very
unsatisfied   satisfied

This question format helps researchers to find out the degree to which a respondent feels "more or less" about something. The numbers may or may not be shown, but they are used for figuring averages.

Yes/No Option

Please indicate if you *have ever been* to Los Angeles by checking one of the boxes below:

☐   ☐
YES   NO

This question format forces respondent into an absolute position.

Ranking Lists

Please rank (1, 2, 3, 4, 5, 6) the following list of duties according to which you feel are most important (low numbers 1, 2, etc.) and least important (high numbers 6, 7, etc.) in your work.

Typing duties   _____   Filing duties   _____
Mail duties   _____   Telephone duties   _____
Ordering duties _____   Accounting duties _____

This question format assists the researcher in separating priorities among a list of activities or items.

EXHIBIT 1–6
EXAMPLES OF UNACCEPTABLE RESEARCH QUESTIONS

Can you identify the problems?

1. Do you think a smart store for nice teen apparel would do well in the mall?

    Yes ☐   No ☐   Sometimes ☐

2. How often do you normally eat out in the evening?

    Very   Once in   Hardly
    often ☐   a while ☐   ever ☐

3. Does the President have your support for the new liberal policy on tax reductions?

    Yes ☐   No ☐

Answers

1. A "smart" store could mean many things to respondents—perhaps well furnished or carrying quality clothing. The reference to "nice" teen apparel is similarly ambiguous. The term "apparel" is a poor choice of word because some people would not recognize it. Using the words "do well" is meaningless since this can be interpreted in many ways—for example, "will fit in," "will be successful," or "will look good." The "mall" should be identified. Respondents checking "sometimes" provide little of value to the researcher.

2. The word "normally" is nondescript and confusing. "Eat out" could be interpreted as a backyard barbecue, formal dinner, or after-movie snack. Even the term "evening" is vague enough to cause confusion. Some people would think in terms of the hours after 4:30 P.M. Others would relate to the time limits in different ways—for example, one week or the whole year. The response alternatives provided are too vague to have any value.

3. This question contains an inherent bias. The use of a prestigious office or title automatically supports the idea being posed in the question. Wording such as "have your support" leans toward the positive rather than the ideal—neutral and objective. "Liberal" policy has a positive connotation. Perhaps the most dangerous aspect of the question is the use of the words "tax reduction," an obvious choice for most people. Avoid using words like "peace" and "safe environment," which most people would support.

For example, take the question, *Do you find meals well done in local restaurants? Yes or No.* This question is totally unacceptable as a valid reserach query, because it is riddled with problems. The word "meals" has many meanings to different people: lunches, suppers, snacks, and so on. The phrase "well done" could refer to the variety, quality, or cooked nature of the product. The reference to "local" restaurants could mean within the neighborhood, town, country, or state.

So you can result in highly unreliable and confusing research results. Every research question should be refined and revised until all difficulties have been eliminated. Obviously, some form of pretesting is necessary before a marketing research questionnaire is administered. Here are a few of the critical rules of thumb to keep in mind:

- Avoid the use of vague or ambiguous words, such as *nice, light, happy, like, small,* and *frequently.*
- Start with more general questions and follow with questions needing more specific detail.
- Each question should provide respondents with a complete range of answer options including categories such as *other, undecided,* and *don't know* where applicable.
- Keep the questionnaire as *simple* as possible; sometimes three or four questions are all that is required.
- Attempt to avoid any inherent *bias* in the order, content, syntax, or inference of questions—neutrality is essential.
- Try to build questions that obtain highly *precise* answers that can be clearly summarized and analyzed.
- Professionally documented questionnaires requiring manual completion usually result in *more reliable* results than orally administered ones.
- Provide some form of *incentive* or reward for people to complete your questionnaire. Movie tickets, discount coupons, or free pens are appropriate.

EXHIBIT 1–7
EXAMPLE OF EFFECTIVE RESEARCH FORM DESIGN

Liability Insurance Questionnaire

1. During this calendar year (19XX) have you been or will you be actively coaching?

    YES ☐   NO ☐

2. Please indicate the *number of years* you have been involved as a coach.

    ☐   ☐   ☐   ☐
    up to   1–4   5–9   10 years
    1 year   years   years   and over

3. Please write the name of the sport(s) in which you are *mainly involved* as a coach below.

    (a) ——————————   (b) ——————————

4. Please circle one of the following numbers to indicate how many coaching certification *courses you have* COMPLETED to date.

    1   2   3   4   5   6   7   8   9   10

5. Please indicate whether you personally are presently covered by an insurance policy which provides *liability protection* while you are performing as a coach.

    YES ☐   NO ☐

6. If you already have liability insurance protection, which of the following coverages are included?
    - *General liability* (i.e., bodily injury and property damage)   ☐
    - *Coaching malpractice* (i.e., errors, omissions and negligence)   ☐
    - *Both of the above*   ☐

7. Assuming such a plan offered $1 million of coverage and protected the coach for all acts of error, omission, and negligence, including bodily injury and property damage, please circle an amount you feel would be a *reasonable* price for you to pay for such a plan annually.

    $10 $15 $20 $25 $30

8. If the Coaching Association were to offer a *liability insurance plan* including both general liability and coaching malpractice coverage, would you be interested in purchasing such a plan?

    YES ☐   NO ☐

Thank you for your assistance. Please place questionnaire in enclosed envelope and mail back to the Coaching Association, ———— Street, ————, ———— 00000.

EXHIBIT 1–8
PRINCIPAL COMMERCIAL RESEARCH FIRMS AND THEIR SERVICES

Audit and Survey Co.—collects retail sales information.

Burgoyne Indexes—profiles of consumer buying.

Canadian Facts—consumer product field research.

Goldfarb and Associates—consumer buying and motivation studies.

Market Facts—retail trends and consumer behavior.

M.R.C.A.—brand preferences using consumer panels.

National Family Opinion—family product opinion research.

A. C. Nielsen Co.—retail store audits of client products.

R. L. Polk—consumer purchasing behavior data.

Roper Public Opinion Center—public opinion and consumer attitudes.

SAMI—research on the movement of products to retail stores.

Daniel Starch—research into readership of advertisements.

Yankelovitch Associates—public opinion and motivation trends.

Implementing the Questionnaire

The large corporation undertaking a major research project is usually able to assign a number of full-time staff to their project, sometimes for a period of months. The largest firms have their own well staffed marketing research departments, which undertake numerous research studies in a given year. The small business firm, however, is hard pressed to free up so much as one of its employees for even a day or two. An alternative worth considering is to contact a local University or Community College business department, to determine if some senior students or faculty might be able to provide assistance. Management consultants are another consideration if the firm needing the research is able to allocate sufficient funds to pay for their services. In most cases, a small expenditure for such help turns out to be an investment with a huge return—reliable research design and valid test results that can be relied upon.

Selecting the Sample

Perhaps one of the most important considerations of effective marketing research on a small business level is the selection of an appropriate audience. Depending on the nature of the survey, the researcher may wish to have a totally random group of people act as the target group, or perhaps—as is more often the case—some *selective* group may be more appropriate. For example, if you wished to conduct a survey to determine if a sufficient market existed for a proposed teen clothing store, your selective *focus* groups might be teenagers, single adults in their early twenties, and mothers of teenagers. Senior aged adults and parents of young children are unlikely to provide meaningful or at least authoritative input to such a study.

So the purposeful administration of a research questionnaire to a *select respondent audience* is a valid research method, with one qualification. Since most firms are unable to sample the entire universe of people who should have some opportunity to express opinion on a given topic, some form of *limited sampling procedure* is necessary. This is the tricky part. The people chosen to participate in answering a survey questionnaire should be randomly selected—not always as easy a task as you might assume.

For example, if a movie theater wished to survey patrons' feelings toward a certain film, the researcher is faced with the task of choosing a limited number of the audience without showing any bias or favor-itism toward males, females, whites, blacks, orientals, young people, old people, poorly educated, highly educated, rich, poor, and so on. If the theatre owner simply stands at the doorway and picks out the sample group, there exists a very high probability of *sampling error*. The personal choice method invariably reflects the *individual's bias* or *reverse bias* for blondes, blue jeans, freckles, short hair, or whatever.

From a scientific perspective, very little room for personal judgment should exist in the selection of people to answer surveys. The theater owner should likely establish a sampling method based on patrons' ticket numbers. The second halves of theatre stubs should be placed in a drum, spun to assure total scrambling, and then an uninvolved person should be elected to draw a number of sample tickets. Patrons who hold valid ticket numbers and who agree to participate in the survey should be given some small token of appreciation, such as a free ticket to the next attraction. This process should be repeated at each performance over a number of days. Thus the survey questionnaire will have been answered by an *indiscriminately chosen* number of patrons attending the showing over a prescribed time frame.

Such a methodology may seem awkward and complex to many readers operating small entrepreneurial businesses with limited resources at their disposal. Such an observation is entirely reasonable. Perhaps the method need not be so complex; the critical requirement is to assure research integrity as much as possible. Sometimes the small business person is just looking for some confirmation of a need to change the firm's current policies, products, or promotions. For example, support for a planned change to a storefront sign might be achieved by showing the artwork for the proposed sign to a sample of the store's patrons. Such basic approaches to obtaining valuable market opinion are often as accurate as much more sophisticated approaches.

DETERMINING SURVEY SAMPLE SIZE

Under ideal conditions, marketing researchers should obtain the opinions of all the people who might provide information useful in solving the issue being considered. Yet the real world demands that any research activity must be justifiable on an *economic* and *time consumption* basis. Small research projects, such as interviewing each of the twenty customers patronizing a beauty salon on a particular day, may be accomplished with little difficulty. Sometimes a survey may demand that all the potential respondents be contacted; if not, much of the value of the study may be weakened. Other instances, though, involve so many potential respondents, that only a small proportion can be reasonably included in the research study. Whereas a chemical firm selling to twenty paint firms in a local area has a relatively simple research task, a toothpaste marketer with a clientele numbering in the millions faces serious problems in determining a suitable sample size that will assure reliable results.

In some organizations, full-time statisticians use sophisticated mathematical formulae to arrive at absolute numbers, which represent statistically valid sample sizes for given populations. Yet for the purposes of most small to medium-size organizations, *some degree of imprecision is usually tolerable* in most research projects. For example, in the determination of general (simple) opinion on some commonly understood event, a number of generally accepted percentage and real number sample quantities have proven to be reliable. For example, let's say that a person wishes to make a reasonable assessment of the number of people who will attend a well publicized craft show in a community of 60,000 inhabitants. That researcher will likely obtain quite accurate results by randomly surveying (probably by telephone) enough of the population to generate a minimum of 1 percent or 600 respondents from that community. Let's say further that 42 (or **7** percent) of the respondents indicated that they planned to attend. This response would correlate to 4,200 (7 percent of 60,000) of the community's total population (assuming children are included). Statistical purists might decry such a rough computation, but experienced field researchers have proven this methodology to yield results that are about 80 percent reliable. National polls, designed to indicate current popular election opinion throughout the United States, are often based on a sampling of as few as 10,000 respondents, which represents less than 0.00005 percent of the eligible voting population!

To convert the results of a research project to a possibly more meaningful format, you might present the findings in a manner that discounts the "nominal" or anticipated attendance figure of 4,200. Typically, a Lo–Hi (low–high) projected attendance range is given. In this case, the low forecasted attendance would be 3,360 and the high, 5,040. This range accounts for a possible difference of 20 percent on either side of the anticipated patronage figure.

Such estimates may or may not be accurate enough for the organization commissioning the study. The researcher may also feel obliged to qualify the estimate with other variables, such as the state of the weather on the show day. (Good weather often attracts people to outside sporting events, whereas bad weather often helps indoor events.) So to increase the accuracy of the results obtained from a study such as we have outlined, several methods may be employed.

First, the size of sample could be increased. For instance, if you were to include 2 percent of the population, 1,200 respondents would be sought in the random telephone survey. The larger sample might entail the dialing of some 2,000 or more calls and greatly increase the cost. How much greater accuracy might be obtained from such a decision? Experience shows us that a doubling of the sample size usually results only in a 5- to 10-percent increase (from 80 percent up to 84 or 88 percent) in the accuracy of the result. So a researcher should not expect to obtain vastly different results from increased sample size alone.

A variation of this first technique can sometimes be of greater value. Simply conduct second and third samplings of the same population, and then measure the difference (variance) in results obtained from each group. A low variance tends to indicate a high degree of reliability in the research data, whereas large differences in the outcomes usually imply considerable doubt. Field researchers sometimes deliberately plan a number of small sample surveys drawn from a large population to be studied, just to estimate the *standard deviation*, which is a measure of the dispersion or the "scatter" of the various sample values. This deviation shows how the sample results are either bunched together or spread out from the *arithmetic mean*, which is the average value of the samples.

The size of small samples, such as we have been discussing, is usually assumed to be in minimum quantities of 100 contacts or respondents. To determine meaningful the *normal distribution* (or the skewed distribution, as the case may be), ten or twenty of these small samples would have to be processed. So you can see that the application of statistical methods is most appropriate when the actual numbers are relatively large. Most readers of this book are unlikely to need to use such methods on a regular basis, and, for this reason, our discussion shall continue to focus on only those basic, practical concepts that are of more immediate concern.

MARKET TESTING OF NEW PRODUCTS

Once a successful market study has determined a specific, unfulfilled market need, it usually results in a product or service development program to exploit the profit opportunity. Upon completion of such a program, therefore, marketing personnel are often requested to become actively involved with the new product idea once again. As Exhibit 1–9 illustrates, the marketing firm then has an important responsibility to conduct a number of vital tests prior to any full-scale launch of the item into the marketplace. Increasingly, government and public action organizations are placing greater pressure on the business community to demonstrate greater responsibility in the development and manufacture of new articles. In particular, such organizations are questioning the *functionality, performance,* and *cost effectiveness* of a wide-ranging number of consumer goods. So marketing personnel should, more than ever before, prepare a strong defense for their new product development actions.

This defense is best accomplished through the implementation of *concept, performance,* and *commercial* tests. In a more or less standard procedure, larger marketers subject each new product or innovation to these tests and publish the results in their entirety for presentation to external challenge groups if necessary.

As an example, a market test that can be a highly profitable exercise for a small business is to periodically evaluate the effectiveness of in-store displays. Exhibit 1–10 provides an example of the proper method for such experimentation. Note that the example assumes the organization has a number of outlets such that some might be used for "control" purposes. The independent store owner has to use a modified form of this test—but still adhere to sound scientific method wherever possible. For example, the owner of a single clothing outlet might set up two identical racks of mixed ties next to each other and evaluate the sales results over a period of time through the use of a special ticket code. When the sales history of the two racks has been established (and statistically speaking, there should not be a great difference in sales between the two), the owner can attempt to make a change in a single variable, for example, shining a colored light on one rack. While no experiment can be conducted perfectly without some bias or inconsistency, each of us as researchers should attempt to follow the basic precepts of sound research design.

EXHIBIT 1–9
CRITICAL STAGES IN MARKET TESTING OF NEW PRODUCTS OR SERVICES

(1) The Concept Test

Products or services that represent dramatically new concepts or highly innovative styles should be subjected to the critical scrutiny of consumer or business panels. Such an analysis focuses upon the esthetic and practical acceptability of the product in the marketplace.

(2) The Performance Test

Prior to introducing a new product or service to the market, you must subject the offering to a series of rigorous trials, to determine any threat of breakdown, off-specification performance, or danger to the well-being of users. This test should seek to exaggerate the adverse conditions of the marketplace.

(3) The Commercial Test

A limited number of the new product or service should be introduced to a well defined and controlled sector of the market for the purposes of making last-minute refinements to the firm's proposed packaging, pricing, promotion, or distribution system.

EXHIBIT 1–10
EXPERIMENTAL DESIGN TO TEST EFFECTIVENESS OF CHANGES IN A STORE DISPLAY

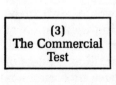

	Pre-Test Period (one week)	Test Period (one week)	Post-Test Period (one week)
Control Stores			
Test Stores			
	Establish per-unit volume norms for test and control stores.	Measure changes in per-unit sales volume in test and control stores.	Evaluate overall variance in performance for control and test stores.

In this example, a chain of stores wished to examine the sales effectiveness of a particular display. One group of stores were selected as control units and no changes were made to the displays. The other, experimental group of stores had the new displays installed to see if any improvement (or deterioration) in sales could be observed. Note that the number of units sold were closely monitored in both groups of stores for a 1 week pretest and 1 week posttest period. Thus, the sales patterns in both groups could be quite accurately measured and the new display's effectiveness tested.

MARKET MANAGEMENT

Management should always have current information on how they are doing in the marketplace. To discharge this serious administrative duty—and to ensure the organization's continued success—management must assess the organization's position within an industry and then formulate appropriate courses of action. Toward this end, marketing people should possess a strong grasp of a number of simple but important measurement methods and concepts.

The Value of Company Records

Be sure to utilize the abundance of market-related data available within your own organization. The data found in company sales records, properly interpreted, can cast a whole new light on marketing problems. Marketing people should be concerned with such items of interest as:

- the *ordering cycle* of customers (when they buy)
- the *average size of orders* from sales territories and from specific types of accounts
- seasonal variations in ordering by type of customer
- sales costs
- freight burdens
- other cost factors by territory and type of client

This kind of data may uncover the reasons for unduly competitive tactics in the marketplace.

Measuring Market Potential

In addition, some very specific measuring methods are available to assist in determining the relative position of the organization within an industry or market. (The proper use of the terms we are about to discuss is a requisite of skilled management.) Too often, the misuse or inappropriate application of these concepts can breed a certain laxness among marketing personnel, who should know better.

The starting point for any measurement of market activity is the determination of *industry or market potential*, which indicates the total universe of potential customers (or purchases) for a given product, in a certain market, over a specified period of time, usually one year. This figure represents the best possible estimate of the total number of units (the quantity of demand) that would be shared among competing industry suppliers. In some circumstances, a market potential number may be easily obtained from an industry trade association or government trade department, if such a figure is maintained for the firm's particular product or service. More often than not, these two sources are able to supply only some of the more mundane raw data from which a market potential figure is derived. For example, you might arrive at a market potential in New York State of 250,000 bicycles for a given year. All domestic and foreign producers of bicycles would be required to compete, through their distributor and dealer networks, for portions of this market or industry potential.

In actuality, the full market potential may or may not be satisfied. On one hand, the industry may have shortfalls in production (strikes, machinery failures, and the like), or distribution-channel members may exercise poor inventory control, thus causing stock shortages and *lost consumer orders*. Conversely, industry sales sometimes exceed estimated market potentials due to consumer fads, product hoarding, or just poor market forecasting.

The first step is to develop the most current estimate of total market sales or market consumption. Business marketers can sometimes estimate market sales according to a simple formula:

$$\text{Market Sales} = P + (M - X) - (I_1 - I_2)$$

where:

- P is the annual total production level in units of all firms within the market.
- M and X are respectively the total markets annual imports and exports in units.
- I_1 and I_2 are respectively the total end-of-year and beginning-of-year inventories of the product, in units, held within the market by suppliers.

The resultant figures obtained from this equation provide the researcher with an estimate of total market consumption in units of a certain product over a specified period of time.

To find total market consumption, small specialty retailers can total all the local store purchases of an item during the year and then add this figure to the difference between the total year-beginning and year-ending inventories of the product held by the various outlets.

Market sales, however, may or may not represent a *close approximation of the total available market potential.* The actual industry sales and the industry potential to sell may show a wide variation. Perhaps, for example, a greater quantity of goods is in demand than the seller is able to supply. In the light of such variation, some rudimentary trend analysis, correlation, or survey technique is often used to modify the market sales figure and thus to reflect a truer picture of the industry's total potential to sell. Sometimes the researcher is able to apply an insider's knowledge of one or more subjective factors; this knowledge has the effect of adjusting the market sales figure into a more realistic estimate of the industry's market potential. Sometimes the market for a given product is highly sensitive to demand-stimulating expenditures of promotional effort and money, so the market potential is seldom an absolute, fixed number. Rather, it is partially a function of the degree of industry stimulation evident at the particular time. More stable markets have smaller ranges of elasticity, whereas highly volatile markets indicate a wide range of sensitivity to stimulation.

A single business firm is rarely able to satisfy all of a market's potential. Indeed, most markets have a number of firms freely competing to capture the largest or most lucrative portion of the available business. Even so, buyers within a given market are often seen to be unhappy or unsatisfied with some aspect of local supply. As a result, you often see either an outside source supplying the market potential or some other good or service substituting for it.

So each individual supplier has a *sales potential* that it is capable of achieving. This sales potential represents the firm's maximum ability to sell, in dollars or units, to a given market over a specified period of time. Thus a small firm marketing photocopy machines in a state or province that has an annual market potential of 1,200 units may only enjoy a sales potential of 840 units. That is, if all facets of the firm's business operations are optimal, *they may* be able to sell as many as 840 photocopy machines.

The reasons for this limitation are generally common among all business firms, as well as among all types of products and services. First, the marketing firm is seldom able to manufacture or distribute a sufficiently broad product range that will satisfy the many different needs and tastes of the entire market potential. Furthermore, the firm is probably unable to communicate with all the market potential to let them know of their particular products and services. Third, competing firms are bound to have some superior selling points that enable them to be assured of certain sectors of the market universe. No single firm is likely to be able to satisfy the price, delivery, credit, service, and other expectations of an entire population.

A company's sales potential figure is arrived at through one of two methods:

1. Surveying existing client needs
2. Discounting the market potential figure

Client Survey Sales Forecast Method. In this method, you accumulate the best estimates of the anticipated needs of existing and known potential customers, to arrive at a realistic sales potential composite. Most larger firms conduct some form of annual survey of customer buying intentions for the coming year. There is a significant difference between a sales forecast and sales potential figure: The forecast represents an objective assessment of order volume that the firm expects to receive, whereas the potential figure reflects the maximum amount of order volume the firm could possibly receive if all factors were favorable. This build-up method of projecting expected or potential sales can usually provide a reliable end product, but it has the shortcomings of being both time-consuming and costly to administer.

Discounting the Potential Figure. A much simpler method of deriving the firm's sales potential is to *discount* the market potential figure according to a number of key independent variables. For example, a firm that has no distribution for its product in the New England and Middle Atlantic states may readily ascertain that they have lost the ability to access 15 percent of the national market potential for an item. So the sales potential is quickly reduced to a figure representing only 85 percent of the national market potential. Additionally, the firm's inability to produce the product in several popular sizes could again limit sales potential. After applying four or five of these important detractors to the national market potential figure, the firm might arrive at a sales potential that represents only some 20 percent of the total market potential.

Why must the sales potential figure be so accurate? The reason is that it provides a benchmark against which the firm is able to meaningfully assess its performance. When a firm totals the actual unit sales of an item at the end of a year, it is then able to compare this figure to the sales potential that existed for that year. The resultant number, expressed as a percentage, represents the firm's *sales penetration* or the degree to which they were able to satisfy their sales potential. Many companies regard sales penetration data as *the key indicator* of selling performance. The share of market, or *market share*, held by an individual firm is another measure of relative well-being sometimes studied by marketing personnel.

Exhibit 1–11 presents an example. The garden tractor manufacturer sold 20,000 units or one out of every five units of market potential for a 20-percent share of the market. In the highly competitive farm and garden machinery industry, our firm appears to have done exceedingly well. But, as is often the case, the company's sales penetration rate of 40 percent seems to leave something to be desired. In effect, the sales penetration figure tells us that the firm only did 40 percent as well as it might have, if conditions were optimal, certainly leaving room for improvement. On another occasion, the figures might well appear in some quite different perspective, such as a 5-percent share of market and a 90-percent sales penetration rate.

Whether sales penetration or market share is the better indicator is an ongoing question. An important aspect of this comparison is the degree to *control* which rests with the selling firm to improve its performance. Obviously, a far greater number and variety of influences shape the firm's resultant market share figure. To a very significant extent the share of market held by a firm will, in the long run, be proportional to the company's share of industry advertising, sales, and other marketing expenses. Thus the individual firm—or brand—is to a great degree at the mercy of the resource allocation expended by directly competitive firms and products. Sales penetration, on the other hand, is a more realistic measure of the firm's *actual achievement compared to their maximum ability to achieve.*

MEASURING SMALL BUSINESS MARKET PERFORMANCE

This topic is of vital concern for the small independent store, typically an owner-operated retail outlet.

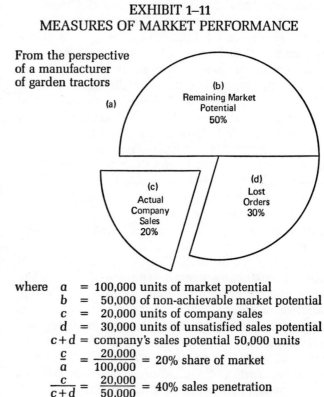

EXHIBIT 1–11
MEASURES OF MARKET PERFORMANCE

From the perspective of a manufacturer of garden tractors

(a)

(b) Remaining Market Potential 50%

(c) Actual Company Sales 20%

(d) Lost Orders 30%

where
a = 100,000 units of market potential
b = 50,000 of non-achievable market potential
c = 20,000 units of company sales
d = 30,000 units of unsatisfied sales potential
$c + d$ = company's sales potential 50,000 units
$\frac{c}{a} = \frac{20,000}{100,000} = 20\%$ share of market
$\frac{c}{c+d} = \frac{20,000}{50,000} = 40\%$ sales penetration

Whereas the larger chain store organization or manufacturer is able to afford the services of a full-time market analyst, who may enjoy numerous resources and extensive computer facilities, the very small business operator must "sweat it out" over the kitchen table late in the evening. However, the little business has just as great a need for solid planning expertise. Unfortunately, the operator of the smaller enterprise sometimes operates at a disadvantage. The independent entrepreneur is often so caught up with the daily turmoil involved in keeping the firm afloat, that little time is available to step back and examine the business' real nature and position, along with the direction it is taking.

The following techniques are valuable to small business people in measuring market performance:

1. Seek out a distinct market position.
2. Calculate the share of market controlled.
3. Determine how well the business is known.

A Distinct Market Position

If six shoe stores were operating in a 40,000-member community, you might feel tempted to suggest that the local market was *saturated*. Upon closer scrutiny, however, considerable latitude for additional competition might be discovered. One of the six existing stores may be focusing attention on work, safety, and hiking boots. Two stores might belong to national chains and might be attempting to sell a complete range of moderately priced footwear. Two of the remaining stores might cater solely to women's footwear needs. The sixth store could be an orthopedic specialty shop with custom-built or adapted shoes to help people with severe foot disorders. Opportunities suddenly reveal themselves. The community has no children's shoe store! Neither has it any specialty athletic shoe retailers or any stores catering to nurses and to other professionals. A brief survey might indicate that a substantial number of people travel to neighboring communities for these needs.

The key point is that, although a number of similar businesses coexist within a given market, *each one has chosen to adopt a particular position relative to competition.* Yet the generalist store is normally only able to satisfy the most basic requirements of the consumer. More often than not, the entry of specialist retailers severely affects one or more segments of the generalists' business. A small store manager should look at the business from the perspective of the client and ask: "Do we convey the image of serving some clearly defined market need relative to the competition's offerings?" If the answer to this question is no, then the firm should make itself *more clearly distinguishable* to its various publics.

Share of Market

Small independent retailers often wonder how much of the available business they are getting. Typically, a number of competing specialty shops and departments of a few generalist stores carve up the total business done in a neighborhood or community. Each one desires to increase the size of its particular piece of the pie—but a fundamental problem exists. No one seems to know the size of the pie!

Several solutions to this problem are available. First, most business types have some sort of trade association to which they belong. Such associations often collect, analyze, and report back a variety of industry statistics to their membership. One such statistic, which the retailer could simply calculate, is the *average sales per employee.* Another is the industry's *average sales per square foot or meter.* Armed with this information, a small store owner can develop an approximation of the total sales in the area based on the total number of people em-

ployed or the space utilized by all competing stores. A little less reliable but quicker estimation method, which uses the same rationale, is to calculate the average amount of sales dollars per employee necessary for your business to maintain a moderately successful business year. Then use this number to calculate the total amount of business that would likely sustain the total number of employees working in all of the competing businesses. You might wish to use both these methods and compare results of the percentage shares of market arrived at each way.

How Well the Business Is Known

Many retailers take for granted that most of the eligible buyers within the trading area know about their business. As long as the level of sales and profits of the organization are enough to satisfy the owners' expectations, no one really worries about the business' public image. Surprisingly, however, any business—profitable or otherwise—can be the victim of an inadequate public relations effort. A key concept to remember in this regard is the difference between store *recognition* and store *recollection.*

Recognition. In this instance, the litmus test is to find out how many prospects in your prime market potential recognize your business's name when asked which of a number of firms supplies a given product. Using the research questionnaire design techniques discussed earlier, such a question might appear as:

Which of the following Centerville flower shop names do you recognize? (You may check more than one.)

Faye's Flowers	☐
Heidi's Boutique	☐
Karen's Place	☐
Mother's Garden	☐
Pride Plants	☐
Zappeda's Nurseries	☐

The number of positive responses to such a question, compared to the total number of questionnaires administered, should give the small business a reliable estimate of the recognition of their store name. In a large city, 10 or 15 percent positive answers of those polled might be regarded as quite satisfactory, whereas you might expect more like 90 percent in a smaller community.

Of course, the data gathered in relation to your organization should be related to the results obtained on competitive stores. If a 30-percent recognition rating received for your business is, say, twice as large as that of a leading firm, you should be exceedingly pleased with your performance on this criterion. Thus a firm is able to calculate not only whether a large enough percentage of the population recognizes it as a supply source, but it can also gauge the degree to which it is recognized in comparison with competitive businesses.

Recollection. The measurement of the marketplace's ability to *recollect* your store or firm name is another measure of public awareness. Note that actual recollection is a far more demanding task than the requirement simply to claim recognition of something. Essentially, the recollection question goes beyond simple association of a product or service with a group of given business names. Recollection taxes respondents' memories by requiring them to access and retrieve information stored in their memory banks. Furthermore, the question of recollection forces them to discriminate among those business identities that are foremost candidates for the particular good or service. The following research question is typical and appropriate:

If you were going to buy some flowers, list as many Centerville shops as you can that they could be ordered from:

Sometimes such a general approach is not enough to trigger viable answers from respondents. Under such conditions, the researcher might have to move on to what is known as *aided recall,* that is, a question in which some form of help is given the respondent. Often, the researcher provides the respondent with each of the firm's logos, trademarks, or advertising themes to see if such information generates immediate recollection results.

No universal statements can be made to link a business' popularity or notoriety with its success. But some reasonable evidence seems to indicate that the organization that is well known (for good reasons!) encounters less *sales resistance* in the marketplace.

TACTIC 1 SUMMARY

Everything in this first chapter focuses on the need of business people to *know their markets* before embarking on substantial investment programs. Marketing people commonly think of this first step as the proverbial "ounce of prevention" that pushes the odds a little closer to be in favor of correct decision making. For well thought-out marketing plans— those with a high probability of success—you must have a comprehensive understanding of all the factors influencing the purchase behavior evident within a particular market. As you accumulate more and more reliable market information, the directions that the organization ultimately takes will more and more likely recognize the critical interests of its customers. Who buys our products? What characteristics do buyers have in common? Why do they give us their business? What other products would they be willing to buy from us? These are the day-to-day questions posed by marketing people who realize that the survival and future of the enterprise rests largely on the firm's ability to maintain an intimate knowledge of customer needs and wants. The first step to marketing success, therefore, must always be the total understanding of all factors shaping the making of decisions within the market environment being considered.

The information accumulated from such research must then be interpreted in light of your knowledge of accepted buyer behavior patterns—which is the subject of Tactic 2.

GOOD READING

Babbie, Earl R., *Survey Research Methods.* New York: Wadsworth Publishing Co., Inc., 1973.

Enis, Ben M. and Keith K. Cox, *Marketing Classics,* 2nd ed. New York: Allyn & Bacon, Inc., 1973.

Ferber, Robert, ed. *Handbook of Marketing Research.* New York: McGraw-Hill Book Company, 1979.

Kress, George, *Marketing Research.* Reston, Va.: Reston Publishing Co., 1979.

Livingstone, James M., *A Management Guide to Market Research.* New York: MacMillan, Inc., 1977.

O'Dell, William F., *The Marketing Decision.* New York: American Management Association, 1968.

Schaffir, Kurt H. and H. George Trentin, *Marketing Information Systems.* New York: Amacom, 1973.

Wilson, Aubrey, *The Marketing of Professional Services.* McGraw-Hill Book Company (UK), 1972.

FREE PUBLICATIONS

The Nielsen Researcher Publication
Marketing Research Group
A. C. Nielsen Company
International Headquarters
Nielsen Plaza
Northbrook, Illinois 60062

May Trends
George S. May International
111 South Washington Street
Park Ridge, Illinois 60068

Marketing Research Facts and Trends
MacLean–Hunter Research Bureau
481 University Avenue
Toronto, Ontario MSG IW8

MSU Business Topics
Michigan State University
East Lansing, Michigan 48823

Readers should write to the above addresses on their letterhead and request that they be added to the mailing list.

VALUABLE SUBSCRIPTION PERIODICALS

Marketing Information Guide
224 Seventh Street
Garden City, New York 11530

Industry Week
Penton Plaza
111 Chester Avenue
Cleveland, Ohio 44114

Journal of Small Business Management
West Virginia University
Morgantown, West Virginia 20506

Journal of Marketing Research
222 South Riverside Plaza,
Chicago, Illinois 60606

SOME KEY RESEARCH DIRECTORIES

Encyclopedia of Business Information Sources
Gale Research, Book Tower
Detroit, Michigan 48226

Thomas Registers of American Manufacturers
1 Penn Plaza
New York, New York 10001

Rand McNally's Commercial Atlas
Western Road
Ossining, New York 10562

Standard and Poor's Register
345 Hudson Street
New York, New York 10014

Financial Post Survey of Markets
481 University Avenue
Toronto, Ontario

Wenco International Trade Directory
Box 4623
Portland, Oregon 97204

Marketing people should attempt to build a meaningful library of business research materials. Write to any of the above and request an information brochure or sample of their publications before purchasing.

Understanding Buyer Behavior

TACTIC 2

Grace is given of God,
but knowledge is bought in the market.

ARTHUR HUGH CLOUGH
1819–1861
The Bothie of Tober-na-Vuolich
Chapter IV

People and organizations are willing to spend money only if they believe they can satisfy some particular need or desire. This second stage in the Marketing Tactics for Profits model is designed to enable you to better understand the many forces influencing customers' buying decisions.

Two primary factors differentiate the nature of commercial buying from that of consumer buying. First, since the business sector possesses no intrinsic market demand of its own, industry must rely on demand generated by the forces of consumer and government purchasing. Secondly, the almost totally rational nature of commercial market transactions is unique to the industrial marketplace. In contrast, the nature of consumer marketing depends to a large extent on the effective promotion of a unique idea or innovation to a fickle public whose expression of needs shows constant change.

THE NATURE
OF MARKET DEMAND

Marketers of commercial goods tend to live in a world entirely apart from marketers involved in satisfying consumer wants and needs. A company that produces valves, for instance, might see its markets as chemical, petroleum, food, and adhesive processing companies. In contrast, the toy company producing or distributing novelties may see its major market as children aged three to thirteen. To a significant extent, industrial product suppliers often assume an ongoing constant demand for their goods, irrespective of consumer marketplace realities. This attitude is totally erroneous, of course, because the demand for any commercial good is the result, direct or indirect, of either a consumer or government purchase.

While long-term buyer–seller relationships occur only infrequently in the consumer sector due to consumers' constantly changing buying preferences, business buyers and sellers are known to form more permanent alliances. Not infrequently, large companies map out their future expansion plans in close cooperation with their suppliers, to assure themselves of a continuous flow of needed materials. Occasionally, two or more supplying and consuming firms build new facilities in close proximity to each other to effectively share supplies or resources.

Elasticity and Inelasticity

The demand for most business-directed goods is generally regarded as *inelastic*, such that a large change in price will result in only a small change in the quantity demanded. (See Exhibit 2–1.) A wire and cable manufacturer, for instance, has little control over demand in its marketplace. Such firms are secondary manufacturers, because they provide the products used in the construction of other products, which in turn rely on demand from an entirely different marketplace. The demand for telephone and communication cable depends on the ability of a communication company to sell its service to the public.

EXHIBIT 2–1
HOW TO MAKE MONEY FROM AN UNDERSTANDING OF PRICE ELASTICITY

	An Elastic Market might order…	An Inelastic Market might order…
At the normal selling price of $10	1,000 units for a sale value of $10,000.	1,000 units for a sale value of $10,000.
At a reduced selling price of $9	**1,500 units for a sale value of $13,500.**	1,020 units for a sale value of $9,180.
At an increased selling price of $11	700 units for a sale value of $7,700.	**970 units for a sale value of $10,670.**

Different results might be incurred as a result of a marketer increasing or decreasing a product's price. Some markets exhibit a high degree of sensitivity to changes in price and are termed *elastic*. Other markets may be *inelastic*, such that fairly significant changes in selling prices result in virtually no change in customer orders.

Our illustration shows that, under elastic market conditions, the marketer can benefit from substantially increased sales by reducing their selling price by a modest 10 percent. Under inelastic market conditions, the firm can also increase sales revenues, but by increasing selling prices. This result is due to the market feeling that there is substantial value in the product or service offering even at the higher price, and so customers do not reduce their ordering.

The essential lesson is that a complete understanding of the buying behavior of customers for various products may reveal opportunities to make minor adjustments in selling prices that will have large payoffs in increased sales.

The nature of a marketer's business determines, to a significant degree, the behavior of its demand. Companies whose orders come from firms that produce short-lived consumer fad products can naturally expect wide fluctuations in demand. Yet a noteworthy goal of most businesses is to achieve an orderly stable rate of growth, and to accomplish this, firms attempt to involve themselves in markets with *consistent purchasing characteristics*.

The position of any firm should also be studied to determine its place in the supplier chain relative to the ultimate consumer. Marketers may sell their companies' products and services to consumer goods manufacturers, to other industrial firms, or directly to the public. Marketers buried deep in the supply chain are *less sensitive to abrupt changes* in consumer buying than those that serve the consumer directly. To illustrate this point, assume for a moment that consumer buying trends indicate a sudden distaste for breakfast cereals. The consumer product manufacturers of cereals would suffer immediate, perhaps devastating, losses. But cereal packaging suppliers would incur far less of a setback. Cereal producers might represent only one of twenty different industry markets served by the packaging supplier. Deeper into the supply chain, a logging firm supplies raw materials to several paper manufacturers, which in turn sell their products to a host of packaging fabricators. A solitary decline in the demand for cereal packages would scarcely be felt by the myriad of secondary and tertiary suppliers of pulp, wax, and industrial chemicals used in the production of paper.

More often than not, the commercial material firm is able to develop an inherently stable order flow through the *deliberate diversification* of industries served. Giant oil refineries and primary chemical producers—deep in the supply chain—are often so far removed from the realities of the consumer marketplace, they may not notice any significant change in their volume of business, despite some rather dramatic change in consumer demand for, say, telephones.

Derived Demand

Yet not all sales transactions can be traced so easily back to their consumer product sale origin. The purchase of obscure machines used to produce a variety of intermediate products in a given supply chain is rarely seen to be connected with demand from the consumer sector. The oil used to lubricate the machine, the can used to hold the oil, and the employment of the person who does the oiling all result, in the final analysis, from the purchase of some product by a consumer. This is commonly referred to as the *direct derived demand process*. Profit-conscious marketers should take careful note of the following demand-related characteristics:

- *Price elasticity:* Individual consumer and industrial products exhibit varying degrees of sensitivity to price changes. Each type of organization must experiment to determine if selective price increases or reductions will result in favorable outcomes, such as a greater order volume or total profits.
- *Market leadership:* All organizations must determine if they will benefit or suffer from being the market innovator. Should they be the firm to introduce the new products, offer the lowest prices, try some trendy promotion, or perhaps just position themselves as a middle-of-the-road supply source?
- *Supply situation:* Business people should examine the relative volatility or stability of the market in question. Excess supply normally brings about increased competition and lower market prices. General exceptions to this rule are highly differentiated product offerings or commodity goods.

The automotive industry provides the classic example of the progressive movement and transformation of goods. The impact of derived demand is staggering when you consider that close to half of all steel and a quarter of all plastic materials produced are incorporated in automobiles in one form or another. Similarly, the purchase of this book creates a direct demand for paper, ink, type, adhesive, and cloth, as well as an indirect demand for binding machines, paper cutters, collating, and labeling equipment. In turn these items create secondary and tertiary demands for steel, rubber, plastics, lubricants, and so on. Marketers should therefore carefully monitor the well-being of their clients' customer markets or sources of income as any significant change can have a snowballing effect.

CHARACTERISTICS OF MARKET TRANSACTIONS

A firm's sales volume to any single market rarely remains stable indefinitely. Indeed, certain products may follow more fickle demand patterns than others. This irregularity is due, in part, to an absence of brand loyalty among consumers of many products. Also, industrial markets are often highly sensitive to rapid technological change and to product specialization. How well a firm supports policies that proliferate style innovation and reciprocal buying

behavior has a dramatic effect on its overall *stability of operations.*

In the case of most capital goods, a considerable amount of *presale* and *postsale* service is required. The need for service is especially great for goods installed on a lease contract basis, where the responsibility for setup and maintenance rests with the seller. The marketing of both consumer and industrial products is affected by the seasonal and cyclical nature of the end-user's business. For example, steel for bridges is commonly ordered in the late fall and winter because the finished bridge is normally erected in the warm months of spring. The steel demand from automotive production follows a similar pattern. Electronic components are ordered in large quantities during the summer when appliance manufacturers concentrate their efforts on building up finished goods inventories to meet the autumn-to-Christmas order boom.

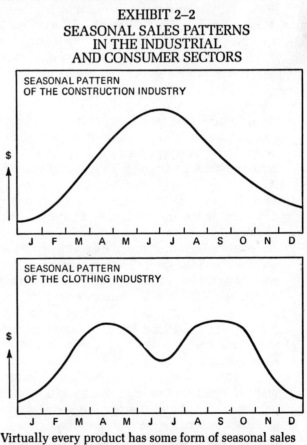

EXHIBIT 2–2
SEASONAL SALES PATTERNS
IN THE INDUSTRIAL
AND CONSUMER SECTORS

SEASONAL PATTERN OF THE CONSTRUCTION INDUSTRY

SEASONAL PATTERN OF THE CLOTHING INDUSTRY

Virtually every product has some form of seasonal sales pattern. Knowledge of these patterns enables marketers to more effectively forecast sales and to time new product entries. Retail and brand managers should monitor these patterns closely.

Marketers in all types of business have a fundamental responsibility to satisfy customer-established wants and needs, because doing so assures broad acceptability of their products or services. Machinery producers must guarantee their equipment for certain periods of time. Each shipment of raw and fabricating materials must meet established physical specifications and perform satisfactorily in their production applications. Consumer product marketers must adhere to stringent safety and performance criteria established by government and consumer protection groups. Their failure to provide effective surveillance of essential market needs can result in a shift in market preferences without their noticing.

Simply stated, *sales declines* are commonly seen as a result of users' finding new product sources with better or additional benefits than products they previously used. The rate of a sales decline is a function of several factors, including the degree of supplier loyalty involved, the consuming firm's dependence on the long-term reliability of the material, and the purchaser's confidence in the alternative supply source. Foremost among the list of marketing support activities that encourage client patronage are:

- *Total product knowledge:* Any organization should attempt to establish itself as the market's most competent supplier. This goal is best achieved through ongoing programs of product research and employee technical training. Knowledgeable marketing personnel inspire client confidence in the firm's reputation and advice.
- *Helpful, courteous staff:* Any organization should also take great care to ensure that staff who have client contact are properly informed on the fundamentals of consumer behavior, on coping with buying objections, and on the importance of exhibiting sincere interest in people's problems. Marketing personnel must be able to empathize.
- *After-sale service:* Even in the face of severe price competition, an organization will be well received by the marketplace, if it is known for its genuine concern for the customer's welfare after the sale has been made. Effective delivery, installation, and repair services are important requirements for success.

Offsetting Sales Resistance

Once a customer adopts a competitive product or service and purchases it on a regular basis, marketers encounter substantial difficulty in changing the established buying behavior. Exceptions to this rule occur when the purchaser, for some reason, cannot obtain the product normally used or when the regular item is faulty. Normally the procedure for selling something to an established purchaser of competitive products requires numerous discussions and written communications, just to reduce the factors causing sales resistance. Although this procedure in itself rarely produces a sale, negotiations clear the way for a physical test or instore trial of the seller's goods. In most business sectors, trial orders are normally supplied at "no charge" or at the lowest volume price. Occasionally, the potential customer and supplier come to an agreement to share the cost of the materials; in some large-scale programs, such as in the aerospace industry, the agreement to share costs may even include those expenses pertaining to production time, labor, testing, and so on.

Buying Criteria

Purchasers of day-to-day business supplies are motivated to buy from *less sophisticated criteria* than those firms buying a large value of component parts, installations, or fabricating goods. The machine shop that requires a drum of lubricant will usually continue to buy from their regular source if the price remains competitive, the delivery rapid, and, the sales representatives friendly through regular visits and other communications methods. Such *order predictability* is not evident when the value of a firm's purchases represent a signficant financial outlay. Corporate purchasing policies often preclude the establishment of automatic ordering procedures in an effort to achieve a lower price or some other preferential advantage.

EXHIBIT 2–3
THE NATURE OF CUSTOMER SATISFACTION

Consumer Satisfaction

$$S = f(n, q, p)$$

where S = degree of consumer satisfaction,

f = a function of...,

n = the number of goods or services purchased or consumed, in relation to personal expectations,

q = the quality of goods or services purchased or consumed, in relation to personal expectations, and

p = the price paid for the goods or services purchased or consumed, in relation to personal expectations.

Business Satisfaction

$$S = f(c, p, r)$$

where S = degree of business satisfaction with a purchase,

f = a function of...,

c = the cost of goods purchased or consumed, in relation to the organization's expectations,

p = the performance of goods purchased or consumed, in relation to the organization's expectations, and

r = the reliability of supply of goods purchased or consumed, in relation to the organization's expectations.

Note: The factors and relationships provided in these two models are for illustrating a general hypothesis. They are not intended to represent any definitive construct. Readers wishing to gain a further insight are suggested to consult the following texts for expanded coverage of this topic: James McNeal, *Dimensions of Consumer Behavior* (New York: Appleton-Century-Crofts, 1969) and C. E. Block, and K. J. Roering, *Essentials of Consumer Behavior* (Hinsdale, Illinois: The Dryden Press, 1976).

THE ESSENTIALS OF CONSUMER BEHAVIOR

"Consumer behavior" is somewhat of a misnomer. A more apt description is *buyer behavior,* because the purchaser of a given item is not necessarily the consumer/end-user of the item.

Most studies of consumer—or buyer—behavior are based on psychological and sociological motivation. Essentially, we are concerned with the factors that permit and cause individual buyers to direct their purchasing behavior in certain ways. Central to the marketing concept is the notion that sellers should address themselves to consumer needs and wants. On the surface this orientation appears to be a rather simple task, but, in today's complex marketing environment, even the most astute marketers are challenged to understand consumer buying behavior.

Broadly speaking, two general fields of study—economics and the behavioral sciences—attempt to offer the bulk of explanations for buyer behavior. The classical economics model portrays consumers as totally rational decision makers, as the possessors of full knowledge of any given product's benefits and detriments. In reality, however, consumers are unable to avail themselves of complete information, and, even if they were able to, their emotional side would likely prohibit an absolutely logical buying decision. In Exhibit 2–4 a number of the essential considerations in the analysis of both consumer and industrial buying behavior are illustrated.

EXHIBIT 2–4
MAJOR FACTORS
AFFECTING PURCHASE BEHAVIOR

In Consumer Buying Behavior

• Educational attainment	• Disposable income levels
• Nature of occupations	• Level of social activity
• Ethnic origins	• Media exposure
• Marital status	• Regional economic climate
• Age distribution	• Shopping accessibility
• Sex differentials	• Dominant lifestyle patterns

In Industrial Purchasing Behavior

• Size of industry	• Market stability
• Number of sales potential	• Need for assured supply
• Strength of competition	• Duration of contracts
• Level of technology	• Nature of order cycles
• Purchasing influences	• Existence of reciprocity
• Price sensitivity	• Prevalent economic climate

The Package of Needs

While answers to the question, "Why do people buy?" may remain a mystery, marketers are often able to analyze enough characteristics about a given market to develop a deliberate and effective marketing program. Perhaps the most fundamental principle you should keep in mind is that, when something is purchased, the item has likely satisfied not one but a *package of needs* that the consumer perceives as important. The strength of a consumer's need package is weighed against the product's or service's *benefits,* as claimed by you the seller. Social class, family structure, group conformity, peer and reference groups, mobility factors, and cultural customs—these are only a few of the significant influences on buyer behavior, that is, on the package of needs.

Reference Groups

In particular, groups that influence a person's buying and other behaviors are called *reference groups.* Most people are members of a number of groups in which they play different roles. In effect, such groups are frames of reference by which individuals attempt to measure themselves. When a marketer discovers that certain reference groups relate to specific types of products, the firm should stress those groups—those people—in their promotional messages. Reference groups may be isolated by occupational category, income, geography, housing type, education, or simply family size.

Social class is another discriminator of buyer behavior that is largely determined by an individual's income, education, and family background. Magazine publishers, automotive manufacturers, and certain food marketers have long recognized that wide variations in purchasing behavior exist among members of different social strata. Some long-standing arguments that these variations were caused solely by contrasting income levels have been largely dismissed. On the contrary, studies have shown that definite *class* preferences exist in the choice of nominally expensive products such as beer, motion pictures, books, tobacco, and coffee brands.

Family versus nonfamily purchases also reflect significant differences due to the influence of peer groups. Some decisions are made as a result of the consultation and the interaction of family group members, while others appear to be independent in nature. The influence of children cannot be overlooked, as parents attempt to compromise their own desires with those of other family members.

Psychographics

Perhaps the most interesting area for consumer research is in the subject of *lifestyles,* or *psychographics.* The primary elements of lifestyles are age, mobility, leisure, status, conformity, type of work, educational pursuits, and life attitudes. *Psychographic research* attempts to categorize groups or individuals according to the way they live.

One of the most common lifestyle discriminators affecting many marketers is the degree to which certain consumer groups are *active* or *passive,* measured essentially by their level of involvement. People whose lifestyles are active provide a fertile market for swimming pools, additional automobiles, instant foods, entertainment, and sports equipment. Their more passive counterpart provides an improved market for insurance, books, music, furniture, garden equipment, television, crafts, and tools. (See Exhibits 2–5 and 2–6.)

Individual consumers tend to perceive products and advertising messages differently. This sort of reaction is the central reason why buyer behavior is often an enigma for market analysts and researchers. Definitive correlations between reference groups, social class, lifestyles, or any number of consumer classification mechanisms and their encumbent behavior is at best imprecise. Despite all other logical factors, individual buyers will often *disregard, distort,* or *block out* a marketer's attempts to communicate if the message is neither relevant nor in keeping with their expectations.

What then should the marketer do? At this point in our understanding of buyer behavior, there are no

---

EXHIBIT 2–5
KEY FACTORS IN PSYCHOGRAPHIC PROFILES OF YOUR MARKET

Activities	Interests	Opinions
Work	Family	Themselves
Hobbies	Home	Social issues
Social events	Job	Politics
Vacation	Community	Business
Entertainment	Recreation	Economics
Club membership	Fashion	Education
Community	Food	Products
Shopping	Media	Future
Sports	Achievements	Culture

Source: Joseph T. Plummer, "The Concept and Application of Life Style Segmentation," *Journal of Marketing,* Vol. 38 (January 1974), pp. 33–37.

The Rationale: Research has shown that market segments possess certain common characteristics made up of their activities, interests, and opinions. Typically, an effective marketer might discover that most of the business clientele are college-educated career women who are active in sports, who have traveled extensively, who watch little television, who are fashion-conscious and committed to liberalism. Such in-depth probing to discover how customer markets *think* and *behave* go beyond earlier simple segmentation, which focused mainly on basic demographic information. The better marketers understand customer attitudes (reflected in their lifestyles), the more able they are to predict the type of appeals that will generate positive responses.

The Method: The determination of meaningful psychographic profiles is based on comprehensive research. This can be accomplished by formal studies of population cross-sections of a given market or, in smaller organizations, by an analysis of sales transactions and other internal records.

EXHIBIT 2–6
TWO COMMON PSYCHOGRAPHIC PROFILES AND THEIR IMPLICATIONS FOR MARKETERS

Profile 1

Linda—the career-minded city mother: Age 26, married, one child, leases modern townhouses, employed typically by government or corporation in administrative function.

She combines her better education and urban opportunities to provide higher income. She is more interested in her out-of-home activities than she is in providing comforts and services to her family.

Marketing Implications

Linda:
• would like to take a trip around the world;
• does not like household chores;
• would rather purchase children's clothes than make them;

• does not believe a woman's place is in the home;

• has a personal savings account;

• desires to be as mobile and free as her husband, to come and go as she pleases;

• believes occasional separate vacations contribute positively to marital harmony;

• spends considerable time and money shopping for clothes, makeup, and books;

• enjoys visiting art exhibits and musical concerts;

• dines at a quaint restaurant as a weekly "must";

• is interested in politics and major sporting events;

• drinks in moderation;

• does not attend church;

• is unwilling to get involved in volunteer social work groups;

• attends evening classes at a nearby college;

• plays tennis or golf most weekends;

• seldom views television.

Profile 2

Carl—the striving achiever: Age 42, married, three children, owns renovated old home in town, employed as computer marketing specialist with large financial institution.

He places great emphasis on being up-to-date and able to readily adapt to change. Money is central in motivating him to greater effort.

Marketing Implications

Carl:

• is typical of the hard-driving, business-oriented male;

• has come up through the system the hard way;

• has held a number of jobs with a variety of office equipment manufacturers;

• rarely takes time for vacation, preferring to talk the family into weekend excursions;

• an authoritarian personality, places a low value on fostering personal friendships;

• spends many nights at the office and gives little consideration to the needs of his wife or children;

• believes strongly that technology can solve most of the world's problems;

• does not enjoy working with his hands and avoids situations that may require manual work;

• is a heavy purchaser of personal services;

• an avid junk food consumer, watches Monday night football undisturbed and alone with a few bottles of his favorite beer and cheese-flavored corn chips;

• belongs to a number of service organizations for the business contacts, but resents contributing time to community projects;

• distrusts churches, subscribes to all popular news and technology publications; and

• does not want his wife to work.

Reproduced with the permission of Irwin-Dorsey Limited, publisher of *Profile Canada: Social and Economic Trends.*

absolute laws governing, determining, or predicting consumer decisions. Current evidence appears to support the view that marketers must first identify the need structure of uniform groups of consumers and then design convincing promotions with an appropriate appeal in that direction. Individuals within any target group may have different or the same need structure. The primary goal of the marketer should be to ascertain those common and *highest-priority needs* within each major buying group. This approach largely overlooks causal factors such as social class, education, or income, in favor of influencing current states of mind toward given products, values, themes. Once defined, the marketer must attempt to develop a reflective mirrorlike product, a communications response that consumers *identify immediately* with their need sets. An important aspect of this development program is the *position* of the marketer's response relative to competition. In this regard contemporary marketing programs should concentrate on *different* need-satisfying motives from those that the competitor is focusing upon. This different emphasis provides consumer buyers with a real alternative in their decision-making process.

CONSUMER BUYING TRANSACTIONS

Consumer buying behavior offers a radical contrast from that of the professional buyer in a manufacturing or retail organization. We know that much. But consumer behavior is largely unpredictable because of the vast number of variables shaping the purchase decisions. Contrast this with the largely rational decision process of a full-time commercial buyer whose production department has stipulated a need for a precise number of cardboard containers of a certain dimension, weight, and strength. The commercial buyer's responsibility is simply to fulfill the internal request at the lowest price and best delivery. By comparison the individual consumer is recognized as a fickle being, one who may arrive at the department store with only a vague notion of some intent to buy.

Some market analysts contend that the largest proportion of consumer buying is *unintentional* in nature, the result of *habitual shopping* without predetermined goals in mind. Just getting out of the house has, for many, become synonomous with a tour of the local shopping plaza or mall. There, the individual comes under the nearly hypnotic suggestion to buy, from the influence of an impelling kaleidoscope of color and sound. Such routine exposures, usually reinforced by some rewarding experience or purchase decision, represent an *effective behavior-conditioning process* that leads to subsequent shopping trips. The expenditure of money then becomes a pleasurable experience, or at least one not associated with punitive outcomes.

EXHIBIT 2–7
MAJOR FORCES SHAPING BUYING DECISIONS IN THE EIGHTIES

1. The continuing increase in educational attainment levels means more knowledgeable, discriminating purchasing.

2. Greater discretionary time resulting from reduced work hours means even greater demand for leisure products, travel, and recreational services.

3. Ongoing inflationary pressures on the cost-of-living means greater acceptance of do-it-yourself involvements in home renovations, furnishings, and decoration.

4. An older, more mature population means purchase decisions will reflect greater conservatism in the search for value and for lifestyle satisfaction.

5. Growing societal emphasis on self-fulfillment means greater expenditures on exciting adventures, travel, and personal products.

6. More working-age women holding career positions will reinforce the idea of smaller families but will provide for greater levels of disposable household incomes.

7. Higher incomes attained by traditionally lower-paid blue-collar workers will lead to far greater experimentation in long-standing white-collar values such as wines, ethnic foods, and the theater.

8. Large numbers of women reaching the end of childbearing age will result in a minor boom of "last-chance" babies, which will sustain a multitude of previously "dying" products and services.

9. Reduced availability and higher cost of energy resources will establish conservation consciousness as a permanent ethic in the national psyche, leading to broad-scale acceptance of small autos, energy-saving appliances, and solar and other conventional energy alternatives.

10. The rapidly expanding electronic technology will bring about a profound change in consumer buying transactions, for example, homeshopping by TV, electronic transfer of funds between merchants and banks, and nearly instantaneous market research capability.

Some consumer behavior authorities argue that consumers exhibit essentially reasoned or purposeful decision behavior, but that the consumer requires some form of memory-jogging stimulation. This process results from media advertising messages, and it is typified by the consumer who returns from a shopping trip for one specific item—with many additional items that he or she had not set out to buy. In this view of consumers behavior, store environ-ments or *atmospherics* (Kottler) are known to have a significant influence on the selection and value of consumer purchasing behavior. Store space allowances and counter configurations, decor style and color, soft music, and subtle lighting are all important environmental considerations for retail management. Neat merchandise displays and wide aisles are congruent with high-quality products and services, whereas discount store shoppers fully expect a collage of assorted stock through which they can hunt for bargains. The availability of sales staff is another factor that must be determined by the nature of the product, by the image of the store, and by the expectations of clientele. Prospects entering an expensive jewelry store, for example, do not expect to be pounced upon by a high-pressure, commissioned salesperson, but neither do they expect to have to wait in line to be served. Sales personnel should be reserved, conveniently accessible, and prepared to be of assistance in the selection process, but they should not radiate *signals of anxiety*. Contrast this with the selling process encountered at many car dealerships where the rule of thumb seems to be to prohibit the prospect from leaving the lot at any cost. Still other retail businesses, notably the discount mart, offer little or no sales personnel, and shoppers are left to fend for themselves.

Discrimination Processes

Purchasing decisions are often characterized as the result of learning and *discrimination processes*. Let us examine, for example, some of the evaluative criteria used by the consumer in selecting an appropriate store in which to shop. To a large extent, the number of criteria included in this process depends on the relative value or importance placed on the purchase. A consumer wishing to buy a new camera will consider many more factors than one considering the purchase of a ballpoint pen. A few of the most common criteria considered by the consumer are product choice, price, store convenience, service availability, the quality of store personnel, and the credit policy.

EXHIBIT 2–8
SOME USEFUL CONSUMER BEHAVIOR QUESTION FORMATS THAT WORK

Even small organizations need to better understand their customers' buying behavior. The following questions can be modified for use in a broad variety of settings. But first a suitable preamble must be developed, to briefly acquaint the person being approached with the purpose of your solicitation. For example:

Good morning, sir. My name is _____
_____. I'm the _____ [title] of
_____ [the organization]. We're conducting a
study of customer buying, and I'm wondering if you would
be willing to help us?

To Measure Consumer Awareness

We have a number of *super specials* advertised in the store,
and I'm wondering if you can tell me what some of these
items are?

[Researcher then records list of items cited for later comparison to the actual items.]

To Measure Consumer Preference to a Proposed Change

I have a number of printed cards in my hand with the
names of different types of goods we are considering
adding to our store. Would you please sort them according
to that you would most like us to stock, down to the one
that is least desirable?

[Researcher then records the order of preference of the
cards provided.]

To Measure Why Consumer Buys at Your Store

On this piece of paper your will find a list of the most
common reasons people shop at certain stores. Would you
please choose the three main reasons you decided to come
to our store today, marking them one, two, and three according to importance?

[Researcher then records the priority list drawn from items
such as handy location, friendly staff, low prices, and so
on.]

Ideally, this type of research should be conducted after
people have concluded their purchases. The research data
obtained is enhanced if additional information on the respondent can be obtained—age, marital status, occupation, area lived in, and similar pertinent data.

Readers should also be aware that consumer discrimination is a *major goal* of marketers—convincing people that a particular product, service, or
sales outlet offers particularly unique benefits over
alternative offerings. Through the discrimination
process, consumers are able to demonstrate *selectivity* in their choices of what they feel to be satisfying purchase experiences. The processes by which
marketers attempt to make their offerings stand out
from others must be based upon the highest priority
needs of the specific group of people to whom they
wish to sell. Remember, too, that not all purchase
decisions are made by a single individual; marketers
often must convince couples that their offerings are
the best alternatives. Increasingly, consumer product
marketers find themselves addressing a more demanding type of client than in the past. Nearly 50
percent of all North American households are now
child-free, a status which has profound implications

for marketers. These "empty-nesters" have more disposable income than other households and are therefore more interested in acquiring objects of greater
permanence and value for their homes. Whereas
family households shop for utilitarian value, non-
parent markets look for good taste, polish, and
pizazz. Thus, retailers must provide an appropriate
shopping experience if they are to capitalize on the
needs of a particular market segment.

Store Image

The dimensions of these elements for a given
store, taken as a composite result in what is commonly referred to as *store image*. A store image need
not be considered only in terms of good or bad.
Generally speaking, consumers perceive a retail organization in a *much broader array of contexts*, such
as friendly, thrifty, uncluttered, exciting, warm, comfortable, busy, drab, or helpful, in comparison to
competing stores. No single organization can expect
to satisfy all people's expectations of them and
should not try to do so.

Retail stores should seek rather to develop an
image that is *consistent with preferences* of its major
sales potential. A children's shoe store for example,
might develop an image of caring for the health of
children and of providing qualified professional
counseling to parents on the type of shoe best suited
to their child's feet. In a marketing context, the store
should attempt to see itself more as a provider of
comfortable, healthful footwear for young people
than as a volume seller of children's shoes.

The conscious design of a store interior to accom-
modate maximum product exposure, efficient customer flow patterns, protection against pilferage, and
fast check-out service is an art not easily mastered.
Entrepreneurs entering the retail business for the
first time would be wise to enlist the support of a
specialized retail consultant and interior designer to
ensure successful layout, furnishing, and decorating.

In-store purchasing behavior is one of the least
researched areas of retail merchandising. Consumers
are normally attracted to a particular store out of
either habitual patronage, the outlet's established
reputation for product selection and price, or a
specific promotion. Where two similar retail outlets
are available, the consumer may be attracted to one
over the other for the most subtle of motives. The
store's name, its tidy exterior, or a friend's recommendation are common discriminators that influence patronage.

Perhaps the strongest influence of all is the consumer's past shopping experience at a particular

outlet. Was that experience rewarding or punishing? Long lines at check-out counters, limited size or color choice, discourteous sales staff, and check-cashing hassles are only a few of the experiential factors that dissuade the buyer from returning to a certain retail store. Consumers invariably return to shop at those outlets in which they *have confidence, feel comfortable,* and believe *they received fair value* for their money. These feelings make the customer's visit a totally rewarding experience!

Specialty Stores Versus Scrambled Merchandising

Certain consumer purchases lend themselves to specialized retail store types. For example, the purchase of a sewing machine is unlikely to be made at a discount chain store, for reasons that are not complex. The consumer has difficulty in perceiving the discount mart as a *credible* supply source. High staff turnover, unrecognized brands, and uncertain servicing ability are not in keeping with the nature of an expensive and relatively sophisticated consumer purchase. The age of discontinuity in which we live is exemplified by the rapid and concurrent growth of two essentially opposite trends:

1. *specialty stores*
2. *scrambled merchandising*

Specialty stores attempt to offer consumers a direct alternative to an often impersonal and sometimes confusing shopping experience in large department and discount stores. They offer a single line of goods addressed to discriminating buyers who crave personal attention and product selection. Low prices are rarely associated with specialty stores, which prefer to emphasize product quality, shopping environment, and good customer service. The most common forms of specialty retailers with which we are most familiar are camera shops, health food stores, sweater boutiques, and pizza parlors.

Scrambled merchandising is a phenomenon whereby many stores, previously regarded as specialty in nature, abandon their original single product lines in favor of a highly diverse product mix encompassing many dissimilar goods. Thus the corner drugstore of old embarks on *merchandising tangents,* which only a few years ago would have been considered bizarre. Consumers in most parts of North America are no longer shocked to see the local pharmacy selling electronic calculators, hair dryers, or lawnmowers. Neither is it unusual to see food supermarkets carrying patio furniture, sporting goods stores offering automotive accessories, and jewelry stores selling a line of barbecues.

Scrambled merchandising came about when specialty stores became less inclined to remain polarized within a limited product framework. Marginally profitable specialty stores in particular saw the need for expanding their market audience, and they sought out additional products that would attract increased patronage. Initially, such diversions were kept within the realm of products complementary to their existing offering. As time passed, however, the relationship between new product additions and the original store concept widened. Today it is truly difficult for any store to establish a rigid product policy—*flexibility* and *innovation* are the key strategems.

Consumer's Self-Concept

In as much as the consumer's self-image is an important consideration in buying transactions, the elements that shape the consumer's *self-concept* psychological construct became important also. Individual consumers often perceive the purchases they make in terms of their symbolic value. Many consumer transactions are clearly a result of a certain harmony between individuals' perceptions of themselves and their perceptions of what the product expresses, or stands for.

Marketers should be well aware of the powerful influence of product styles that represent status symbols, most of which has been artificially created by clever media campaigns. A given product may imply youth, poverty, feminity, or elegance to any number of people. More often than not, however, the smart marketer will *reinforce a particular theme* throughout a single advertising campaign, because consumer audiences learn to identify the product's symbolic message. If the symbolic expression agrees with the individual's psychological set or self-concept, a purchase is likely to ensue. Exhibit 2–9 outlines a number of the key rational and emotional factors shaping the purchase decision. You might evaluate which combination of these most affects your particular business.

Individuals' self-concepts are shaped by their awareness of their feelings, perceptions, and evaluation of self-worth. Their self-concepts are, in effect, how they see themselves. For example, with other factors being constant, a professional athlete who perceives himself as a rough, masculine figure will likely identify well with products whose promotional theme implies the symbolic values of robustness, good health, and energy. Beer commercials, more than any other product category, have been highly successful in creating *stereotypical brand images*, to appeal to a broad number of highly selective target groups—young sophisticates, newly marrieds, the "jock" set, and so on. Each brand theme is skillfully designed to provide viewers ready identification with known self-concept profiles.

EXHIBIT 2–9
KEY PERSONAL FACTORS SHAPING PRODUCT CHOICE

Ten of the Most Important Rational Concerns

• Conservation	• Leisure
• Durability	• Nutrition
• Economics	• Population
• Energy	• Serviceability
• Functionality	• Toxicity

Ten of the Most Important Emotional Concerns

• Color	• Risk
• Culture	• Sexuality
• Fashion	• Status
• Peers	• Self-concept
• Religion	• Taste

Lastly, an important consideration that pervades all consumer buying is the notion that people attempt to *maximize their satisfaction* by continuing to acquire additional units of any good or service until they feel that some other buying alternative offers the hope of greater satisfaction. Remember to reinforce each and every consumer on their excellent purchase choice!

BUSINESS PURCHASING METHODS

Most large manufacturing and retailing organizations employ professional purchasing personnel. Occasionally, the purchasing department has a staff of buyers, each responsible for the procurement of specific types of goods or materials for a particular division of the company. The company requiring a central purchasing authority usually buys thousands of different items for production, operating, or resale purposes. The purchasing department's tasks include the establishment of product supply sources, the attainment of the best possible price and delivery, the investigation of freight and customs tariffs, and the avoidance of duplication of orders from various company departments.

The purchasing job is not an easy one. Purchasing is subject to extreme pressures from production and sales departments, as well as from senior management. Few people understand the internal workings of purchasing departments. Purchasing agents themselves have taken steps to upgrade their profession through professional associations and education programs. In many firms, purchasing personnel are regarded as key members of the executive decision-making team. Purchasing managers are normally required to:

- establish qualified material suppliers and maintain a continuous product information and supplier evaluation system.
- negotiate with suppliers to obtain the most satisfactory supply agreements based on quality, delivery, and price.
- determine appropriate ordering systems based on economic order quantities, cash flows, and practical aspects of supplier services offered.
- improve existing supply arrangements by renegotiating terms of sale, credit, delivery, order size, and price.
- maintain effective internal communication, advising on new product developments, material supply status, and cost allocation.

Purchasing Authority

Sales representatives must determine if the purchasing employee has the *ultimate authority* to buy a given product. Some subtle probing often does the trick—asking the buyer if there is anyone else that you should contact with product information. Sometimes the decision-making structure requires multiple sales contacts with several key individuals, each time the salesperson visits the client.

For example, a sales representative for a company marketing felt-tipped marking pens might have to check with the employees using the pens, to be sure they are satisfied with them. The salesperson might then seek performance approval from a departmental supervisor at the client firm, who will notify the firm's purchasing department. An additional formal sales presentation to the buyer may be useful.

Contracts

As a seller, you may be requested to sign binding contracts. Large retailers often require a contract when purchasing consumer goods, to maintain continuity in prices and supply. Similar contract requirements are found with petroleum firms selling crude oil to export clients, with mining concerns selling ore to refiners or steel producers, with vegetable farmers selling crops to food processors or canners, and with forestry firms selling to lumber and paper-making concerns.

A contract may favor the buyer or the seller, depending on whether the document's supply and consumption criteria are couched in positive or negative phrasing. For example, a statement such as "the purchaser agrees to pay" is regarded as a positive supply commitment in favor of the seller. Other variations in contractual stipulations may be represented by statements such as "the buyer agrees to purchase" or "the buyer is prohibited from." In either of these cases, the seller has probably secured an advantage. On the other hand, a negative supply statement is represented by "the seller will not change the," which usually supports the position of the buyer. The number and relative importance of preferential clauses, which place an obligation on either the supply or consumption of a product or service, determine the contractual bias in favor of a buyer or seller. Consult an attorney with regard to appropriate legal phrases satisfactory for use in your particular area.

Trading Relationships

For their essential materials, most businesses attempt to secure two or three sources of supply, classified as *primary, secondary,* and *fringe* suppliers. The purpose of multiple supply sources is to provide security against supply interruption caused by strikes or breakdowns occurring at the seller's producing facilities. Of course, this task becomes increasingly complex if the firm purchases thousands of different products. A buyer may also encounter difficulty in attracting *alternate supply sources* if the product being bought is of a highly technical or specialty nature.

Many marketers are adverse to negotiating on a single-order or a "one-shot deal," for fear of alienating their long-established regular customers. (See Exhibit 2–10.) Each partner in a trading relationship attempts to seek out the safest and most economic situation based on its degree of leverage. Special prices, delivery, or credit terms that are offered to a single-order account may represent a legal infraction and involve the marketer in a costly lawsuit. Important factors in market transactions that cannot be overstressed are the legal commitments, constraints of purchase, and sales order conditions.

Offers-to-Purchase

Any legal purchase order is an *offer-to-purchase* the specified goods or services according to certain terms and conditions. The purchasing firm normally

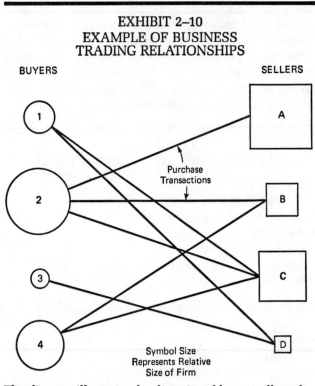

EXHIBIT 2–10
EXAMPLE OF BUSINESS
TRADING RELATIONSHIPS

BUYERS
SELLERS

Purchase Transactions

Symbol Size
Represents Relative
Size of Firm

The diagram illustrates the diversity of buyer–seller relationships found in a typical market situation. Notice how the giant firm 2 attempts to cover itself against short falls in supply by buying from three sources, sellers A, B, and C. Seller A, the largest of the supply firms, has the largest portion of buyer 2's purchasing requirements but is highly vulnerable to a major setback should this relationship terminate. Small buyer 3 probably has a high trust relationship with the equally small supply firm D. The nature and extent of buyer–seller relationships are kept confidential in some industries. However, in industries where a large amount of patronage information is available, such an exercise can be of great marketing value.

EXHIBIT 2–11
HOW TO IMPROVE PROFITS
IN TOUGH BUSINESS TIMES

- Promote shopping by telephone and free delivery service to save customers the cost of travel and shipping expenses.
- Prune the existing product line of poor selling goods and reallocate promotion efforts to hot items.
- Cut back on out-of-pocket expenses for travel, entertainment, samples, office maintenance, and the like.
- Reduce inventories and accumulate volume orders to achieve improved production efficiencies.
- Evaluate the cost of servicing the smallest accounts and attempt to combine their orders for extended time needs.
- Be more promotion-conscious; ask supplier for ad allowances; look for direct response from each advertising dollar.

mails or gives to the seller's representative a standard purchase order form. Buyers commonly type in those standard terms and conditions that they know are agreeable to a particular seller— "net 30 days; steel drum packaging; F.O.B. Atlanta," for example.

But the buying firm may also view other terms and conditions as mandatory in any of its purchase agreements. These are commonly printed on the face or reverse side of the purchase order, and constitute part of the buyer's offer-to-purchase conditions. A typical example of such a condition might be: "The purchaser reserves the right to return any or all goods to the seller within thirty days of receipt of merchandise, for full and immediate credit, without cause, notice, bonus, or handling charges." Such a condition may directly conflict with the seller's policy of accepting returned goods only when they do not meet the stated quality specifications.

The onus is upon the marketer to evaluate all offers-to-purchase, ensuring that the terms and conditions of both parties are in agreement. A seller normally signifies acceptance of a purchase order by giving the buyer an order acknowledgment; thereby, both parties become bound by the terms and conditions of the contract. Contractual negotiations, resolution, and documentation of a purchase order may take less than an hour or as much as several years, as in the case of large defense contracts.

Some situations may permit sales representatives to *circumvent the conventional documentation process*; they may book orders by recording the terms and conditions themselves. In some lines of business it is an accepted practice to write the order detail on a sales order form and present it to the buyer for a signature approval. The completed sales order form represents the selling firm's legal offer to sell. Operators of new businesses should ask a variety of firms for copies of their sales order forms to assist them in the design of their own.

The emphasis of transactional responsibility can shift from seller to buyer throughout the course of any order negotiation period. Many purchasing departments are structured in such a way that all *initial selling contacts* must be done through the purchasing director. Sales personnel who violate the system may find themselves in jeopardy of being blacklisted.

The purchasing authority for goods of lesser value, such as operating supplies and accessory items, is often delegated to the individual department who submitted the original request. Department managers are sometimes held accountable for negotiating a satisfactory price and selecting a suitable supplier.

In addition, the purchaser of operating supplies, even for a large firm, hardly justifies a highly paid executive's time, especially when viable alternatives such as automated ordering and systems contracting are available. In *systems contracting*, an independent middleman firm takes over the responsibility for stocking and maintaining the supply of *all* high-consumption, general supply items of a large client firm. But *internal* purchasing control systems have also become increasingly sophisticated in recent years.

Vendor Analysis

Vendor analysis is a performance rating method designed to evaluate supplier capability based upon measureable criteria such as financial stability, production capacity, technical competence, delivery reliability, and quality control. Exhibit 2–12 illus-

EXHIBIT 2–12
VENDOR EVALUATION FORM

VENDOR'S NAME:	MAIN PRODUCT:			
Item	Performance Rating			
Favorability of Price	1 Poor	2 3 Acceptable	4 Excellent	5
Delivery as Requested	1 Poor	2 3 Acceptable	4 Excellent	5
Suitability of Product	1 Poor	2 3 Acceptable	4 Excellent	5
Packaging Acceptability	1 Poor	2 3 Acceptable	4 Excellent	5
Competent Service	1 Poor	2 3 Acceptable	4 Excellent	5
Technical Support	1 Poor	2 3 Acceptable	4 Excellent	5
Sufficient Inventory	1 Poor	2 3 Acceptable	4 Excellent	5
Cooperation in Promotions	1 Poor	2 3 Acceptable	4 Excellent	5
Evaluator:	Date:			

trates a typical evaluation form that a firm might use periodically to assess a seller's performance on an on-going basis. *Value analysis* is an internal system of investigation used by purchasing departments. It is designed to identify and to implement cost and quality improvements through improved product specifications, inventory control, order expediting, packaging, and transportation methods. Professional purchasing management have done much to reduce the adversary relationship, traditionally prevalent between sellers and buyers. A new spirit of cooperation appears to be growing as marketing and purchasing people become increasingly sensitive to the expanding dimensions of their respective roles. Mutual *understanding* and *compromise* have replaced much of the antagonism of old, generated by steadfast policies and opportunistic bargaining.

TACTIC 2 SUMMARY

You should now have a good understanding of the major contributing factors that govern consumer and commercial purchasing behavior. Draw from this knowledge those significant factors that you deem to be the most important in influencing your key markets. For example, if marketing research (Tactic 1) reveals that your primary target market consists of business executives, apply your new understanding (Tactic 2) of reference groups, rational motivation, and risk analysis to develop an appropriate marketing appeal. If you are marketing to a consumer goods target audience, psychographic analysis and familial influences certainly will be key considerations.

There appears to be a rather distinct emphasis on certain factors affecting buyer behavior in each of the consumer and commercial sectors. Such a division is by no means absolute. While research has shown that elements such as color, design product names, brand loyalty, and personal experiences are of paramount importance in determining consumer product choice, they may also be hidden persuaders behind an industrial buying decision. Factors such as education, social status, financial means, and peer pressure cannot be overlooked in either the consumer or the commercial sector. It is important that you as a marketer fully appreciate that your buyers may not really recognize what their chief motivation is in purchasing certain goods. Through experience, however, you may be able to develop an accurate explanation for your major customer's buying behavior. As a result, your marketing programs will yield high dividends.

Be aware that your organization's ability to change consumer purchasing behavior is likely to be very slight. Instead, the greatest gains are made by experimenting and monitoring the behavior patterns of your major customer groups, so that more refined (perfected) marketing campaigns can be developed. Methods for developing effective products and services are discussed in Tactic 3 of the Marketing Tactics for Profits model.

GOOD READING

Bennett, P. D. and H. H. Kassarjian, *Consumer Behavior.* Englewood Cliffs, N.J.: Prentice-Hall, Inc., 1972.

Block, C. E. and K. J. Roering, *Essentials of Consumer Behavior.* Hinsdale, Ill.: The Dryden Press, 1976.

Enis, B. M. and K. K. Cox, *Marketing Classics,* (2nd ed.). Boston: Allyn & Bacon, Inc., 1973.

Marquardt, R. A. et al, *Retail Management,* (2nd ed.) Hinsdale, Ill.: The Dryden Press, 1979.

Myers, J. H. and W. H. Reynolds, *Consumer Behavior in Marketing Management.* Boston: Houghton-Mifflin, 1967.

Robertson, T. S. *Consumer Behavior.* Glenview, Ill.: Scott, Foresman & Company, 1970.

Walters, C. G. *Consumer Behavior.* Homewood, Ill.: Richard D. Irwin, Inc., 1978.

KEY REFERENCE ARTICLES

Baltera, L., "Focus Selling Efforts on Lifestyles, Retailers Told," *Advertising Age,* January 26, 1976.

Britt, H. S., "Applying Learning Principles to Marketing," *Business Topics,* Spring, 1975.

Frankel, M. "What Do We Know About Consumer Behavior," in *Selected Aspects of Consumer Behavior,* Washington, D.C.: National Science Foundation, 1976.

Henry, W. A. "Cultural Values Do Correlate With Consumer Behavior," *Journal of Marketing Research,* May, 1976.

McGuire, W. J. "Some Internal Psychological Factors Influencing Consumer Choice," *The Journal of Consumer Research,* March, 1976.

Plummer, J. T. "The Concept and Application of Lifestyle Segmentation," *Journal of Marketing,* January, 1974.

Villani, K. E. A. "Personality/Lifestyle and Television Viewing Behavior," *Journal of Marketing Research,* November, 1975.

VALUABLE SUBSCRIPTION PERIODICALS

Journal of Marketing
American Marketing Association
222 South Riverside Plaza
Chicago, Illinois 60606

Journal of Purchasing
National Association of Purchasing
11 Park Place
New York, N.Y. 10007

Psychology Today
PO Box 2990
Boulder, Colorado 80323

Journal of Applied Psychology
American Psychological Association
1200 17th Street, N.W.
Washington, D.C. 20036

Commercial News
3181 Fernwood Avenue
Lynwood, California 90262

Journal of Consumer Research
American Marketing Association
222 South Riverside Plaza
Chicago, Illinois 60606

Write to any of these on your organization's letterhead and request a complimentary copy for evaluation prior to taking out a subscription.

Providing Appropriate Products and Services

TACTIC 3

*Don't sell me industrial fuel.
Sell me controlled heat, speed,
production, quality, and greater profits ...*

From poem of the North Thames Gas Board
London, England

Large increases in business profits can be achieved through effective product planning. The introduction of appropriate new goods or services into a firm's existing product mix can multiply money-making opportunities for the enterprise. Hence product planning is the third Marketing Tactic for Profits in which management uses market research information in a continuous effort to maintain a product mix with a high degree of market acceptance. The process places substantial emphasis, not only on the quality and quantity of market information gathered, but also on the expert personal judgment of the business person.

TOTAL PRODUCT CONCEPT

Contemporary marketers now appreciate that most products convey many complex aspects of human feelings, images, status, prestige, and so on to most consumer buyers. With every planned product change, the marketer should view the process as an opportunity to develop a new combination of appeals, to enhance the item's appearance, or to attract new sales potential. Even minor changes in design, color, size, package style, or name have the effect of

creating a new product in the public mind. The promise of whiter teeth, of shinier nails, of sweeter breath or of a better backhand are powerful stimulators to buy. The essential marketing rule is to *sell customer benefits*, not product features. Any new product development idea should first be examined in light of how well *concepts translate into meaningful client benefits*. Sometimes these benefits are difficult to identify, or to explain, as in the case of a small animal or sports logo sewn on the pocket of a summer jersey. Such subtle little touches are seen to be very positive contributors to shirt sales to both men and women.

The concept of *total product* is important to small business people and yet easily overlooked. Essentially, the concept means that the product manager or developer should look beyond the tangible or obvious aspects of a given product or service, and envision the total *enjoyments* or *satisfactions* that might be derived by consumers.

For example, only the naive shoe manufacturer or retailer would believe that tennis players' primary concern is to purchase shoes that will be long-wearing. Nothing could be further from reality. A more realistic order of priority might be the shoes' appearance, their general comfortable feel, the amount of apparent rubber underfoot to absorb shock, the appeal of the shoe's name, price, and even the uniqueness of the tread design! You can see, then, that the development or consideration of a new tennis shoe involves a number of thought-provoking criteria. A new shoe with pink and purple stripes on the side might be a poor seller only because those colors clash with the area's "accepted" tennis coordinates. Even the shoe box should be designed for maximum consumer impact; such matters as action drawings, special instructions, guarantees, and so on should be well thought out in terms of their potential impact. The same conceptual approach applies to the restaurant business. The entrepreneur who starts a new restaurant with an almost exclusive concern for good food, and little else, will likely run into serious sales difficulty. Again, the reasons people patronize a particular restaurant rarely have to do with any single product characteristic. Rather, each patron has a number of *underlying motives* and *expectations* that the establishment must, more or less, seek to satisfy. Typically, these might include a relaxed atmosphere, a unique menu, comfortable seating, fast service, large helpings, friendly personnel, and low prices. No one restaurant product is going to be ideal for everyone, but the owners' critical task will be to *modify and to refine* their customer benefits to satisfy the broadest possible target audience. The interior colors used, the music played, and the uniforms worn by staff are as much a part of the total product of the restaurant as their steaks, salads, and wine list.

Monitoring Customer Needs

Periodically, small business managers should solicit the opinions of their customers to measure attitudes toward their existing services and uncover unsatisfied needs. This sort of feedback is commonly referred to as "taking the pulse" of your market. For focusing on the product change process, the following explanation of the major types of new products will prove helpful:

- *Modified products* are those in which one or more features or benefits have undergone change such that the goods or service are able to expand the firm's sales potential.
- *Imitative products* are those which one firm may add to its offering to suggest newness, but in fact the products are substantially the same as those offered by competition.

- *Original products* are those that represent some truly unique approach, for which the firm knows of no substitute offering that is equal in customer benefits or satisfactions.

People concerned with new product development need to take a constructive, innovative attitude toward the task. The organization must steadfastly commit itself to servicing the specific needs of certain groups of clients, despite pressures from purchasing, engineering, manufacturing, or other departments to conform to organizational prerogatives. Based on the identification of some unfulfilled customer need or want, the firm should establish some distinct product objectives. Such statements of intent might be tied to improvement in the tread design of a tennis shoe marketed by the firm. Or, to use our other example, perhaps the restaurant has found that it requires considerable improvement in the speed of its service. The process by which either of these objectives is achieved is really immaterial, so long as the consumer recognizes improvement in the changed product and this recognition results in the desired outcome.

The impetus for new or changed products can originate from a variety of sources. In a retail store, the salesperson, the store or department manager, the division head, or the buyer may recognize the need for change. Often, this awareness comes about when a great deal of slow-moving merchandise, lost sales, or returned goods becomes apparent. Sometimes the business makes a point of recording customer complaints, and some commonality of concern becomes evident. Occasionally, inside salespeople are the first to recognize that some product problem exists. A common customer com-

---

EXHIBIT 3–1
MOST COMMON CAUSES
OF NEW PRODUCT FAILURES

1. Insufficient market analysis
2. Incorrect estimates of market potential
3. Poor timing in introduction to the market
4. Lack of effective prototype evaluation
5. Insufficient initial promotion
6. Improper distribution channels
7. Unexpected competitive reaction
8. Poor technical service backup
9. Higher-than-anticipated production costs
10. Long development delays, causing late market entry

EXHIBIT 3-2
CONCEPT TEST FOR NEW PRODUCT

This exhibit is meant to illustrate the basic mechanics of a product concept test as it would be presented to members of a test panel. Note that the given information attempts to provide an objective description of the item, with sufficient information for the respondent to form their own mental portrait.

Given Information

The product being considered is thick brown syrup that replaces powdered forms of instant coffee. The syrup can be added to hot water or cold milk, and it dissolves completely without residue left in the cup. This new proposed product (tentatively titled *Caffette*) has the advantages of indefinite shelf life and the elimination of floating particles on the drink surface.

Questions

1. Is the concept clear and easy to understand?
2. Would this product satisfy some real need of yours?
3. Do you feel the product has strong selling features?
4. Would you buy this product?
5. Do you feel a lot of other people would like this product?
6. What improvements do you think would help this product?

---

plaint with regard to available sizes, colors, or designs may also be a signal that some change is in order.

Whereas larger firms often rely on *product planning committees* for the change process, a small enterprise must be highly resourceful in any new product program. Under such circumstances, the use of external engineering, development, or consulting firms may be beneficial in providing an unbiased opinion. In nonprofit organizations, the need for product evaluation and renewal programs is just as critical. To attract audiences to swim events or music recitals, the basic entertainment product must often be enhanced with contests, celebrity appearances, token giveaways, and other attendance benefits.

Not all new product introductions become success stories. Readers will readily identify with many of the product failures in the following list: Arctic Cat snowmobiles, Rely Tampons, Campbell's Red Kettle Soups, Dupont's Corfam, Bricklin automobiles, Revlon's Super Natural hair treatment, Ford's Edsel, Listerine Toothpaste, and Easy-Off Cleanser. Most of these items were the victims of poor product planning, insufficient market analysis, or technical default.

KEYS TO EFFECTIVE PRODUCT MANAGEMENT

Successful marketing companies continuously audit the firm's progress by examining their degree of operational effectiveness. Several of the criteria for such a review are as follows:

- The speed with which the firm reacts to changing market conditions
- The number of successful new product introductions made during a specific time period
- The consistency with which the firm is able to maintain profit growth

One effective system for introducing a new product is to overlap each new product's life cycle onto an established product's cycle. In this way, the company can capitalize on the cumulative building block effect of the overlapping markets, with *increased profit potential* in a shorter time span. This system demands of the marketer an increased flow of new product developments and greater attention to new product phasing.

Some products have *seasonal variations* or *fluctuations*. For example, a company supplying spark plugs or other parts to an outboard motor producer falls into this category. In such cases, the industrial supplier relies on the customer's market performance in a business based on a seasonal demand pattern. In addition, however, a larger cyclical demand model is evident. Other marketers have products whose volume is cyclical, caused by factors other than derived seasonal demand. A marketer selling vinyl sheeting to an above-ground pool producer is one example; a manufacturer that supplies a

---

EXHIBIT 3-3
PRODUCT LIFE CYCLE OVERLAP

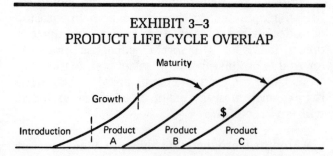

Every product and service goes through a normal life cycle with identified stages of development. An essential key to effective marketing management is the preplanning of old and new product life cycle trajectories. This enables the firm to plan for the future by preparing new products in anticipation of declining market acceptance of mature goods.

middleman wholesaler is another. The sale of outboard motors has a significant relationship to the sale of cottage properties, the rise in discretionary income, or recent weather trends. But swimming pool sales exhibit cyclical behavior based on new home construction, disposable income levels, or peaked curves of the world Olympic years. These cyclical themes are represented by a modulating curve of longer duration than one depicting seasonal fluctuations. And the wholesaler's reorder cycle is determined by a combination of ninety-day or six-month forecasted sales and limitations on total inventory value.

When the purchaser is not committed to any one supplier, another variable affects the fluctuation in demand for the supplier's goods. The supplier has no guarantee that it will get the next order. Producers of operating supplies such as cleaning compounds, lubricants, brooms, mops, and paint are often in this situation when dealing with multiple channels of distribution in each geographic market served.

PRODUCT TIMING

Companies entering the marketplace "late"—that is, after the competition has its products in the growth stage—have a particularly difficult task to become market leaders. Competitors may have as little as a one-month, or as much as three- or four-year advance, on them in the marketplace. The late entry firm should realize the strengths and weaknesses of the market leader in the areas of marketing, technology, and production abilities. Occasionally the market leader will not have strong marketing abilities, perhaps achieving its market position in the absence of legitimate competition. In this case, late entry firms have a relatively simple skirmish on their hands. In cases where the market leader obtained its position through substantial marketing prowess, the later entry firm has to exhibit an intensive marketing program to compete effectively. In either case, your approach should be to analyze the competition's strengths and weaknesses in relation to the needs of the key market audiences. Capitalize on the deficiencies or voids in the competitor's offering.

Often, leading marketing firms are faced with situations where an extension of a product's life cycle, even in its decline stage, becomes desirable. The reasons for extension are usually related to the delayed introduction of a new product or to the requirement for maintaining a certain volume of orders to cover overhead. The strategy of lengthening a product life cycle is accomplished by introducing *product and price innovations* that will enhance the attractiveness of the offering and act as an inducement to continued patronage.

PRODUCT RENEWAL

Products that have reached market maturity can sometimes be revitalized through minor or major innovative actions. The change or addition of colors of an item represents a relatively minor innovation that requires little modification of production methods. The addition of a select number of alternative colors offers less of a threat in the event that other modifications are made to the product. A line of screwdrivers could be extended to include a magnetized version with a different colored handle. A line of metal office desks might be offered with woodgrain laminate top and hidden casters in the legs. Many of these changes actually represent little or no increase in costs, but the product can be sold at higher prices and life cycles extended.

Changes in packaging, although more effective in the marketing of consumer products, is another product innovation that has significant merit for industry. One marketer of power saws lengthened the product's life cycle by offering a special promotion of "giving" the saw purchaser an electric drill for only $5 extra at the time of ordering. The price of the drill was self-liquidating. But the promotional appeal caused many thousands of the new saws to be sold over a one-year period and generated replacement parts sales for some five years after. Always plan some extra or bonus inducement to make your product or service more attractive to buyers.

PRODUCT OBSOLESCENCE

A product that outlives its usefulness to the marketplace is termed "obsolete." The two basic causes of product obsolescence are (1) an unacceptable style or (2) outdated technology.

Style

Style obsolescence is most commonly associated with consumer products, particularly women's fashions. The impact of style is often overlooked in the design stage of new industrial product development, but there is little doubt that it is a powerful motivational factor in the purchasing process. Consider the relative importance of style in each of the following purchasing situations:

• A secretary selecting a new typewriter

- An executive selecting new office furniture
- A production supervisor selecting a new machine
- An architect selecting elevators for a proposed building complex.

All other purchasing factors being relatively equal, *style* could be a major determinant in the selection of one product over another.

The two major considerations of product style are *functionality* and *resistance to obsolescence*. In some industries, whole markets have been swept away from a producer virtually overnight. Brushed aluminum has hurt stainless steel. Plastics have penetrated markets traditionally held by paper, wood, and metals. And self-coating steel has hurt the paint industries. Today, producers of wooden boats are an oddity as fiberglass strengthens its hold on that industry. And glass milk bottles became a rarity when polyethlene jugs and bags proved themselves superior. In each of these cases, the quantity of the consumer product demanded has remained relatively stable, but, for one or more reasons, the nature of the product has undergone dramatic change.

Technological Obsolescence

Technological obsolescence may be viewed in a dual perspective, as performance exhaustion or as technical default. Every product reaches its own point of technological obsolescence sooner or later. A product that becomes obsolete due to performance exhaustion is one whose operational ability has ended due to mechanical fatigue.

EXHIBIT 3–4
FACTORS INFLUENCING NEW PRODUCT TECHNOLOGY

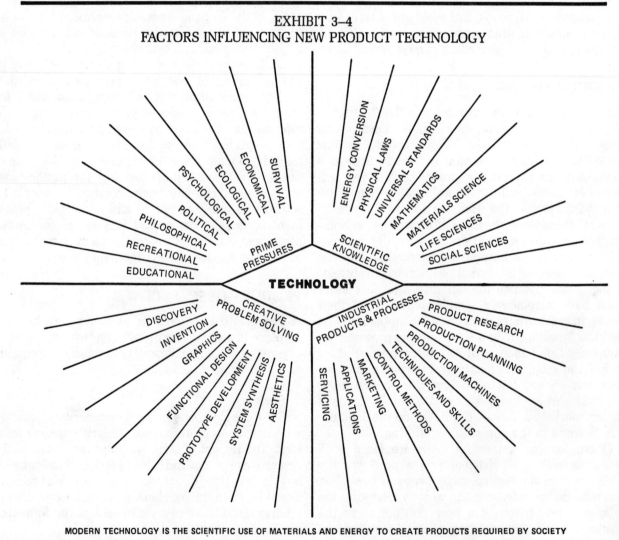

MODERN TECHNOLOGY IS THE SCIENTIFIC USE OF MATERIALS AND ENERGY TO CREATE PRODUCTS REQUIRED BY SOCIETY

Reproduced with the permission of Mr. D. E. Loney, Faculty of Education, Queen's University.

Performance Exhaustion. This sort of obsolescence is governed by factors that establish the durable life of an item. Engineers know that the steel frame of a ten-year-old automobile or bridge, may have only half the strength of the original. Similar deterioration, through oxidation, wear, and molecular activity, occurs in almost every product.

Product development specialists have a critical task to determine the appropriate amount of durability to build into a product. As a general rule, greater durability means greater costs, which must be absorbed by the customer. So economics play an important role in moderating a marketer's idealism to build invincible products. Many products have unnecessary durability designed into them. Most people would agree to a generous durability safety margin in passenger aircraft. A fabric manufacturing company, however, might object to paying for twenty-five-year durability in a machine the firm is certain to discard in seven or eight years.

Technical Default. This second type of technological obsolescence must also be considered by marketers. It involves the rate at which a new technical development provides an improved performance alternative to the marketplace. Technical default provides product development with its greatest challenge due to the accelerating rate of technological change. Frequently a product development department finalizes its plans for a product only to find a new, more appropriate technology presenting itself. Management must then decide whether to carry on with its original plans and risk an early technological obsolescence, or delay the project in the hope of capitalizing on the new technology and thereby gaining a competitive edge in the marketplace. The key words here are "in the hope," which denote the possible introduction of a new variable; perhaps the redevelopment period will be too long or the costs too great.

Planned Obsolescence

"Planned obsolescence" is the term used to describe a marketer's efforts to deliberately design a certain longevity or usefulness into a product. Of the primary factors affecting product obsolescence—style acceptance, performance exhaustion, and technical default—only performance exhaustion is to any great degree controllable by a manufacturer, in terms of the *predicted product life termination,* under given conditions. Style obsolescence and technical default are, by and large, vagaries of the marketplace and only marginally controllable by most marketers.

The term "planned obsolescence" often takes on a derogatory connotation in the consumer sector due to the concomitant visibility of rapid style change and the vast selection of product models available. Some consumer advocates have deplored the rate of technological innovation that has brought us remote control television and pushbutton everything. What few outside the marketing sphere understand is that technical innovation is the result of companies striving to satisfy consumer needs or wants in a competitive environment. A free enterprise system actually fosters the manufacturing and marketing of high-quality products at the lowest selling prices by reason of the competitive market environment. If you are in the position of developing some tangible new product, the anticipated (technical, physical, style) life built into the item should be enough to satisfy customer value expectations for a given expenditure. The market provides a strong safety mechanism to thwart the continued sale of items giving poor value—that is, the customer's power to purchase or reject any item.

Industrial product planning, because of its derived nature, is subject to all the same uncertainties that affect the consumer product sector. In addition, most marketers must contend with the ever-present threat of watching a market evaporated by a changing technology and by a host of competitive suppliers. The fact that some products have a relatively limited number of users is not always in its favor. The requirements of one customer may represent 25 or 30 percent of a company's sales of a given product. In some industrial fields, there is an equal number of suppliers and customers for specific goods, a balance that creates severe competition.

UNIQUE PRODUCT OFFERINGS

A company wanting to purchase fifty portable electric drills will select the product offering the greatest number of beneficial features, all other things being equal. A drill offered with variable speed, a nonconductive handle, a heat-dissipation mechanism, a chemical- and cut-resistant cord, and lightweight carrying case will certainly be more salable than one not having these features at the same price. Often, the cost of including these features in a new product is very little, but a company offering them in a product at the same price as a competitor's goods without these advantages has a significant edge in the market. A purchaser may even be willing to pay a premium for the goods due to the points of differentiation.

Even when the change in the appearance of a product is negligible, proper promotion can create a need for the product in a customer's mind. Some new but common products, for instance, have developed a unique aura about them, simply through the proper use of an effective trade name.

Also, the use of color in products is often ignored by marketers. Some firms feel that color is not practical in their goods because the industries that they serve are interested only in efficiency, durability, or value. Where competitive products show little difference in product performance, price, and service, even the professional business buyer is likely to select an item based on the satisfaction of some emotional criteria.

All other factors being equal, the visual impact of a product differentiated by its unique color is often a *powerful purchasing motive*. Industrial machinery, tools and accessory equipment can be given a distinct identity, setting the product apart from a competitor's drab goods. Even replacement parts and operating supplies, which are traditionally black or grey, can be regenerated. For example, a black rubber automotive fan belt may be given a new image by the addition of a red stripe. A heavy industrial machine may be given added glamour by the use of colored controls, levers, instrumentation cases, or instructional decals. In this regard, you can safely say, with little reservation, that consumer product marketers hold a higher degree of sensitivity to the value of color and brand names. Just imagine the impact of a return to the widespread use of black only in the production of automobiles, toys, and housewares. Color choice presents the prospective buyer with *positive options* that are difficult to resist. The selection of appropriate product colors, like the determination of an esthetic design, is a critical issue, and it must ultimately be decided by marketing personnel equipped with conclusive market research data.

MARKETING PHYSICAL AND ADVISORY SERVICES

Virtually all businesses and consumers utilize some form of external services. For example, engineering firms design new production facilities, interior designers plan new office arrangement, maintenance companies attend to office cleaning, gardening, or painting. Professional services are offered by psychologists, dentists, architects, and others. Tatoo salons, weight-reduction clinics, hair stylists, in-stant tanning shops, and computer dating agencies are often seen to offer aggressive marketing programs to capitalize on their highly specialized services. During the past twenty years, by far the largest growth sector of the economy has been in personal and business services, and this trend is projected to continue throughout the next decade. If you are thinking of starting a service-type business (or currently operating one), you will find the information in this section valuable.

Physical Service

A *physical* service company provides customers with tangible, sometimes visual proof of a task having been accomplished. Physical services are most often concerned with altering the form or composition of the customers' materials, or with supporting the customers' operations in a maintenance sense. Physical service companies are most often single-line firms and channel their abilities in one direction, such as building cleaning, fabric, coating, duplicating, or packaging. Firms specializing in the collection and disposal of chemical by-product waste, independent office cleaning, and decorative finishing of metal products are only three examples of physical services. Because physical service firms provide tangible or visible evidence of their work, they seldom encounter as high a degree of *price resistance* as do *advisory* service companies. But since the competition in physical services is often more intense than in advisory service areas, they generally enjoy *lower gross margins* on a given volume of sales revenue.

People involved in offering physical business services should price each individual job separately. Usually a formal contract is required when dealing with an industrial manufacturing client, but it is seldom necessary when doing business with smaller retail or professional concerns. Many firms have the ability to sign long-term contracts and to carry out a needed physical service on a continuous, uniform price basis.

Advisory Service

An *advisory service* company or institution undertakes no processing of material, but rather provides assistance to customers through research, planning, consultation, and advice. Advisory services are often looked upon as counseling and information-giving processes. Since most advisory services really *sell time*, some customers, on occasion, offer resistance to advisory fees for which they can see no tangible goods. Most small consulting operations can be run from the individual's home or apartment. This is a particularly valuable consideration for the individual who is just starting up a consulting service and who wishes to keep the monthly overhead down.

A pertinent example of an advisory service is the marketing consultant, who offers an independent counseling service to businesses. This consultant, through research, analysis, and experience, offers a professional and unbiased opinion to a particular marketing problem and suggests alternate courses of action.

For entrepreneurs wishing to start their own businesses with a limited capital outlay, the establishment of some form of advisory service may be their answer. The key qualification necessary for success is the principal's expert knowledge of a particular facet of business or other activity. A given consultant might, for instance, advise business firms on improvements to their organizational structure, accounting systems, public relations, or marketing strategy. A common fallacy is that consultants require all sorts of formal academic qualifications. Such is not necessarily the case. While some large management consulting firms specializing in complex business consulting assignments may prefer to hire college graduates, CPAs, and the like, a tremendous demand exists for small business consultants whose educational roots lie in their breadth of practical experience.

People with expertise in machinery maintenance, industrial safety standards, business record systems, or personnel relocation procedures often possess a gold mine of valuable information that can be readily marketed to those in need of such services. Income tax, real estate, and computer consultants provide commercial advisory services in the same way that flying, dance, and charm instructors provide consumer services. Exhibits 3–5 and 3–6 illustrate a

---

EXHIBIT 3–5
TWENTY-FIVE SMALL MONEY-MAKING BUSINESSES THAT CAN BE OPERATED FROM YOUR HOME OR APARTMENT

1. Tutoring public or high school students
2. Measuring homeowners' electrical usage
3. Making distinctive house numbers
4. Shampooing carpets and rugs
5. Offering a car interior cleaning service
6. Providing a landscape design consulting service
7. Selling and servicing fire extinguishers
8. Starting a lawn and garden maintenance service
9. Producing mobiles from scrap plastic and metal
10. Becoming the neighborhood car insurance agent
11. Offering basement clean-out service
12. Restoring antique guns and swords
13. Teaching a foreign language in your home
14. Obtaining printing contracts for a commission
15. Making costume jewelry for sale worldwide
16. Producing fancy candles for Christmas trade.
17. Arranging artificial flower displays for all seasons
18. Painting stripes in parking lots and sports fields
19. Offering a bookkeeping service in your community
20. Starting a summer hobby school for children
21. Becoming an agent for a wallpaper manufacturer
22. Writing political speeches for local politicians
23. Designing book covers for local publishers
24. Starting home security checks for vacationers
25. Measuring sound and light intensity in industries

EXHIBIT 3–6
TYPICAL BUSINESS OPPORTUNITIES

In Advisory Services

- Financial counseling
- Relocation assistance service
- Automotive appraisals
- Credit investigations
- Office systems consulting
- Physical fitness coaching
- Urban planning advice
- Designing political campaigns
- Real estate evaluations
- Apartment-finding service
- Vacation planning advice
- Wedding organization consulting

In Physical Services

- Mobile truck wash
- Washroom sanitation
- Automotive waxing
- Landscape maintenance
- Ski repair and storage
- Window polishing
- Office renovations
- Furnace maintenance
- Boat and trailer repair
- Racquet restringing
- Refuse collection
- Furniture refinishing

---

number of typical business opportunities in the service sector.

The cost of advisory services is usually assessed on a per-job basis. An interior design service, for instance, may stipulate either a flat fee or an hourly rate. For service in the planning of a small group of offices, it might estimate a charge of $500 to $2,000. On a large business complex development, the firm may charge by the hour—say $25 to $100 per hour. Occasionally the designer may quote a price based on a sliding scale, such as 5 or 10 percent of construction or renovation costs.

Most advisory service sales are made on a person-to-person basis. Frequently many hours of discussion with a potential client are necessary before a suitable contract is reached. Such costs as the telephone, mailing, and travel expenses of personnel working for the advisory service firm must be negotiated. Advisory and physical service sales are rarely consummated at the first meeting with a client. The key ingredient in closing an advisory service order is *trust*. This trust factor can only be achieved through the establishment of a *proven reputation*. in turn, a good reputation is commonly seen to be the product of a successive record of *positive accomplishment* without moral blemish. Whereas the physical service firm is able to show an immediate tangible proof of performance, advisory services firms function in a somewhat grayer milieu and, as a result, need to accumulate a file of impeccable references.

In either the advisory or physical service industry, a company must operate as a marketing organization. The decision of a service organization to purchase new equipment to offer a different or improved line of service must be based on market research as exhaustive as any manufacturer would employ.

PRODUCT RESEARCH METHODS

New product and service ideas are most often generated from sales personnel whose up-front contact provides them with the best exposure to customer problems and requests. In larger industries, manufacturing and product development departments often submit new product ideas as well. Many of their suggestions take the form of innovations to existing products, packaging, and transportation methods. All new product ideas should be carefully analyzed before a proposal is decided to be worthy of implementation. Marketing research must be performed in order to fairly assess the merits of any proposal. The completion of most marketing research studies may require as little time as one week or as much as several years, depending on the nature, depth, and scope of the information required.

Companies cannot determine the right direction in which to move by guessing, averaging, or intuition. (See Exhibit 3–7.) If a product research study uncovers an unfavorable market climate, too little volume potential, too many competitors, and so on, the firm should turn its attention to another alternative. Yet, if a study indicates that a *viable market situation* exists (a growing need, few suppliers, or the like), the business should examine the anticipated risk, profit potential, and probable return on invested capital should they move ahead. In addition, the company must base its decision on projected cash flow estimates, resource utilization,

marketing benefits, and the probability of success. Some large marketing organizations apply empirical values to these standards, for use in a quantitative model, to determine the proposal's chances for success in relation to established development projects. The wise marketer, large or small, will examine the results of any proposal on a revenue-producing basis.

EXHIBIT 3–7
PRODUCT STRATEGY GRID
FOR PRODUCT ANALYSIS

	High Market Share	Low Market Share
High Growth Potential	Firm should carefully maintain marketing support programs and thwart competitive efforts Ideal = 50% of products offered or more	Firm should increase promotion and distribution to capitalize on growth opportunity. Ideal = 20% of products offered or more
Low Growth Potential	Firm should maximize selling prices to obtain best profits. Ideal = 20% of products offered or less	Firm should phase items out and replace them with products having better potential. Ideal = 10% of products offered or less

How to Use the Grid

Examine each of the firm's products or services according to the two criteria, the *growth potential* and *marketing share held* by the item. For an overall analysis of how the firm's existing product mix is doing, calculate the percentage of products that fall into each cell category. An organization with fifty percent or more of its products in a high-growth/high-market share situation is usually very strong. All organizations should attempt to minimize the number of low-growth/low-market share products in its total offering.

The Product Strategy Grid illustrated here is based on the Portfolio Matrix Concept developed by the Boston Consulting Group.

Rational analysis of customer/market requirements simplifies the seller's task in determining which products, which sizes, which styles, and which colors to offer. Rigid specifications are established from the required performance data gathered by marketing personnel. Designs are drawn up for approval, and prototypes are built for the product testing stage. At this point a manufacturing firm has likely spent about one half of the total investment amount that will be needed. Once again, a formal management decision must be made before a company becomes committed to customers and suppliers. A positive decision usually requires approval of the firm's president or owner before large capital expenditures are made.

EXHIBIT 3–8
MAJOR NORTH AMERICAN CENTERS
OF MERCHANDISE TRADE

Readers may wish to write to any of the following organizations for free information on upcoming trade shows. Attendance or participation at trade exhibitions usually results in considerable exposure to producers and distributors who may be of assistance.

Atlanta Trade Mart
240 Peachtree Street, N.W.
Suite 2200
Atlanta, Georgia 30303
404–688–8994

American Furniture Mart
American Mart Corp.
666 Lake Shore Drive
Chicago, Illinois 60611
312–787–4100

Chicago Trade Mart
Merchandise Mart Plaza
Room 830
Chicago, Illinois 60654
312–527–4141

Cleveland Merchandise Mart
420 Prospect Avenue
Cleveland, Ohio 44115
216–771–5566

Dallas Apparel Mart
2300 Stemmons Freeway
Dallas, Texas 75207
214–637–1970

Dallas Home Furnishings Mart
2000 Stemmons Freeway
Dallas, Texas 75207
214–748–6832

Dallas Trade Mart
2100 Stemmons Freeway
Dallas, Texas 75207
214–748–6832

Oak Lawn Plaza
1440 Oak Lawn Avenue
Dallas, Texas 75207
214–631–0600

Kansas City Trade Mart
250 Richards Road
Kansas City, Missouri
64116
816–842–5939

California Mart
110 E. 9th Street
Los Angeles, California
90015
213–620–0260

Los Angeles Home Furnishings Mart
1933 South Broadway
Los Angeles, California
90007
213–749–7911

Los Angeles Trade Mart
712 South Olive Street
Los Angeles, California
90014
213–622–7538

Pacific Design Center
8687 Melrose Avenue
Los Angeles, California
90069
213–657–0800

Miami Trade Mart
777 N.W. 72nd Avenue
Miami, Florida 33126
305–261–2900

Midwest Merchandise Mart
800 N. Washington Avenue
Minneapolis, Minnesota
55401
612–339–8788

New York Gift Center
225 Fifth Avenue
Room 123
New York, New York 10010
212–MU5–6377

New York Merchandise Mart
Madison Ave. and 26th
Street
New York, New York 10010
212–889–6540

Western Merchandise Mart
1355 Market Street
San Franciso, California
94103
415–552–2311

Northwest Home Furnishings Mart
121 Boren Avenue North
Seattle, Washington 98109
206–623–1510

Seattle Trade Mart
1932 First Avenue
Seattle, Washington 98101
206–622–3860

Montreal Place Bonaventure, Inc.
P.O. Box 1000
Place Bonaventure
Montreal, Quebec H5A 1G1
Canada
514–395–2233

Canadian National Exhibition
Toronto, Ontario
416–366–7551

Mexico Mart
Izazago No. 89
Mexico City, Mexico
585–0709

Once marketing management decides that a new product idea is valid and essential to the growth of the firm, a virtually irreversible process is set in motion. The firm will likely proceed to purchase all the necessary equipment, as well as to hire and train the needed personnel. Marketing departments will plan their marketing programs: package design, pricing strategy, promotion, distribution, and planned management of the product's life cycle. At the manufacturing stage, a final check is made of the production quality after machine setup has been completed—sometimes accomplished by sampling one or two firms with which the company has longstanding relations. Even minor technical problems should be caught and corrected before the product is introduced to the marketplace. An opening inventory, usually large enough to satisfy the forecasted first three months of demand, is prepared with especially stringent quality control measures in force. Even so, the aware marketer may opt to take a further precaution—a *careful physical inspection* of all units prior to their being sent to customers on their first orders. In many industries—particularly the electrical, automotive, pharmaceutical, food, and furniture trades— the reputation of the firm is challenged with the introduction of each new product. Many marketing organizations have policies whereby sales representatives are instructed to be at the customer's side when the first delivery of a new product is made.

Ownership of New Product Ideas

While you might generally assume that employees who have new product ideas will have a natural desire to see the item developed by their employers, they are usually under no such obligation unless they have previously assigned their invention rights to the company. Many large companies require employees to sign a document (or contract) at the time

47

of their hiring, waiving rights to discoveries and assigning ownership of all inventions, copyrights, and patents during the person's tenure with the firm, in return for some nominal consideration. Some firms use the suggestion box system to foster the flow of ideas; almost all companies offer tangible rewards for any ideas accepted and instituted. The use of cash awards is particularly successful in many business concerns to stimulate innovative and cost-saving ideas.

Product Standards

Hundreds of different performance standard tests and specifications can be found in almost every industry. The plastics industry, for example, is continually concerned with tensile strength, flame retardancy, and ultraviolet degradation. The paint industry must constantly attempt to upgrade their products scrubability, drying time, and coating coverage. Some of the more common types of performance criteria for various component and fabricating goods are as follows:

• Abrasion	• Mildew
• Impact	• Migration
• Tensile	• Permeation
• Chemical	• Reflection
• Ultraviolet	• Scratch
• Electrical	• Bounce
• Gloss	• Compression
• Friction	• Adhesion
• Slip	• Shrinkage
• Tear	• Evaporation
• Puncture	• Expansion
• Torque	• And so on
• Stretch	

Each manufacturing business is obliged to observe certain government- or industry-imposed standards of performance and longevity. The standards arrived at for a given product must also be established by an examination of the end-use demands to be placed on the item. Tennis balls, for example, must conform to five separate *standards of excellence* to receive United States Tennis Association (USTA) approval. The most signficant of these requires that balls dropped on concrete from a height of 100 inches must bounce between 53 and 58 inches. Each manufacturer must monitor its own production to ensure that standards are being maintained, in addition to submitting samples to the Association for testing.

Performance testing requirements become more onerous for products that may pose some threat to human life. Food, drug, toy, automobile, and appliance companies are especially susceptible to *rigorous inspection* due to their intimacy with each of our lives. The coloring used in a toy must have Food and Drug Administration approval to avoid endangering young children. Of equal concern are the bacteria levels in our food and the chemical additives used to control them. Virtually every new product has some aspect on which an attack might be launched. Radiation emissions, metal fatigue, and residual chemical transfers will remain topics of human concern for decades to come.

Today, a successful new product development is one not only that is acceptable to the marketplace, but also that conforms to the social values of society. Marketing personnel have a large responsibility in the analysis and disclosure of all pertinent information concerning the potential use of a product. A salesperson for an electrical wire company, for instance, should attempt to find out where switch-producing customers are selling their goods. The general-purpose wire being used in the switch device may be totally unsuitable for extreme temperature applications. An irate boat owner in Miami and an equally disturbed snowmobiler in Winnipeg may be the result.

In any discussion of product standards the central issue is not business ethics. Rather, it concerns a *heightened awareness* among marketing, manufacturing, and technical personnel, to the increasing necessity for diligent examinations of all the variables surrounding new product development decisions. The accountability for developing the general performance, safety, and durability standards for new products often falls on the shoulders of marketing personnel due to their close contact with potential users. In concert with the manufacturer's various technical specialists, the marketing person is often called upon to endorse a new product's physical, mechanical, chemical, or other properties. Distributors and retailers also play an important role in providing background information on buyers, purchase methods, packaging, transportation, and so on. The information in Exhibit 3–9 represents only a few of the typical areas of concern that might have to be researched and responded to in a new product development.

DETERMINING AN APPROPRIATE PRODUCT MIX

Any business enterprise should constantly review its product mix offering in relation to the needs and

EXHIBIT 3–9
CHECKLIST OF PRODUCT CHARACTERISTICS TO BE EVALUATED FOR PROPOSED NEW ARTICLES

Toxicity	Flaking	
Color Transfer	Impact Strength	
Cold Cracking	Displayability	
Flammability	Light Sensitivity	
Odor Transfer	Adhesive Properties	
Melting	Staining	
Drying Out	Stackability	
Fading	Color Selection	
Wicking	Static Electricity	
Fingerprinting	Ease of Use	
Unit Weight	Shock Resistance	
Unit Volume	Surface Texture	
Ease of Handling	Instructions	
Stress Cracking	Warnings	

wants of customers, competitive actions, and profitability. An infinite variety of alternatives are available to people responsible for determining the firm's product mix offering. The firm may, for example, attempt to assert itself as an industry leader in a limited number of product types, by expanding into a multiplicity of product variations. Alternatively, the same firm may take an entirely different approach, limiting the variety of any particular product offered, but embarking on a course of action that would facilitate the penetration of new markets, with products representing a radical departure from their normal business specialty.

Product Mix

The *product mix* of a company is the sum of its product offering, usually consisting of one or more product *lines*. *Product lines* are any group of closely related products whose differentiating characteristics relate to size, color, style, model, or performance standard. Since most companies want to offer more than one line of products, a firm manufacturing hand tools, for instance, will usually produce lines of screwdrivers, hammers, and pliers. A company

that has only one line of goods is referred to as a "single-line producer" or "middleman." Single-line manufacturers frequently offer a narrow, small product mix, such as a company that produces only plastic rulers.

The single-line approach depends to a great extent on the depth to which the producer has developed the line of goods. A firm that offers a single product line has chosen to *specialize their production* to satisfy the particular needs of one or more markets. When a company is the market leader in its field, it may be loathe to risk the possibility of diluting their marketing efforts through the introduction of additional products. Such a policy may be considered particularly prudent in situations where the organization possesses limited financial, production, marketing, or other resources. Hence, companies that offer single-line product mixes are normally able to involve themselves in more *intensive product development* programs, whereas firms with multiple-product line mixes must necessarily allocate their technical and other resources in a more conservative manner.

Expansion, Contraction, and Diversification

Product mix expansion involves the addition of one or more lines of goods. A marketer that expands its product mix does so to increase the sales penetration of the existing customer market, to protect its market against a competitive offering, or to facilitate entry into a new market sector.

Product mix *contraction* involves the deletion of one or more product lines from the firm's offering. A company that makes a decision to contract its product mix does so to withdraw from an unprofitable market, to reduce manufacturing costs, or to place increased emphasis on developing more profitable product lines. For example, the advent of an allocation or rationing economy brings about severe shortages of many process materials and component parts. To satisfy customer demands, a firm is often forced to eliminate those products in a line for which there is a material shortage; a concentrated manufacturing effort is then permitted on those items in the line for which there is no material shortage.

Product mix *diversification*, the seemingly natural desire of most aggressive marketing organizations, is the planned development of an extensive product offering to satisfy market needs and organizational goals. Yet profit-conscious marketing management must look at new product proposals objectively with respect to their real contribution to the organization. The criteria for product line diversification involve one or more of the following objectives:

- An increased rate of sales and profit growth
- Greater stability to seasonal fluctuations in many markets
- The desire to increase penetration of a profitable market

For example, a manufacturer of red and white striped soda straws might readily gain access to new customers if it is willing to produce *custom* color combinations for restaurant chains. Similarly, a producer of gasoline engines sold to snowmobile manufacturers may find new sales potential in the chain saw, cultivator, marine, or all-terrain vehicle industries.

Rarely, however, is a marketer able to achieve equal sales success in many diverse markets. Under normal circumstances, business concerns develop their strongest sales position by serving a limited number of market segments. Most wire and cable companies, though publicly acknowledging themselves to be in a competitive business, are essentially serving a few distinct markets with products whose only resemblance is in name and basic function. One wire and cable company serves major appliance manufacturers. Another finds its product specialization in selling high-tension power transmission cable to government and hydro agencies. A third firm focuses on residential wiring and electricians' supplies.

When a marketer feels sales are maximized in a given market, a search for other *accessible markets* commences. This search is usually confined initially to potential markets that require:

1. minimum modification of existing products and
2. only slight deviation from current distribution methods.

When these criteria are maintained, cost and risk factors remain low. Small companies, in particular, are not advised to deviate far afield from their primary business concern, in the pursuit of new product developments.

BRANDING IDENTITY

In a competitive market environment, sellers are continually attempting to show some differentiating characteristics in their products, so that consumers develop preferential behavior toward their goods over competitors'. The development of a distinctive brand is one way of evoking this preference. A *brand* can be described in any name, term, symbol, or design that serves to provide a special identity to a seller's goods. *Brand names* are groupings of words or letters that can be spoken. *Brand marks* are symbols or special lettering and colorings used to distinguish the goods. Both producers and retailers can establish branded goods if the marketing situation so warrants. Producers such as Nabisco, Quaker Oats, IBM, Citgo, Omni, and Turtle Wax all have brand names that most readers recognize. Retail organizations such as Sears, J.C. Penney, Fayes Drugs, Safeways, and A & P Stores also have established a number of house brands to exercise some degree of *market control*.

Generally speaking, the goodwill of a customer is seen to be directed towards the originator, not the reseller, of the brand goods. Sometimes the real differences in the physical attributes of two competing products are far less than the brand promotions would have the consumer believe. When a certain brand is able to support its claim to being truly unique in some aspect, the product will likely have a greater following of loyal consumers. *Brand allegiance* might be regarded as the key objective of most consumer goods marketers. Most consumers or industrial buyers feel confident in purchasing a known brand because they feel that they can count on a certain *consistency of quality*. A short summary of some of the reasons why any business may benefit from establishing a brand name program is as follows:

- Branding inhibits competitive price comparison analysis.
- Branding suggests large-scale acceptance of the goods.
- Branding provides a focal point in advertising programs.
- Branding reduces a middleman's substitution of other products.
- Branding implies a consistency of product quality.

House Brands

A small retail business may feel insecure in its first attempt at starting a house brand, because of the longstanding reputation of producer's brands that they have sold for some time. Yet by establishing their own brand names on goods that are not highly differentiated from the established best sellers, they

EXHIBIT 3–10
STEPS IN CONSUMERS' BRAND AWARENESS

1. Not aware of brand—virtually no chance of sale
2. Aware of brand—slight possibility of sale
3. Not considering brand—fair opportunity to sell
4. Considering brand—good odds on making sale
5. Brand is first choice—excellent prospects to sell

may be able to expand their gross profit margins with no loss in unit volume. For example, a small men's clothing store might be selling twelve dozen pairs of national name men's executive length socks each months with a $2-per-pair gross profit margin. By instituting a program of buying socks in a comparable quality from a local hosiery mill, with their store designed SOFTAYR labels affixed, gross margins of $3 might be attainable. So with little fanfare, the retail operation may be able to phase in its own brand and achieve an additional $100 or more revenue each month. Such product policy changes should be thought out with care. Obviously, if the retailer's clientele ask for specific *nationally advertised* brands of goods, the owner must take great care that no sales volume or customer patronage is lost due to inappropriate changes in the firm's product offerings.

Brand Protection

Protection against the use of brands by others is an issue with few absolutes. One difficulty is that businesses often attempt to establish brands that become common language in the public domain. But if the general public uses the brand word to describe a general class of goods or services, the brand name becomes *generic*. This is what has happened with the names aspirin, thermos, ginger ale, shredded wheat, cellophane, and nylon, all of which are now used widely. The brands Coke (Coca-Cola Company) and Kleenex (Kimberly–Clark Company) have become so popular in everyday language that their producers must wage an ongoing battle to maintain legal protection. Under common law, the ownership of any brand is based on the priority of use; the person who first uses the brand commercially is regarded fundamentally as the owner. In the United States, the Lanham Act provides protection for brand ownership by permitting individuals and companies to take formal steps to register their trademarks through the U.S. Patent Office (Washington). In Canada, similar protection is granted under Copyright and Trademark legislation; applications are processed by the Bureau of Intellectual Property,

Department of Consumer and Corporate Affairs (Ottawa).

EXHIBIT 3–11
HOW TO SELECT
A NEW PRODUCT NAME

- The name of a new product, service, or store should suggest some aspect of product qualities or customer benefits: Softouch, Coldspot, Fastrak, Lovecraft.
- The name should be easily pronounced and readily identified: Crest, Javex, Mustang, Selectric.
- The name should be distinct and imply success: Kopy-Kats, The Athlete's Foot, Trak-2, Musak.
- The name should not have any peculiar or distasteful translation in another language: Cue, Pantano, Wad.
- The name should be easily displayed on the product (not too long or difficult to read).
- If copyright or trademark protection is to be sought, the name should avoid the possibility of confusion with other similar well-known names: Hilton, Arise, Promise, Medalist, Disney.
- If copyright or trademark protection is to be sought, the name should not be purely descriptive: Custom Blended, White-N-Foamy.
- The name should not imply benefits that the product cannot fulfill: *Lemon* soap containing no lemon; *One Year Shine* when such a guarantee is hard to uphold; or *Buttery Bread* that has no butter in it.

Finding the perfect brand name can be an exasperating task for marketers. Sometimes the ideal answer can be found by listing all the perceived client benefits. A few of the most outstanding brand names developed include Bausch and Lomb's *Soflens*, Procter and Gamble's *Pampers*, and General Food's *Shake'n Bake*.

GENERIC (NO-NAME) PRODUCTS

We are all aware how accelerated levels of inflation have led to exaggerated grocery bills in recent years. As a result, consumer action groups and concerned citizens have actively sought out avenues to save money on good shopping, while maintaining nutritionally sound family diets. One result of these pressures has been the widespread introduction of unbranded generic foodstuffs in plain wrapper packaging. Generic products have some appeal to all consumer market segments, but they have been most strongly accepted by young, better educated, middle- and upper-income groups. No-name goods seem to have two major selling advantages for their purchasers—lower unit price and an apparent image of no frills, no additives.

Ostensibly, such food items as orange drink, canned peas, pork and beans, tomato juice, and toilet paper are supposed to be of the same "quality" as nationally branded goods. In practice, however, the manufacturers of many no-name products use them as outlets by which they can channel off-standard, flawed, experimental, and extended versions of their firstline goods. All such products must still conform to meeting government health and other regulations that may be in force. The chief difference lies in the producing firm's ability to maintain an *adequate margin of profit* while providing some minimum level of good taste, appearance, and performance for the consumer. As a general rule, the manufacturer of branded merchandise is unlikely to be supportive of no-name products because they do not permit for *brand differentiation* and the promise of ongoing consumer loyalty.

Most of the large food chains have joined forces with the consumer to exert pressure on grocery suppliers for increased availability of generic goods. Retail margins of profit are seldom affected, whether the product is a well known national brand or unknown generic. In fact, retail chainstores have a vested interest in seeing a greater proliferation of plain label packages because such a trend might increase their ability to control product costs. Such a trend would seem to undermine the price arguments of branded goods suppliers that certain brand items must cost more due to the large consumer following generated by a large-scale media program. Manufacturers would be required to submit their lowest price quotation on goods that they knew were of marginal quality, but that they were obligated to supply in order to remain in business. The *all-generic scenario* would see chain stores tendering bids for requirements like:

> Tomato juice—2-liter cans; minimum 18-percent real tomato content by weight; maximum 1-percent by weight of salt, stabilizers, colorants, and preservatives; 12 cans to a case; minimum order, 10,000 cases.

The challenge for national brand manufacturers is to *maintain* consumer demand for their products. Several alternatives are available to national branders:

1. The industry can *ignore* the intrusion of generic products and hope that its market losses will be minimal.
2. They may attempt to *increase advertising* expenditures in an attempt to maintain brand loyalty. One course of action might be directly competitive advertising that compares the performance or ingredients of various branded and unbranded goods.
3. National brand firms can actively *pursue the*

production and supply of generic products in order to hedge their bets.

The most interesting, and probably most likely, alternative is for national brand firms to attempt to squeeze generic producers into playing a smaller role. This strategy could be executed by reducing the price differential between branded and unbranded goods, so that most consumers would stick with the safety of the national brand. Such a strategy, combined with some obvious product improvements in taste and with some clever sales promotion offers, could severely limit the growth of generic products throughout the eighties.

PRODUCT FLEXIBILITY, AN ESSENTIAL

Companies tend to change their product mixes in response to economic conditions. They diversify their product lines extensively during periods of expansion, but this trend reverses itself as a new emphasis towards profitability on every item becomes apparent. As business conditions tighten, companies begin to examine their costs and to investigate methods to maintain or increase profitability. One obvious area open to examination is the extensive product line that features many nearly duplicate goods; product line simplification and a new awareness of profit on individual items become priority items. Some of the factors surrounding a company's decision to *contract* a product line include:

- Short production runs that necessitate expensive machine setup times
- Inventory stockpiling of slow-moving items contributing to high-cost burden
- Disproportionate advertising and sales expenses to maintain a minimum sales volume
- The advent of an allocation economy that prompts firms to focus on their most profitable items.

A useful economy measure which supports productivity is the creation of a number of *private brands*, items bearing the dealer's brand identity rather than the manufacturer's. In this way, unit volume objectives can be retained while eliminating much of the costs associated with extensive promotion and distribution. Sometimes *return on investment* (ROI) is difficult to calculate for a specific product or product line due to the difficulty in accurately allocating overhead, production, and marketing costs. In such cases, companies examine the profit contributions of certain products as opposed

EXHIBIT 3–12
SATELLITE PRODUCT DEVELOPMENT FOR EXPANSION-ORIENTED ORGANIZATIONS

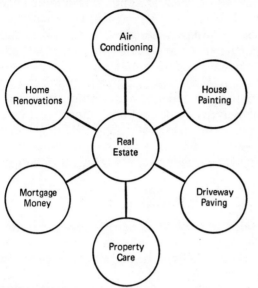

The Goal
Rapid, low-risk expanson of products and services offered by a real-estate firm.

The Concept
Expansion into areas that complement the central operations of the enterprise.

The Process
1. Brainstorming marketing personnel for ideas on new products that can be sold to existing customers.
2. Asking customers what additional products or services they would like to see the organization offer.
3. Selecting option with low investment requirements, large profit margins, and long-term growth potential.

to another product's contribution, both in light of the time and money spent in promoting the goods. Let's examine a few of the most common difficulties you are likely to face in making product decisions:

1. small volume
2. slow-selling goods
3. disproportionate product sales
4. changing market conditions
5. volatile markets

Small Volume
Short production runs are nightmares for manufacturing managers. Charged with the responsibility of producing consistent quality goods at the lowest possible costs, the short or small run can send costs skyrocketing. The production manager's complaint in this regard is a valid one, and each case must be reviewed separately to determine its profit situation. Some companies meet with their customers in an attempt to resolve the problem. If the marketer is able to negotiate a modified order-scheduling process with the client, the results are likely to benefit both parties. Sometimes the customer places fewer but much larger orders, or the marketer plans future order dates in advance with the customer. Another solution to the small order problem is simply to discourage the purchase of the item. Other variations of this same theme include the suspension of prepaid delivery on small shipments or an increase in client discount benefits on larger orders.

Slow-Selling Goods
Slow-moving products are often seen as unprofitable. Inventory costs are high. Purchasing authorities claim the average cost of inventorying goods for one year amounts to some 25 percent of the cost value of the merchandise. The elimination of slow-moving items saves valuable time, space, and frustration, and it frees large sums of money for other use. The amount of advertising and sales time spent on slow-moving or unprofitable lines is often not proportional to their contribution on a revenue or profit basis. Sometimes these goods represent the most difficult products in a line to sell. The same amount of sales time spent on other products may bring greater rewards with less effort.

Disproportionate Product Sales
In many firms, some 80 percent of sales revenue is derived from 20 percent of the product mix offered for sale. A naive logic would assume that 80 percent of the products should be eliminated because of their inferior contribution. Yet this viewpoint neglects to evaluate the less tangible attributes of minor selling goods. Every business has products that bring in steady but modest sales income. Such products have often passed their sales peaks, but they retain a loyal following of buyers unwilling to compromise their brand choice. Many of these goods indicate a high return on investment for the marketer. In all likelihood, product development and production machinery costs have been paid for. Sales and advertising expenses are minimal because, in a promotional sense, all sales potential has been exhausted. These humble revenue contributors may really represent the most profitable items in the firm's product offering.

Changing
Market Conditions

Some companies experience drastic fluctuations in sales because of the *seaonal nature* of the markets they serve. A marketer of marine hardware selling chrome-plated lamps, handles, horns, and trim receives orders in the early autumn for delivery throughout the winter months when boat producers are active. Spring and summer months often bring about a dramatic decline in order volume. To overcome this difficulty, the company might adopt a diversification strategy and incorporate in their product mix hardware for kitchen cabinets, automobiles, and doors. This strategy will assist the marketer in achieving a more *consistent flow of orders.*

Firms that incur *cyclical variations* in demand, that is, two- or three-year peaks and depressions in order volume, face a similar problem. Although the central difficulty might be traced to the nature of the firm's major markets, an effective remedial prescription often relies upon *increased product mix diversity.*

Volatile Markets

Firms involved in producing goods sold to *rapidly changing high-technology industries* must accept the consequences of serving volatile markets. Companies producing glass, metal, and plastic parts for the aerospace, automotive, and electronics industries are in this category. The quest for technological superiority results in continuing demands for stronger, more lightweight, longer-lasting, and cheaper materials, and it places great pressure for change and innovation on suppliers. Manufacturers are cautioned to examine the volume of business accepted from any one company or any market composed of similar companies. Under few circumstances should a seller allow any single customer's purchases to exceed 20 percent of total sales revenue. Should a firm lose an order contract, should the customer experience a strike, or should the competition come up with a startling technical innovation—the company relying heavily upon a single market could experience a severe revenue decline. Such firms should diversify their product lines and clientele to create a more stable, *predictable business climate.*

These five problems are common to marketers in both the consumer and industrial sectors, to retailers as well as to distributors and manufacturers. Larger, established organizations must take care in *charting* their various products, so that management is able to have a clear picture of each item's status in relation to the various markets and distribution channels served. Failure to do so results in inadequate attentiveness to product aging, withering sales, and opportunities to innovate faltering goods. The smaller firm, in particular a small retailer or wholesaler, must often take a more pragmatic approach to product management. Goods or services that have received reasonable promotional efforts (investments), and that show little indication of shorter-term profit contribution, should be deleted from the firm's offering in favor of items having a greater payoff potential.

TACTIC 3 SUMMARY

The third tactic to marketing success requires the business or nonprofit organization to develop, monitor, and sustain products and services appropriate to the needs of their various publics. Throughout the chapter many of the difficulties and pitfalls of product development were emphasized. Short production runs, product obsolescence, untimely introductions, and rapid changes in customer needs were highlighted as significant problems for marketers.

While obviously a well developed new product or service can generate *profitable sales volume* for the firm, inefficient product development programs will not only negate profits that might otherwise have been made, but significant losses can also be recorded. Sometimes such losses are buried in general marketing expenses and not easily identified. Ideally, you should take care to be well organized enough so that each new product development is budgeted for at the time of program approval and so that ongoing expenses for labor, materials, research, and testing are recorded and monitored with care.

Be aware of priorities and the organization's *limited resource capability.* A small firm that takes on too many product development projects courts the same dangers as a larger corporation with too few programs in effect. In the first case, the smaller firm is placing too great an emphasis on long-term product prospects and too little on market development. In the latter case, the corporation is sacrificing its future security for an emphasis on immediate gains from market sales. The message here is clear—a *balanced approach* must be achieved. As marketing personnel identify new potential opportunities, each must be evaluated according to its merit for inclusion in a formal product development program.

54

GOOD READING

Booz, Allen and Hamilton, Inc., *Management of New Products*. Chicago: Booz, Allen and Hamilton, Inc., 1964.

Goslin, L. N., *The Product Planning System*. Homewood, Ill. Richard D. Irwin, Inc., 1967.

Kotler, P., *Marketing Management: Analysis, Planning, and Control*. 3rd Ed. Englewood Cliffs, N.J. Prentice-Hall, Inc., 1976.

Luck, D. J., *Product Policy and Strategy*. Englewood Cliffs, N.J.: Prentice-Hall, Inc., 1972.

Spitz, A. E., ed., *Product Planning*. Princeton, N.J.: Averback Publishers, 1972.

Ulman, D. B., *New Product Programs*. New York: American Management Association, 1969.

Wasson, C. R., *Product Management*. St. Charles, Ill.: Challenge Books, 1971.

KEY REFERENCE ARTICLES

Buell, V. P., "The Changing Role of the Product Manager in Consumer Goods Companies," *Journal of Marketing*, July, 1975.

Cunningham, C. T. and C. J. Clarke, "The Product Management Function in Marketing," *European Journal of Business*, No. 2, 1975.

Drucker, Peter, "The Care and Feeding of Profitable Products," *Fortune*, March, 1964.

Dussenbury, W., "CPM for New Product Introductions," *Harvard Business Review*, 45, July–August, 1967.

Kratchman, S. H. et al, "Management's Decision to Discontinue a Product," *Journal of Accountancy*, June, 1975.

Miracle, G. E., "Product Characteristics and Marketing Strategy," *Journal of Marketing*, 29, January, 1965.

Webster, F. A., "A Long-Run Product Diversification Growth Model," *American Journal of Small Business*, April, 1977.

SUBSCRIPTION PERIODICALS WORTH READING

Harvard Business Review
Subscription Service
PO Box 9730
Greenwich, Connecticut 06835

Product Marketing
Med Economics Co.
680 Kinderkermack Road
Oradel, New Jersey 07647

Discount Merchandiser
Downe Communications
641 Lexington Avenue
New York, New York 10022

Marketeer Magazine
1602 East Glen Avenue
Peoria, Illinois 61614

Business Horizons
Indiana University
School of Business
Bloomington, Indiana 47401

New Product Newsletter
Box 191
Back Bay Annex
Boston, Massachusetts 02117

Industry's Products and News
Specom, Inc.
22543 Ventura Boulevard
Woodland Hills, California 91364

Marketing News
American Marketing Association
Suite 606
222 South Riverside Plaza
Chicago, Illinois 60606

FREE HOUSE ORGAN PUBLICATIONS CONTAINING NEW PRODUCT INFORMATION

Alcoa Aluminum Newsletter
Public Relations Department
Aluminum Co. of America
Pittsburg, Pennsylvania 15219

Goodchemco News
B.F. Goodrich Chemicals
6100 Oak Tree Boulevard
Cleveland, Ohio 44131

Maximizing Distribution Advantage

*There are all kinds of employers
wanting all sorts of servants
and all sorts of servants
wanting all kinds of employers
and they never seem to come together.*

CHARLES DICKENS
1812–1870
Martin Chuzzlewit
Chapter 36

The transaction of business between suppliers of goods or services and their customers requires the establishment of effective communication channels between them. Channels that help to facilitate the physical movement of goods are commonly referred to as part of the "delivery system." Members of such systems see themselves operating at the manufacturing, wholesaling, or retailing level. Whereas some business situations permit buyers and sellers to transact their affairs on a periodic basis, most serious marketing efforts require continuous effective communications with the marketplace. This point is the focus of the fourth tactic in the Marketing Tactics model.

CHANNEL SYSTEM CONSIDERATIONS

Marketing channels should be viewed as systems of communication that provide for the distribution of goods or services between producers and ultimate end-users. A *direct marketing channel* is one in which the manufacturer controls all marketing activities, and it normally consists of a single link with buyers. *Indirect marketing channels* are those in which marketing responsibilities are shared with two or more intermediate middlemen interposed between the manufacturer and customer. The firms that constitute a marketing channel for a manufacturer are termed *channel members*. A *channel system* indicates a marketing process that provides for the effective sale and movement of goods from producer to end-user.

The goal of a manufacturer is to design its channel system to provide for the most effective movements of goods to various markets. From a manufacturer's viewpoint, the channel process is seen as an external pipeline leading from its production line to a customer's business operation. In some petrochemical plants, for example, it is not uncommon to see a myriad of real overhead pipelines between two chemical processing plants, each feeding the other with vital feedstocks for conversion to, or inclusion in, finished products. In these channel systems, electronic metering devices monitor and record the daily flow of material, and centralized computers record and compute the metered data for accounting purposes. This sort of process illustrates the *ultimate channel system*. Administration is minimal. Sales revenues are guaranteed by long-term agreement.

The customer is assured of supply. Virtually no promotional expenses are required and competition has been effectively thwarted. No intermediate agent stands between seller and buyer to interfere with the direct distribution process.

Yet only in isolated circumstances is the process represented in this pure, simplified version. A producer may utilize a short, direct channel system for one market and a long, indirect system for another. The design, selection, and *management* of appropriate channel systems is a critical aspect of marketing.

The relative locations of the supplier and its markets—place channel factors—relate to the decisions concerning where, when, and by whom goods and services are to be offered for sale. The location of new manufacturing facilities (place factors) becomes quite important if a company sells direct to an industry through its own sales staff. As a company is located more distant from its major market, its freight costs go higher.

Transportation costs also expand as goods become bulky or heavy. The manufacturer of minute electronic components has a very low unit freight cost no matter where the plant is located. Such firms have the good fortune of being able to bundle thousands of products in a relatively small package, and they can avail themselves of air cargo shipping for rapid delivery service to worldwide customers. Producers of heavy industrial engines, however, have a much more serious physical distribution problem and are required to devote increased energy in this area. Sometimes the use of centralized *staging points* or regional distribution centers aid in the efficient movement of such goods.

Distribution Mix

Distribution mix is a term that denotes the combination of channel systems used by a marketer to promote and physically move goods to individual end-users or to markets differentiated by their geography, account type, or purchasing behavior. Sometimes a marketer finds advantages in using a combination of different distribution systems, such as a direct sale through retailers in one region while using sales agents and commercial wholesalers in another. Do not fall into the trap of adopting a rigid distribution policy when a more flexible approach might result in improved dividends.

You must also make sure that necessary customer service devices are in place which will support clients' easy attainment of ownership *(possession utility)*. Credit plans, technical backup, and free delivery are vital channel services that facilitate the smooth flow of products. Timing is also a critical factor. Manufacturers must preplan production so that sufficient product will be available at a time which coincides with dealer orders. At the retail level, careful attention must be given to factors such as seasonal buying habits, local consumer trends, and even changes in weather patterns that may bring about shifts in consumer demand.

Distribution Philosophies

Some of the well-accepted distribution strategies, which marketers should fully understand, are as follows (see also Exhibit 4–1):

1. Intensive distribution
2. Selective distribution
3. Exclusive distribution

EXHIBIT 4–1
DISTRIBUTION ANALYSIS OF A MARKET

1. What is the geographic size of the market?
2. What is the total market potential in units?
3. How many potential clients are to be served?
4. Where are buyers located within the geographic area?
5. When do buyers place orders?
6. What is the average order size or value?
7. How quickly must orders be delivered?
8. What type of package is best for buyers?
9. Who is the firm's major competition?
10. What services do competing suppliers offer?
11. What is their reputation with customers?
12. What client needs are not being met?
13. Are buyers purchasing from single or multiple sources?
14. What credit terms are offered?
15. What type of organization will serve the market best?
16. Are local dealers required to hold inventory?
17. Is the demand for product stable?
18. What potential for additional sales revenue exists?
19. What types of guarantees must be given to clients?
20. Are buyers willing to enter into long-term contracts?

Intensive Distribution. Many business supplies and consumer goods are marketed on a broad distribution basis. Intensive distribution is sometimes referred to as "extensive distribution" because the marketer seeks to have products sold through the maximum number of distributors or retailers, even though one or more other channel members may be calling on the same customer with the same products in this system. Items such as stationery, cleaning compounds, and confectionery are usually meant to be sold to as many reputable outlets as possible. In the consumer sector, convenience goods such as chewing gum, toiletries, tobacco products, and soft drinks are usually distributed to as many outlets as possible.

Intensive distribution can be detrimental in the marketing of some goods, due to the technical or secretive nature of the product, the possibility of price wars, the entrenchment of competitors, or the impracticability of more than one middleman in the area. Also, the onus for promotion of a product being distributed broadly rests with the manufacturer, as channel members normally tend to resist promotion for a product available to all their competitors.

Selective Distribution. In this system, a manufacturer desires broad market coverage without sacrificing channel quality. This goal is usually accomplished through the establishment of some minimum acceptable criteria relating to credit, facilities, the size of the sales force, and order quantities. Wholesalers or retailers are much more apt to engage in better promotion, carry more stock, and provide better service when they are confident of their relationships with the supplier. Sometimes relatively small but specialized middlemen can be highly effective, even if they are newly established and have limited working capital. Marketers of products such as cosmetics may opt for a selective distribution policy in order to retain a measure of distinctiveness. Some firms prefer the selective approach because they are able to exert greater control of resale prices. From a producer's standpoint, selective distribution has the obvious advantages of fewer sales calls, larger shipments, simplified communication, and greater flexibility.

Exclusive Distribution. Occasionally a manufacturer develops a product or service aimed at a highly specific segment of the market. Often a product directs itself at a selective high-income bracket of the consumer market, thereby eliminating the greater percentage of individuals from its potential market. In cases such as this, it would be a waste of time and money to attempt to woo the lower-income groups. The producer therefore establishes a channel system of exclusive distribution whereby the channel can concentrate on the market target. Often the exclusive channel, agreeing to inventory a large dollar volume of the producer's goods, requires some form of guarantee that the expenditures in time and money will not be neutralized by the entry of other channels carrying the same product. Exclusive dealerships or

distributorships often prohibit the middleman firm from handling competitive product lines, and they place greater requirements on the firm to provide technical or other services. Automobiles, major appliances, and farm machinery are commonly distributed through exclusive distribution channels.

Considerations in Establishing a Channel System

The result of a successful *place factor formula* is the efficient movement of goods or services to where they are needed. All decisions concerning place factors relate to the location of marketing facilities and the selection and use of marketing specialists, wholesalers, retailers, transportation carriers, and warehouse storage agencies. Managers must carefully select place elements because, once established, they are difficult and usually costly to change. Yet, because of the *innovative and rapidly changing nature of markets*, it is wise to approach the channel decisions relative to these factors with a flexible outlook. Manufacturers often use combinations of distribution channels in a given geographic area, such as a single city, state, or province, or they may use the same or different types when approaching the total national market.

The most effective distribution approach is to adopt a selling system that suits the particular character of an individual market area. For example, a large geographic region containing only a few large accounts is best served from the marketer's head office, whereas another region of similar size with a large number of diverse sales potential normally requires a custom-designed channel system.

Products of a highly technical nature or those requiring regular servicing are best handled directly by the manufacturer in order to give the customer direct service. Also, the manufacturer can better handle the disruptions in a customer's operations should some product failure occur. A product that tends to be sold to a specialized industry may be best sold through a wholesaling middleman who serves that industry with many products. A good reputation and knowledge of the market may provide more rapid acceptance of the product, and local warehousing facilities may result in a greater volume of sales than a more direct marketing approach by the industrialist. Experience indicates that the greatest sales volume and the highest degree of customer satisfaction are both usually obtained through the utilization of the producer's own sales personnel. But the considerations of travel time and other expenses involved in personal selling might make alternate channels in different situations more feasible. Ultimately, marketing executives should invoke either some form of value analysis or rational examination of pertinent factors in their channel system deliberations.

Time strategies are of paramount importance in launching a new product. A new camera, for example, should be introduced to dealers in July and August. In this way orders are processed and dealer inventories satisfied by early October in order to capitalize on Christmas buying.

Many firms' timing strategies involve longer time frames than others. The launching time of a new product must coincide with the time the market deems *appropriate for evaluation*. A producer of automotive lights that has developed a new high-intensity lamp for winter recreation vehicles must realize that a manufacturer's adoption of the product for snowmobile models will likely be introduced to the public one or two years hence.

The importance of effective delivery schedules as timing factor cannot be overemphasized. Manufacturers should run periodic checks on their distributor and dealer delivery systems to ensure that product movement is both efficient and in accord with client requirements. Warehouse and delivery personnel have, on occasion, been known to unconsciously favor handling certain goods and avoiding others because of bulk or weight factors. Such problems may continue undetected and seriously detract from an otherwise strong marketing program.

Direct Factory Sales

A business whose market *reach* is primarily confined to a local setting has little need for extensive distribution operations. Goods are manufactured and stocked in a factory warehouse adjoining the firm's production facilities. Company sales personnel solicit orders directly from accounts in their respective territories and fill them from the factory warehouse inventory. A company producing boilers located in an urban center, for example, uses direct factory sales. The firm has a small but highly specialized sales force calling upon architects, industrial engineers, construction companies, and manufacturing industries.

Such firms process orders in two broad categories: *standard specification goods*, which are filled from stock, and *custom orders*, which require a special production run. Custom orders are normal fare for companies supplying blow-molded (blister) packaging, such as plastic toothpaste, suntan lotion, shampoo, and food packaging.

Some of these custom producers utilize a system of dual distribution: They channel products through wholesale container houses that sell from stock, and they also maintain a technical sales force to solicit large custom orders from major food and cosmetic manufacturers.

Direct selling places the responsibility for promotion, inventory, and technical expertise on the manufacturer. Such responsibility provides the marketer with a *substantial degree of control*. Sometimes customers view the marketer who sells direct more confidently than those within the industry selling through intermediate channel members. A sales branch or an independent wholesaler is always able to pass the blame for an inventory shortage on a supposed failing of the manufacturer.

Sales representatives who sell for direct marketers usually require a greater degree of *technical expertise* those those selling for independent middlemen, because direct sales forces are product-specialized and because technical problem-solving is a priority. The manufacturer's sales representative is the communications vehicle for the transmission of company policy, product knowledge, and corporate image. If a sales representative establishes a reputation for technical competence, reliability, and cordiality, the client perceives the company in a similar context.

Direct factory-to-company sales permit the marketer to gain an intimate knowledge of their markets. When a competitor changes a price or introduces a new product, the marketer receives almost *instantaneous feedback* from the sales force or from a loyal account with which it shares a close rapport. Marketing research is made infinitely simpler and more reliable as a result of the close relations of *the buyer–seller association*. Artificial barriers to the realization of new product opportunities are minimized. In some instances, the client–marketing researcher relationship is as informal as that which exists with the firm's sales representative.

Regional Distribution Systems

Because specialized regional marketers often require more positive control of their markets due to the technical nature of their business offerings, the use of distributor middlemen offers them no real benefit in the long run. A distributor arrangement may result in initial sales penetration of a market but generates severe *communications strain* on the firm's resources. Businesses engaged in custom products of a technical nature have a sufficiently difficult time communicating requirements between the client, themselves, and subtrades, without the additional strain of communicating technical data through numerous middlemen.

So certain firms are able to justify the use of separate, company-owned branch sales and warehousing on the basis of cost savings. Most likely, such firms' early growth stages were completed with the help of strategically located distributors or sales agents. But, once the business reached a certain size, marketing management decided that a more specialized, concentrated effort was needed. This sort of effort can best be attained with the establishment of company-owned distribution. Hence most firms that employ their own sales force for direct sales through regional distribution centers are relatively large.

The decision to stock goods regionally is made only after a number of considerations are weighed:

1. The quality of service provided by previous channel systems must be reviewed. Any decline in earlier performance is viewed unsympathetically by customers, and it provides the competition with an important leverage point.
2. Cost analysis must indicate savings that can be passed on to clients in the form of lower prices. Increased costs may be justified only on the basis of increased sales potential or market shares.
3. Market evaluation of purchasing trends should be able to demonstrate that larger volume orders are attainable through the use of regional distribution centers rather than by alternate systems. Showroom promotions and technical clinics can provide valuable support to the sales force.
4. The suitability of alternative channel systems must be judged on the basis of their expected *contribution to the firm's long-germ objectives.* Company-owned distribution centers offer the marketer tighter control of promotion, transportation, and pricing.
5. The resources of the firm, including both financial and personnel aspects, must be taken into consideration. The new distribution center will require a core of experienced staff. Sufficient operating funds must be appropriated, in addition to capital investment requirements.

USING INDEPENDENT DISTRIBUTORS

Most distributors can be regarded as full-service merchant middlemen. The term "full service" indicates that the distributing firm assumes most of the marketing, credit, billing, collection, and inventory functions normally associated with the producer. This type of arrangement is exceptionally tidy for a manufacturer who finds it difficult to serve a particular market. Distributors are classified into three distinct categories: (1) general merchandise, (2) single-line, and (3) specialty types.

General Merchandise

A distributing firm whose product offering is extensive, including many unrelated lines of goods, is described as "general merchandise." Such firms view their entire business operation as a single profit center with virtually no limit on the type of goods they are willing to supply. General merchandise distributors are found most often in smaller communities, particularly those remote centers that are unable to support single-line and specialty middlemen.

A typical product mix offering by a general distributor might include: lubricants, work clothing, machinery, fire fighting devices, lighting products, truck parts, cleaning chemicals, work sleds, office supplies, electrical wiring, and plumbing components. The broad spectrum of product lines suggest the number of markets being served: government agencies, manufacturing plants, mining camps, energy utilities, schools, construction firms, electrical contractors, equipment repair concerns, and a miscellany of retail dealers.

Single-Line Distributor

This sort of distributor offers a product mix of closely related goods, and usually serves fewer end markets. Such a firm, for example, offers a complete line of plumbing supplies including pipe, fittings, valves, and joining materials. Most frequently, the single-line distributor has developed its product offering to correspond to a *vertical market segment,* such as construction, mining, aeronautics, or electrical engineering.

Single-line distributors operate in a well defined trading area. For example, a firm might establish itself to supply shoe component materials to a particular region's population of boot, slipper, and moccasin manufacturers. Their trading area might be limited to a fifty-square-mile-rectangle and some forty to sixty potential accounts.

Specialty Distributor

This distributor is an intensive marketer of a highly selective product offering that is usually one fragment of a complete line of goods. Firms in this category market a technical product that requires considerable knowledge in a scientific field. Whereas a single-line distributor might market a wide range of common industrial gases—such as propane, oxygen, and acetylene—the specialty distributor would typically be concerned only with the supply of an exotic gas such as krypton.

Specialty distributorships are most common in the densely populated area of the United States and Western Europe due to the sizable market potential. As a general rule, the establishment of a specialty distributorship to supply a singular product, is uneconomical in most sparsely populated regions. Yet just because you find a number of major industrial factories around a given community, you may not assume that an independent distributor operation might satisfy some unfulfilled market need. Many large manufacturing concerns represent little more than *assembly operations*, purchasing their component parts and fabricating materials in large volume from well established supply sources outside the country, on a direct importation basis.

As a general rule, specialty distributors enjoy a *larger margin* of gross profit than single-line or general merchandise middlemen, usually on account of the significantly greater amount of market development and customer service effort necessary. For example, a distributor or ultra-sensitive flow metering and analysis devices for chemical processing industries is rarely able to conclude a sale in two or three customer visits—the way a general merchandise distributor obtains orders for uniforms, fluorescent lamps, or paint. The attainment of a single specialty product involves perhaps ten customer visits, twenty letters, and a dozen or more telephone conversations.

The specialty distributor must develop a high degree of technical competence. Some specialty middlemen have been known to become more expert in product application than the principals they represent. For example, a producer of specialty metals must be most knowledgeable in the physical, electrical, and chemical properties of their product, in addition to the demands and constraints that may be placed on the material in a finished form. Many metals are suitable for the exterior trim of office buildings, but some will perform better under conditions of salt air and extreme temperature fluctuations than others. So the specialty metals distributor might develop a *particular expertise* in recommending trim specification to architects and builders. In a sense, such distributors offer less prejudicial advice, considering the fact that their firms probably per-

form a similar middleman function for several different producers.

DISTRIBUTION AGREEMENTS

The full-service distributor establishes the business close to a market that can be readily served with the product lines required. Most distributors tend to emphasize the offering of goods with characteristically high turnover and repeat sales. General merchandise distributors rarely achieve the degree of sales penetration that single-line or specialty distributors enjoy. This condition results from the greater dilution of marketing effort with their more diverse product offering.

In a true sense, then, distributors must have a full grasp of the marketing concept in order to survive in today's competitive markets. They must be able to research markets and interpret data to ascertain if a group of customers have sufficient needs and wants that are not being filled. The element of *sufficiency* is a critical one to business, as the decision to proceed with an expanded manufacturing or distribution program hinges on management's appraisal of a market's profit potential.

So the manufacturers, or *principals* as they are called, should place the responsibility for the sale of their goods to a specific geographic or customer market in the hands of a competent distributor. Correspondingly, the manufacturer should allow the distributor a substantial discount from the list price to provide a margin of profit in payment of services provided. Most distributors thus become authorized representatives of the producer whose products they sell.

In broad terms, each party receives several key benefits from the association. Simply stated, the producer receives effective sales representation and local stocking facilities, while the distributor is granted a *protected trading sector* and an adequate profit margin.

The protection of the distributor falls into two categories: (1) revenue and (2) representation.

Revenue Protection
This sort of protection takes effect when the client wants to bypass the distributor. Orders and inquiries received directly by the principal are relayed back to the distributor as an accepted practice or unwritten contract. Occasionally, a particularly large or disgruntled end-user/customer will demand to bypass the producer's distributor and attempt to conduct business on a direct basis. The client's threat to

discontinue purchasing the product is frequently good enough reason for the principal to comply with such a request. Under this circumstance, it is not uncommon for the producer to negotiate a settlement with the distributor affected by the policy change. This entails, for example, a monthly rebate to the distributor equal to a part of the margin of profit that it would normally achieve on the customer's purchases. In this way, a substantial confidence is established between the producer and distributor. Obviously, had the distributor not been demonstrating satisfactory performance, such an offer would not be made, and in all probability the producer would seek to terminate the representation agreement.

Distributors also seek revenue protection from the drastic loss of business due to the manufacturer's unilateral and uncompetitive price increases or from stock shortages or poor quality.

Representation Protection

This type of protection refers to the distributor's requirement to be assured that it is the sole authorized agent of the principal, selling to an agreed-upon market. The distributor must also be assured that no other agents of the principal will be permitted to engage in selling, promotional, or bidding activities outside their respective market franchises.

When a manufacturer enters into negotiations for representation with a distributor, the distributor must be made aware of any prior agreements, contractual or understood, that concern its marketing activity. *House accounts* for example, are particularly sensitive in the producer–distributor dialogue. A house account is a captive customer of the manufacturer, one that is exempt from consideration as a client of the firm's distributors, wholesalers, or agents. For example, most manufacturers of paint, fasteners, locks, and adhesives, for instance, consider major automotive producers to be house accounts, despite their extensive channels of distribution to other industries. A customer is classed as a house account because of a longstanding personal relationship, a special requirement for close technical liaison, a reciprocal trading arrangement, or the client's volume importance to the marketer.

Another assurance sought by distributors is that of equal position. The term *position*, in this particular context, describes the attainment of a certain level of trade or middleman status. If one distributor has a greater position than others in relation to the producer, that distributor would then have greater *lever-

age to buy at the lowest cost, with the best delivery, and the longest credit terms.

Categories of position are far from absolute. Although a distributor that receives a 25-percent discount can be said to hold a better position with a manufacturer than a much smaller jobber receiving only 15 percent, the distinctions become far more obscure when comparing the position of a number of distributors only. A new distributor may feel confident in its position that provides a 30-percent margin and net forty-five days credit terms. The firm would be horrified to learn, however, that rival distributors were enjoying 35-percent margins, freight allowances, and 90-day credit terms.

EXHIBIT 4–2
METHODS OF COOPERATION
AMONG SMALL FIRMS THAT CAN RESULT
IN INCREASED PROFITABILITY

- Joint investment in specialized or general-purpose equipment that the individual firm might not be able to afford or utilize fully on its own.
- Shared knowledge about changes in consumer purchasing trends, credit plans, effective display techniques, transportation rates, and government legislation.
- Cooperative promotional ventures such as the shared funding of the cost of bringing a special entertainment event to a shopping area or dividing the cost of booth space at a trade show.
- Combined purchasing or distribution programs for the purpose of achieving economies of scale in ordering from a single supplier or transporting goods.
- Trading market research information or sharing mailing lists of high potential customers saves time and money.
- Sharing costs associated with establishing a joint toll-free 800 number for direct ordering.
- Firms that publish a catalog of their merchandise should arrange for reciprocal swap of advertisements with other catalog producers to expand their sales potential.

Characteristics of a
Suitable Agreement

Such are the dynamics of a competitive business world. The distributor operation possesses a *highly fluid marketing character*, one that demands the dropping of slow-moving products, the addition of new high-potential items, and a continuous search for a better position. Exhibit 4–3 lists a number of the comprehensive services offered by a well established distributor.

The manufacturer and distributor must have a unique relationship involving *complementary objectives* and *mutual trust*. Typically, to consider a

EXHIBIT 4–3
CHECKLIST OF VITAL DISTRIBUTOR FUNCTIONS

Use this checklist as a guide to evaluating a prospective distributor. You may wish to use a simple checkmark (√) or numerical score (0–5) to indicate performance on each item.

	Function	
1	Intimately familiar with target market	
2	Markets complementary lines of goods	
3	Has sufficient and active sales force	
4	Is able to provide suitable storage	
5	Shows desire to take on the line	
6	Has established customer relationships	
7	Capable of ordering in bulk	
8	Credit checks out satisfactory	
9	Maintains accurate inventories	
10	Reputation for honest dealing	
11	Willing to engage in market research	
12	Enjoys co-op promotion programs	

The use of checklists for evaluation purposes helps make the assessment process more objective. You may wish to change some of the items shown above to suit your particular needs.

distributor a favorable partner to a producer, the distributor:

1. must be located in key market area,
2. must have a good reputation for fair dealing and excellent service,
3. must have a good credit rating,
4. must have adequate warehouse and showroom space,
5. must be a marketing organization with an effective sales force,
6. must have product lines that supplement or complement the manufacturer's so that a sale from another line makes it desirable or necessary for the buyer to purchase one of the marketer's products, and

7. must be willing to cooperate fully in promoting the line, including sharing costs in some cases.

The producer who finds a distributor with all these attributes is fortunate indeed. If most marketers were to analyze their present distributor arrangements, they would find that perhaps only several of these conditions are in effect.

MANUFACTURERS' SALES AGENTS

Often called "the last of a dying breed," sales agents are a dynamic part of marketing. They are independent sales representatives who have chosen a career of representing one or more firms with lines of related products in return for a predetermined sales commission, usually 10 percent. The process for becoming a sales agent commonly follows a familiar pattern. A person involved in marketing in a certain field becomes disenchanted with compensation, the petty corporate politics, or the promotion of an incompetent as an immediate superior. As a result, the individual sets out to become established as an independent agent representing one or more producers (sometimes distributors) in a given market region.

The term "agent" means "to be a representative of." For example, travel agents act as representatives for airlines and hotels, while entertainment agents represent either the entertainers or the theater. The most attractive aspect of acting as an independent manufacturer's agent is the opportunity for earning a substantial income without a large capital investment. For the experienced salesperson, one who is intimately familiar with one or more markets, the risk factor can be minimal. Longstanding buyer–seller relationships often grow into close personal attachments, providing a natural vehicle for future sales as an independent agent.

Although the typical sales agency firm is small, usually one to ten employees, the range of goods handled is often extensive. A sales agent operating alone, on 10-percent commission, will probably lose interest in a product line that does not generate $25,000 to $50,000 of yearly sales revenue. A three-person agency, with a higher overhead, might set the cut-off point much higher.

The individual who decides to become a manufacturer's representative should know one or more markets well. Obtaining permission to represent various firms in a given field is often a relatively

EXHIBIT 4–4
ILLUSTRATIVE LETTER USED TO
FIND A DISTRIBUTOR

Pat Wright, Marketing Manager
Marshall Electronics Corp.   November 10, 1982
2500 Allen Ave.
San Diego, California

Dear Mr. Wright,

   The purpose of this letter is to introduce our company
so that you might wish to consider distribution possibilities
for the state of California. We are the nation's leading
manufacturers of CRT filters which have broad application in
the computer, telecommunications and office automation industries.

   As you may be aware, our previous distributor in your state
has entered into a joint venture with a foreign firm to produce
goods similar to the ones they sold on our behalf. I have
enclosed technical brochures on several of our most popular
products for your examination.

   Please feel free to give me a call should you be
interested in pursuing this further.

Yours truly,

Jay Walker
President

Box 1000, Centerville, Maryland 02511

Marshall Gift Distributors

April 16, 1984

Ronald Morgan
Marketing Director
Abby Cutlery Products
500 Smith Street
Ottawa, Canada

Dear Mr. Morgan,

Recently I read an advertisement outlining your products in COOKINGWARE Magazine. The purpose of this letter is to inquire whether you presently have satisfactory distribution in our state.

Our company has only been established for two years but can boast of some 300 active retail accounts on our books. We represent White Oaks China, MICA Candles and Heritage Placemats. We feel your line of quality cutlery would compliment our range of gift products.

If you feel you would like to discuss this matter further please write or call me at your convenience.

Yours sincerely,

Wanda James
Marketing Assistant

1 Center Ave., Little Lake, Florida 01162

EXHIBIT 4–6
CLIENT SERVICES OFFERED BY A DISTRIBUTOR

- Purchasing
- Inventorying
- Repackaging
- Delivery
- Drop Shipping
- Showroom
- Direct Mail
- Educational Seminars
- Technical Support
- Sampling
- Credit
- Billing
- Market research
- Co-op Advertising
- Personal Selling
- Trade-Show Participation

Examine distributor operations thoroughly. Caution is the order of the day when you are looking at the possibility of appointing a distributor to market your goods or services. Many of the apparent services offered by a distributor firm may carry additional hidden charges. Some distributors follow a policy of attempting to sign on as many new representation agreements as possible just to "try out" the goods in their product mix. Be careful to negotiate clear agreements on returned, damaged, and lost merchandise in your discussions. A distributor who is willing to take on your product without the requirement for adequate technical training of their sales force should fall under suspicion.

simple matter, especially for established sales representatives with *sound reputations.* If permanent representation has not been established in the area, the manufacturer may provide enthusiastic support. If the agent sells goods, the firm will honor the commission arrangement. If no goods are sold, agents receive no return on their substantial investment of time and effort. So, when total compensation is based on orders, the aspiring sales agent must have the capability of moving goods or face zero income. Exhibit 4–7 lays out an examination of a typical order transaction involving a manufacturer's sales agent.

The most common use of sales agents is by the furniture manufacturing industry. Agents sell goods to retail and wholesale levels and earn between 5 and 15 percent of the net revenue of the sales made. Often, the firms that sell to the furniture manufacturers use sales agents as well. These companies supply foam, springs, buttons, fabrics, castors, packaging, and labeling for furniture products. Many other sales of consumer goods are made to wholesale

EXHIBIT 4–7
EXAMINATION OF A TYPICAL ORDER TRANSACTION

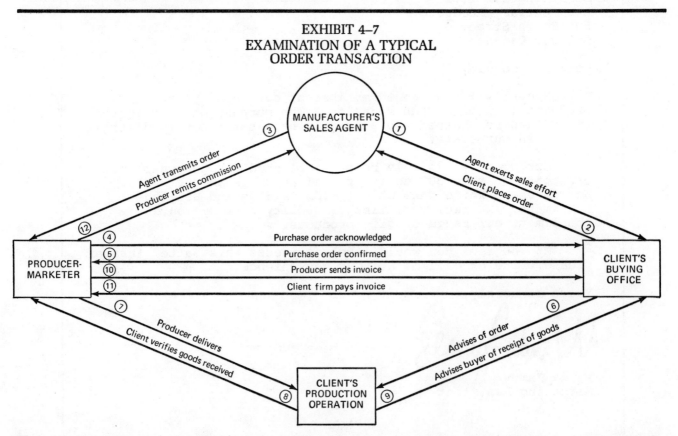

The schematic model shown above is designed to illustrate the various processes involved in obtaining an order through the use of a manufacturer's sales agent. Activities in completing the order have been numbered so the reader can follow the normal sequence of events.

and retail levels by sales agents, particularly those located in areas distant to the home market.

Sales agents are particularly helpful to *seasonal* businesses, the bulk of whose sales are made during a three- or four-month period of the year. Products such as boats and accessories, baling twine, Christmas ornaments, camping gear, portable power saws, and fire fighting equipment are examples. Companies producing such goods find the costs of maintaining a salaried selling force excessive. On the other hand, it is doubtful if good personnel could be retained permanently if they were paid on a straight commission basis. The advantages of employing established sales agents becomes obvious. The company pays out only *selling expenses* (commission) when sales are made, thereby saving considerable fixed costs. And, since the agents should handle related lines of goods, they have ready access to the proper purchasing contacts. Of equal importance is the agent's willingness to accept the seasonal aspect of the principal's goods and to balance their product offerings with more stable, year-round goods.

Some firms produce goods for which demand is highly specialized but for which the volume and revenue value do not economically permit the maintenance of a permanent sales force. The economics become especially troublesome if the customers are spread out over a large geographical area. The appointment of sales agents to handle goods in a given region is more profitable than other means of distribution. Examples of businesses in this category include automatic car-washing devices, people-conveying sidewalks, institutional furniture, safety and antipollution devices.

Pros and Cons of Using Sales Agents

The sales agent often holds a *competitive advantage* over a stocking distributor. First, the agent is able to justify carrying a manufacturer's single product line and to apportion a considerable amount of time to its promotion. Full-service merchant distributors seek comprehensive product lines from major firms in order to purchase bulk quantities on a consistent basis. Producers seeking a considerable amount of market development work for a single product are not likely to have their wishes fulfilled in dealing with the large merchant middleman. The second, and most obvious, advantage to the manufacturer is the agent's lower margin of profit. As a general rule, a sales agent's services cost a manufacturer only one-third that of a distributor. Finally, many middlemen are able to shield the identity of ultimate customers from their manufacturing principals. This is an undesirable situation for many producers who feel they will lose the pulse of their markets. Sales agents provide no such artificial barriers and permit the producer to make contact with their customers at any time.

Some negative factors of the sales agent concept cannot be entirely overlooked. The sales agent is philosophically adverse to conducting *missionary work in virgin markets*. Even the suggested payment for time spent in this endeavor is not a sufficient inducement for most agents. A typical agency has a total of two or three hundred established accounts in three or four product or market fields. The agency's aim, naturally, is ultimately to sell these accounts all the products they purchase. The launching of a new product that results in doubling the number of account is less attractive than one that doubles the business of existing clients. More accounts means more travel, more bookwork, and higher costs, whereas increased sales penetration in existing markets *provides greater profit opportunities*.

Another drawback of agents in the mind of producers is the loss of control over sales activities. A firm that employs its own selling force is able to give direction, evaluate performance, and correct deviance. Activities carried out by a sales agent are inevitably those that result in the *most immediate return* of a commission check. A manufacturer that passes on sales leads to an agent has no way to ensure follow-up. The agent has no interest in becoming involved in a client–producer credit or billing problem unless it directly threatens the future business prospects of a major account. So many sales managers are hesitant to use agents because no enforcement mechanism exists, short of dismissing the agent, to guarantee that sales policies and procedures are carried out.

Also, agents are usually free to carry lines of goods from competing manufacturers. Producers are sometimes faced with hiring an agent who is well established with a competitive product or who is less established and handling no competitive goods. The agent that handles similar products from two or more principals will select those items from each manufacturer's lines that offer the greatest sales promise. In this way, the agent develops the ideal product mix offering. Occasionally a producer finds an agent concentrating on selling only one item of a large number of the firm's products.

Many accounts desire to purchase a product in small quantities, as they need them. In such a case, a producer will find the costs of physical distribution prohibitive. Satisfying this type of need falls into the domain of stocking distributors, which purchase goods in truckload or carload lots and which are prepared to fill small-order requirements in their limited trading area. Some manufacturers are able to overcome the small order issue by establishing minimum order values with their agents.

THE COSTS
OF DISTRIBUTION

The Typical
Small Distributor

A small distributor handles twenty or thirty product lines, whereas larger resellers may carry over five hundred. The typical small distributor has four to eight sales representatives, revenues of $2 million to $5 million dollars annually, and inventory value representing some 50 percent of its total investment. So the distributor relies heavily on the ability and contacts of its sales force to generate orders.

Of course, the problem with carrying a large number of items is the cost of maintaining an inventory of slow-moving goods. Small distributors or retailers, with few but fast-moving lines, are often able to record higher earnings on fewer sales than the larger reselling firms, whose greater sales revenue results from less frequent orders on a much wider range of goods. Some 40 to 60 percent of its product offering is likely to be what is commonly referred to as "branded merchandise," products whose reputation and identity are well known. Most orders consist of three or more products with a total invoice value of $50 to $500. Exceptions to this range are in the distribution of steel and machinery products where the average invoice approaches $1,000.

Small Orders

Yet a paradoxical aspect of wholesaling is the determination of most distributors to overcome the very reason for their existence, namely, small orders. Perhaps the most important justification of middlemen is their ability to combine the individually small requirements of many end-users, and translate them into an economically palatable form for themselves and for manufacturers. But the high costs associated with small orders force resellers to practice a discriminatory pricing policy. Administratively speaking, the average fixed cost attributed to distributor order processing has been estimated at $6 to $8 for each order handled, regardless of size. So on a comparative basis, costs attributable to process-

ing a $20 order are viewed as unreasonably high, whereas the same cost on a $2,000 order is incidental. Clearly understandable is why many distributors regard *average order size* and *number of small orders* as relevant performance indicators.

A certain conflict of philosophy results from this attitude, however. Many buyers tend to consider the distributor an extension of their materials storage complex. Small manufacturers, in particular, engage in little long-term planning and are prone to run out of stock, even on goods essential to their production. The developing firm is loathe to tie up its capital in process materials and in the facilities for storage, preferring to focus its resources on maintaining a salable finished goods inventory. In a freely *competitive market situation*, a distributor that pursues an aggressive policy to increase order size, places itself at a disadvantage. Other competing resellers are most willing to take over the unwanted business.

Several avenues aid the distributor in alleviating the small order issue. Order processing costs can be reduced by simplifying internal procedures—for example, by eliminating unnecessary paperwork, by automating manual tasks, or by increasing work throughput without a corresponding increase in staff or hardware. Externally, and in a more positive context, the distributor can offer to pay delivery charges or advance more liberal credit terms.

In practice, however, the traditional inducement to increase order size is the size of the trade discount or price structure based on single order unit volume. For example, an industry accustomed to a standard 15-percent discount off list price might typically find the distributor altering its policy to permit only a 10-percent discount on a single order whose list price value is less than $500. Similarly, if a distributor's previous policy was to set a single net selling price on an article regardless of the number ordered, that distributor might be attracted to unit volume price scaling, which provides a distinct price for select order quantity levels. For example, for an order of one to five units, the unit price might be $32; for six to ten units, $28.50; and so on. Suffice it to say that there is no absolute rule regarding the handling of minimum orders, and each individual reseller must establish a policy in light of the firm's unique economic and competitive situation.

Company-Owned Versus
Independent Distributors

Management should *carefully weigh the anticipated costs* of company-owned distribution facilities in comparison with those associated with moving goods through other means. In general, the costs of establishing company-owned distribution often exceed the costs of using independent distributors during the first five years.

Inventory. The costs of inventory must be examined on a regular basis. Research has shown that the costs associated with stocking goods amount to some 25 percent of the purchase value of the firm's average maintained inventory. A firm's average inventory value is commonly calculated by adding together the value of total inventory on hand at the end of the third and that of ninth months of the fiscal year, and then dividing the sum by two. By taking one quarter of this value, the firm has an approximation of its annual costs for carrying inventory.

Another consideration of stock maintenance is the proportionality of inventory to forecasted and actual sales. Exhibit 4–8 shows how a firm can find itself in a poorly coordinated inventory situation. Quite obviously, the company is *overstocked* in products 3 through 10 and *understocked* in products 1 and 2. Surprisingly, however, an examination of many otherwise successful firms would reveal a glaring shortcoming in the ability to match goods on hand with sales needs. Larger firms that find themselves in this situation should look for some form of communications difficulties between sales, manufacturing, and distribution management personnel. In a small firm, such as a local retailer of stereo equipment, more often than not the central problem lies in the overly optimistic or pessimistic bias of the store manager.

EXHIBIT 4–8
ILLUSTRATION OF IMBALANCED INVENTORY SYSTEM (RESULTING IN LOST REVENUES)

Products	Percentage of Inventory	Percentage of Sales
1 and 2	20	75
3, 4, and 5	30	15
6 to 10 inclusive	50	10
TOTALS 10 products	100	100

Sometimes excessive goods are coercively pushed through a channel system by the manufacturer who has found itself in an overstocked situation. An unsuspecting sales branch, distributor, company-owned distribution center, or even retail outlet occasionally find they are the recipients of a supplier's inventory problem. The converse also occurs. Dis-

tribution centers or other channel partners must sometimes accept the wrath of irate customers, when a supplier continually *short-ships* the requested merchandise. If the client is able to obtain goods from an alternate material source, or substitute them with some other product, the supplier incurs *lost sales.* All marketers should keep current records of their lost sales.

Credit and Invoicing. The responsibility for credit and invoicing is another factor in any distribution system. Considerable client ill will can be generated by inadequate communication between the local sales outlet and the head office, if the latter is controlling invoicing, customer accounts, and credit checking. Customers often require to know the status of their accounts and their credit. Needless to say, such information should be made readily accessible, regardless of the distribution method used. Small businesses that find themselves being overloaded with manual recordkeeping should investigate leasing an automated word processing or minicomputer system that can relieve much of the pressures in maintaining sales accounts, inventories, payrolls, and other time-consuming activities.

Overdue Accounts. One additional factor complicating business' small order problems is the difficulty in collecting overdue accounts. The credit limits and terms given to customers depend on the individual firm's policies that have previously been laid down. Yet if the company's credit terms are vague, the invoicing system slack, and the collection controls nonexistent, accounts receivable tie up too much of the firm's investment.

Exhibit 4–9 provides an illustration of *aging analysis* of accounts receivable. In this particular example, some 30 percent of the firm's receivables are over the 30-day normal credit period. This aging

EXHIBIT 4–9
ILLUSTRATION OF ACCOUNTS RECEIVABLE AGING ANALYSIS

	Dollars	Percentages
Receivables outstanding less than 30 days	$5,600	70%
Receivables outstanding 30 to 60 days	1,440	18
Receivables outstanding over 60 days	960	12
TOTALS	$8,000	100%

process is accomplished quite simply by listing all the business's individual accounts receivable at the end of each week or month. At the regular sales or staff meeting, an updated aging of receivables can be presented, so that company personnel have the opportunity to comment on the relative "quality" of the overdue account, as well as to make known any extenuating circumstances.

If a credit and collection system is well managed, the level of a firm's accounts receivable should vary directly with sales volume. The number of accounts overdue and the average value of each overdue account are significant measurements of this proportion. Another important test is to calculate the *average collection period*. To calculate this figure, simply multiply the amount of accounts receivable at the end of a year by 365 days, and then divide the result by the total sales for the year. For example, a firm whose year-end accounts receivable are $5,500 and that had annual sales of $75,000 would record an average collection period of 27 days:

$$\frac{\$5,500}{\$75,000} \times 365 = 26.76$$

The prompt payment of accounts that are due is as much a responsibility of marketing as it is of an accounting department. Tender loving care must be taken to ensure that the seller's credit policies are observed with minimum order disruption or offense to customers. A client whose payment record has been unreliable may be suffering the same difficulties with their own accounts. Sometimes the amount of credit granted a customer has remained unchanged over a period of time while its purchases have increased substantially. Almost all credit problems can be negotiated amicably, and marketing personnel have a vested interest in maintaining the continued loyalty of the client.

Allocating Distribution Costs

If an organization establishes its own regional sales branches, some of the distribution costs may be allocated proportionately among the various sales representatives operating from the place of business. "Allocation" does not mean that individual salespersons must personally bear a portion of the expenses, but rather that a percentage is charged against the income of each sales territory. For example, a typical sales branch might employ three or four salespeople, two secretaries, an order processor, and several warehouse staff. For budget and accounting purposes,

EXHIBIT 4–10
DISTRIBUTION ANALYSIS GRID

A	B
Strawberry Flavor Crystals	Orange Flavor Crystals
67,882 Units Sold	58,962 Units Sold
70% of Available Distribution Achieved	42% of Available Distribution Achieved
970 Units Sold per Point of Distribution	1,404 Units Sold per Point of Distribution

This simple grid provides a quick method to determine which products are really the best-selling items. In this example, the strawberry flavor crystals appear to be the best-selling item. But, if you take into consideration the extent of distribution each product enjoys, it becomes obvious that more units of orange flavor are sold for each percentage point of distribution coverage. This is calculated by dividing the 42 figure into the 58,962 units sold.

The information gained from such an analysis can be valuable in several ways. First, stores that have been resisting stocking orange flavor crystals can be shown that they are missing the opportunity to make sales. Second, the data enables marketers to project estimated unit sales from various clients whose total share of market is known. A firm that had 12 percent of the grocery market should have sales of 11,640 units of strawberry (12 × 970) and 16,848 units of orange (12 × 1,404).

each of the sales territories is charged equally with an amount representing its proportionate share of total costs incurred from office rent, equipment leases, utility and maintenance costs, and expenses attributable to wages and warehouse space. In addition, each sales territory must absorb a variety of variable expenses including sales commissions, entertainment, traveling, and other expenses related to automobile use.

The established branch office staff ratio that has proven acceptable for most industrial concerns is *three outside sales staff supported by two administrative employees*. Constant multiples of this ratio—such as twelve salespeople and eight administrators—are generally considered an acceptable staffing guideline. Naturally, the exact ratio depends on the volume of business and the degree of responsibility of the sales branch.

One vital support staff member is the inside salesperson whose basic responsibilities typically include:

- Telephone order-taking
- Supplying technical, order status, or supply information
- Researching economical transportation methods to various points in the sales branch territory
- Maintaining sales records and inventory data
- Selecting and shipping required samples to customers and potential customers

The three external sales representatives are responsible for customer sales and technical service of the company's products to select markets. One of the three usually assumes a dual role as branch manager and has the added responsibilities of assuring that the branch's overall operations including personnel, communications, and physical facilities are running at peak efficiency.

CONSUMER GOODS DISTRIBUTION

All of us are ultimate consumers because we purchase a wide range of goods and services to satisfy some personal need or want. *Merchandise*, the term used to describe products destined for consumption by ultimate consumers, is divided into three broad categories:

1. Convenience
2. Specialty
3. Shopping goods

Each classification indicates a specific type of buyer behavior.

Convenience or Consumption Goods

These are goods that ultimate consumers desire to purchase with a minimum of thought and effort. In reality, such products are largely *undifferentiated*, although they are often promoted heavily on the basis of branding. Chewing gum, tobacco, film, magazines, toothpaste, razor blades, and ballpoint pens are typical convenience goods. *Extensive distribution* and *national advertising* are the two most significant factors determining the success of a convenience product. Almost all convenience goods are regarded as nondurables, that is, they are purchased for nearly immediate consumption and are unlikely to provide their owners with any long-term asset or redemptive value. Most convenience goods are subject to a high degree of *impulse buying behavior* by the consumer, in this regard the importance of brand recognition becomes vital for the marketer. Extensive distribution through all types of retail outlets is necessary to provide the required consumer exposure to convenience items.

Shopping Goods

This type of merchandise refers to goods that consumers are willing to shop for; they are ready to compare the prices and quality offerings of several manufacturers. Typical shopping goods are furniture, clothing, housewares, garden tools, automotive accessories, and cameras. A higher unit cost, a less frequent need, and a longer investment life contribute to the consumer's more rational purchasing behavior. Shopping goods are often the subject of a *planned buying decision*, although on occasion they result from an immediate desire to satisfy some social or psychological need.

The distribution of shopping goods is an important marketing consideration, but *channel selection* is viewed somewhat more critically than for convenience merchandise. The availability of a marketer's goods must be designed so that the consumer does not perceive the merchandise as "common" and yet so that it does not place an undue strain on the consumer to travel long distances to find them. The stores offering shopping goods are always fewer than those offering convenience goods, and the costs of displaying the shopping goods are always higher. A most significant consideration is that shopping goods are highly subject to *credit buying*.

Specialty Goods

These are items for which consumers are willing to make a special effort to locate in order to satisfy a particular need. Most consumers of specialty goods will *postpone a purchase rather than accept a substitute product*. Often, the consumer is willing to travel a considerable distance, or abide by special seller constraints, such as open hours, in order to achieve satisfaction. These goods feature a high degree of differentiation, high unit cost, and limited selection.

Retail outlets catering to the specialty goods trade tend to be small and to follow the boutique model. Inventories and selection are purposely kept low in order to provide consumers with a *one-of-a-kind impression* of the product offering. Customer service is often exaggerated, and specialty stores seek to build a *selective clientele* by catering to their particular taste. Direct mail promotion, tasteful displays, and *cultured store environments* are integral parts of specialty goods promotion.

RETAILING TRENDS

In recent years, marketers have witnessed a large-scale rationalization process taking place, as consumers continue to adjust their lifestyle philosophies toward a *simpler-is-better ethic*. The many causes of this lifestyle change have their roots in the years of anti-Vietnam war resistance, Watergate, severe energy shortages, the devalued purchasing power of the dollar, and the health and other threats posed by burgeoning technology. Young, college-educated people in particular have been among the most perceptive and vocal opponents of high-pressured, harried lifestyles. This trend has been reflected in the rapid growth of natural pursuits such as backpacking, jogging, meditation, crafts, and so on.

Major changes in the consumer's spending patterns on food have also occurred. Sugar, egg, flour, and butter purchases waned as consumer health consciousness heightened. With both marriage partners working, home cooking declined as fast-food restaurant purchases soared. Convenience food preparations have continued to grow on a straight-line trend while microwave ovens established themselves as a kitchen necessity.

The following are a few of the key lifestyle projections signficantly affecting consumer purchasing behavior in coming years:

- Greater leisure time will support continued growth in sports and recreation equipment, resorts, and services.
- Increasing female labor participation rates will accelerate consumers' disposble income levels, thus providing for greater savings and spending.
- A revolution in electronics technology will bring about dozens of new technical innovations in home computers, video recording equipment, cameras, home appliances, and automobiles.
- Smaller family and nonfamily household units will demand many products in smaller sizes and lighter weights.
- An older, more knowledgeable consumer will place greater deamnds on sellers for technical and performance information about their goods or services.

Beyond these generalities, many marketing observers see an even greater emphasis placed on *personal pleasure, optimum convenience,* and *consumptive satisfaction* in the lifestyles of consumers leading up to the twenty-first century. Look for new merchandising wrinkles like national or *international catalog shopping* by toll-free telephone with universal credit card charge privileges. Even the weekly grocery shopping ritual may undergo a broad-scale change of direction toward *phone-and-deliver* service to alleviate the hassles of parking and check-outs. Far wider use of television as a *shopping medium* is predicted. Tests have indicated high consumer acceptance of shop-by-TV systems, most of which use the telephone for communication with an order-answering service or computer.

Franchising

A well-established distribution technique which has merit in virtually all forms of business is the licensing of a successful *marketing process* to others for a fee. Such distribution agreements usually call for a continuing relationship between the parent company, or franchisor, and the individual outlet, or franchisee. In consideration for the fee(s) paid, the franchisee obtains full access to the franchisor's knowledge, image, trademark, name, and technical support. Automotive dealerships and service stations are the most common forms of franchise in North America (over 250,000 franchisees). Perhaps the most well-known franchise operations are McDonald's Family Restaurants, Howard Johnson's, A&W, Diary Queen, Weight Watchers, Holiday Inn, and Dunkin' Donuts. The same franchising process that has helped the rapid expansion of the fast-food and hotel industries is now spreading to all sectors of business. Some of the newest inroads made by franchise marketing include auto parts, beauty salons, instant printing, employment agencies, income tax services, and daycare centers.

The strength of a franchise agreement lies in the mutual competence of the partners involved. Most franchisors have a proven manufacturing or marketing formula but lack the large financial resources required to expand on their own. Independent franchisees often have sufficient capital for a local operation and the needed entrepreneurial motivation to implement the franchise program. With the franchisor's assured expertise, a franchisee usually finds it simpler and less expensive getting started than going it alone.

Most franchisors have established franchisee criteria which must be met by qualified applicants. The foremost of these standards is always the ability to pay the initial rights fee. This can range from as little

EXHIBIT 4–11
PROFILE OF RETAIL STORE MIX
(SUITABLE FOR AN URBAN COMMUNITY
OF 100,000 POPULATION)

The bracketed figures indicate the estimated average size of population needed to support one retail operation of that type.

Antique/Secondhand	14	(7,000)	Groceries	50	(2,000)
Automobiles (new and used)	17	(6,000)	Hairdressers	75	(13,000)
Bakeries	10	(10,000)	Hardware	25	(4,000)
Bicycles	2	(50,000)	Jewelry	15	(6,500)
Books	14	(7,000)	Laundries	16	(6,000)
Building Supplies	24	(5,000)	Men's Wear	12	(8,403)
Butchers	9	(10,000)	Optical	7	(15,000)
Cameras	2	(50,000)	Painters	30	(3,300)
Candy	15	(6,500)	Pet Shops	1	(80,000)
Chain Groceries	13	(7,500)	Pharmacies	24	(4,000)
Children's Wear	16	(6,000)	Plumbers	32	(3,000)
Dairy Products	3	(30,000)	Real Estate	65	(1,500)
Department Stores	13	(7,000)	Records	10	(10,000)
Dry Cleaners	19	(5,000)	Restaurants	100	(1,000)
Electrical Appliances	19	(5,000)	Service Stations	100	(1,000)
Floor Coverings	25	(4,000)	Shoe Repair	12	(8,000)
Florists	10	(9,527)	Shoes	20	(5,000)
Fruit Markets	6	(16,000)	Sports Equipment	20	(5,000)
Fuel Dealers	14	(7,000)	Stationery	5	(20,000)
Furniture	20	(5,000)	Tobacco	6	(16,000)
Furriers	3	(35,000)	Variety	7	(14,000)
Gifts	7	(14,000)	Women's Wear	24	(4,247)
			Shopping Centers	5	(20,000)

Source: Most of this data was compiled by comparing and averaging the number of various retail businesses in communities of approximately the same size in upper New York State and Southeastern Ontario. Some figures are based on Bureau of the Census and U.S. Department of Commerce data. The data is presented only for comparative purposes.

as a few thousand to several million dollars, depending upon the notoriety of the franchisor and the scope of the franchise agreement. In addition to the fee payment capability of the applicant, the franchisor normally conducts an in-depth analysis of the prospective franchisee's background, skills, and experience.

The greatest benefits to be derived from franchising a successful marketing operation include the rapid deployment of subsidiary organizations and the immediate realization of cash. The wise marketer will draw up an agreement which is clearly nonexclusive, enables enforcement of standards of service, and provides for residual income based upon franchisee purchases, sales, and profits. A characteristic of most good franchise arrangements is the requirement that the franchisee undergo intensive training in the franchisor's operations. In this way the franchisor is able to maintain some form of quality control standards which will help ensure that an adequate level of service is provided by the franchisee.

The Box Store

In terms of conventional retail store trends, two emerging concepts appear to be capturing marketers' attention. Both have been forecast to become dominant retail themes through to the end of the eighties. The first of these trends is the so-called *box store,* a neighborhood convenience outlet devoted to offering a limited range of generic (no-name) products. The concept, first introduced in France, was based upon the *triple-four principle:* four hundred square meters (four thousand square feet), four-hundred products, and four cash registers. These stores are designed to reflect an image of austerity whereby all visible aspects of high cost services are eliminated. Little product choice, virtually no advertising panels, self-bagging, and spartan store interiors are the order of the day.

The high degree of product standardization, along with the lack of significant brand differentiation exemplified by the orthodox box store, has led some observers to suggest that we may be entering a new antimarketing age of *consumer resentment*. Such a new ethic, in favor of *absolute rationality* in consumer purchasing, rejects the traditional merchandising model exemplified by lavish store interiors and the unending proliferation of product styles, colors, sizes, and other influences.

The Super-Combo Store

The second major retailing trend projected to grow in popularity is the super-combo store, a large 50–80,000 square foot outlet with about one-half the space devoted to food and the other half to nonfood merchandise. In theory, the operations of such an outlet are supposed to generate profit only on the nonfood items; the food section is seen primarily as a drawing card to attract people to the store center. Food products can be presented in a generic, bulk, box-store format, while nonfood merchandise might be better received by the public in a more traditional private and commercial brand format.

Fast-Food Stores

The need for retailing *adaptability* is best exemplified in the fast-food industry. The 1980s will see tremendous growth in the trend to eat away from home. Working women, young childless couples, and "empty-nest" mature adults will seek the convenience, adventure, and social experience of new eating places as never before. Look for growth in the concept of fast-food "clusters," which feature a number of diverse limited menu establishments catering to a variety of target groups and tastes. Particularly evident will be large growth in the European deli-type restaurant where people can experiment with the unfamiliar. Watch for a gradual moving away from the staple beef-based burger products to new meat-salad-bun combinations. A more discriminating consumer will gravitate to those establishments offering *clean*, *colorful*, and *comfortable* surroundings. All-you-can-eat salad bars and alcoholic beverage licenses will become nearly mandatory requirements for successful operations, which aim for $1,000 to $1,500 in annual sales volume per square foot of restaurant space. Despite inflationary pressures, economic forecasts project a high degree of consumer willingness to expend funds on personally satisfying indulgences, adventurous experiences, and convenience.

To be sure, the field of retail merchandising is entering a dynamic period of change. The most profitable retail businesses of the future will recognize the growth in specific market segments (older age, singles, and the like), identify their particular needs, and provide an appropriate *satisfying response*.

TACTIC 4 SUMMARY

When a marketing organization secures a comprehensive field representation and product delivery system that assures effective access to its total sales potential, it maximizes its distribution advantage. This objective is rarely achieved due to the continuous changes resulting from new product applications, additional market opportunities, and competitive initiatives.

A channel of distribution should be viewed as a total system in which the component parts should work in cooperative harmony. Sellers must take care in establishing the degree of control they wish to exert over the marketing of the firm's products. Such control is usually determined by the degree of directness built into a channel system. A high degree of control is achieved when the marketer sells directly to end-users; a low degree of control results when it utilizes a number of agents, distributors, local jobbers, and other intermediaries. Most important is the appropriate application of intensive, selective, or exclusive distribution. A faulty decision that results in the use of the improper basic distribution approach invites marketing failure.

The fourth Tactic for Marketing Profits emphasized the vital need of using marketing intermediaries who are able to reach and serve sales prospects quickly and efficiently. Selection of the best channel members to serve various target groups represents only half the distribution decision. The ongoing management of marketing activities that supports optimum distribution performance is the more demanding and far-reaching part of the decision. Never expect that merely "setting up" a new distribution link will bring about automatic sales success. Continuous communication, stimulating incentives, technical training, and close coordination of promotional programs are esential elements of any distribution support package.

Finally, there is the need for a careful monitoring of the costs of distribution, along with the effects of discounts, inventories, and accounts receivable on distribution profits. This point leads us into the topic of product prices, the focus of the fifth Tactic for Marketing Profits.

SOME KEY ASSOCIATIONS

Manufacturers Agents National Association
2021 Business Center Drive
Box 16878
Irvine, California 94406

Small Business Administration
Washington, D.C. 20416

National Retail Merchants Association
100 West 31st Street
New York, New York 10001

American Retail Federation
1616 H Street, N.W.
Washington, D.C. 20416

Retail Council of Canada
74 Victoria Street
Toronto, Ontario

American Management Association
135 West 5th Street
New York, New York 10020

National Federation of Independent Businesses
150 West 20th Avenue
San Mateo, California 94402

National Small Business Administration
301 1225 15th Street, N.W.
Washington, D.C. 20036

Mass Retailer Institute
570 Seventh Avenue
New York, New York 10020

National Venture Capital Assoc.
10 South LaSalle Street
Chicago, Illinois 60603

NEWSLETTERS AND DIRECTORIES OF INTEREST

Mainly Marketing
Schoolmaker Associates
P O Box 339
Coram, New York 11727

Diversified Directory of Manufacturers Representatives
663 Fifth Avenue
New York, New York 10022

Marketing Network
Business Science Associates
2837 B Baycrest Drive
Ottawa K1V7P6 Canada

International Wealth Success
I-W.S., Inc.
Box 186
Merrick, NY 11566

SUBSCRIPTION PERIODICALS

Buyers Purchasing Digest
20 Community Place
Morristown, New Jersey 07960

Industrial Distribution
Morgan–Grampian, Inc.
205 E. 42nd Street
New York, New York 10017

Industrial Distributor News
Ames Publishing
1 West Olney Avenue
Philadelphia, Pennsylvania 19120

Purchasing Magazine
Cahners Publishing
270 St. Paul Street
Denver, Colorado 80206

Channels Magazine
1725 K Street, N.W.
Washington, D.C. 20006

Retailer and Marketing News
Box 57194
Dallas, Texas 75207

Merchandising Magazine
Billboard Publications
1 Astor Plaza
New York, New York 10036

Canadian Distributor and Retailer
Suite 501
1118 St. Catherine Street
Montreal, Quebec

Pricing Goods and Services to Sell

*Everything is worth
What its purchasor
Will pay for it.*

PUBLILIUS SYRUS
Circa 42 B.C.
Maxim 847

The development of new revenue-producing products requires an understanding of the price at which customers will be willing to buy the product. If all other elements are perfect, errors in the calculation of the selling price, product cost, and anticipated profit margin can lead a marketing program into a financially disastrous situation. Simply stated, the best selling price for any product is the price that attracts a profitable order volume and that permits the selling firm to provide all the necessary customer service and support to achieve a satisfied clientele. Such a price is determined largely through the influences of customer needs, competitive product offerings, and the selling firm's internal costs. All pricing objectives are in some way related to the volume of goods and net profit expectations of the marketer.

SIGNIFICANT INFLUENCES ON PRICING DECISIONS

There can be little doubt that pricing is one of the most powerful promotional tools available to business. The image of most businesses as *quality mar-keters* or *price-cutters* is an important factor in the treatment and respect shown to the company in the marketplace.

Contrary to what might be your first inclination, most people are wary of firms that operate mainly on a *price-first* basis. Such firms tend to place other aspects of a marketing program—such as consistent quality, customer service, product warranties, and so on—at a distinctly lower level of importance. At the opposite end of the spectrum are firms that concern themselves primarily with nonprice competition. A gift shop, for example, usually finds success in stressing exquisite or unique selection, friendly and helpful sales staff, special gift wrapping, and so on, rather than low prices or discounts.

The advent of two-income families has boosted average household incomes to a point where price scrutiny is the most critical buying factor only under select circumstances. While on supermarket trips the family remains on a vital price-watch, but while dining at the local burger or pizza outlet they often overlook price as an essential purchase factor. Do not overlook the fact that consumers may evaluate product design and quality, store location, staff friendliness, and facilities as more important considerations affecting the *buy/no-buy decision* than the price of the goods or services provided.

Another critical assessment business persons should make is whether their particular businesses are more susceptible to promotional elasticity or price elasticity. For example, if the firm allocates $1,000 for advertising in a given period of time, will this expenditure bring a larger or smaller increase in volume than if it was made through a price reduction in the goods or services for sale?

Influence on Prices

Few *fixed prices* are apparent in the North American marketplace. With the exception of some government regulated services, such as the post office or residential utilities, most consumer and commercial prices are free to fluctuate according to prevailing market forces. The principal variables affecting prices of products or services may be summarized as follows:

- The degree of competitive price pressure
- The availability of sufficient supply
- Seasonal or cyclical changes in demand
- The costs of distribution
- The products life cycle stage
- Changes in costs of production
- Prevailing economic conditions
- Customer services provided by the seller
- The amount of promotion done
- The market's buying power

The list might easily be expanded by incorporating items concerned with taxation, import tariffs, transportation, inventory costs, and so on. The list represents only a basic inventory of the major consumer and commercial factors. While one factor may be influencing the marketer or merchandiser to increase a given selling price, another factor may be working in an opposite direction.

To a considerable degree, then, any price placed on an article or service is a *compromise* situation, one arrived at by the proverbial balancing act, trading off one price-influencing factor against another. Sellers must constantly ask themselves if the market will perceive a change in price as being commensurate with the current situation. Consumers may be willing to pay a several-dollar higher price for a record album if they are aware there is a limited supply. But music dealers who must pass on $2 higher price on a new shipment of albums, because

of increased plastic resin costs, may have a much more difficult selling task. So the *awareness level* of the marketplace can be said to have a very signficant effect on the acceptance of a price increase.

Another important factor affecting acceptance of upward price change is the *general context* or method by which the change is instituted. Sellers who are able, and who make an attempt, to justify a price change to customers, will encounter less sales resistance than those who unilaterally try to raise a price without explanation.

MARKET CONTROL PRESSURES ON PRICE

Small businesses tend to see themselves as participants in perfectly competitive markets. *Perfect competition* is commonly described as a free market situation that incorporates sufficient buyers and sellers to ensure that no single firm dominates the market. Small manufacturing and middlemen businesses focus a greater emphasis on being price competitive with market rivals than do large enterprises.

To be more realistic, the marketplace is rarely a tableau of perfect competition. A more precise description would be that it is an environment of *monopolistic competition*, lying somewhere between the extremes of monopoly and perfect competition. A single firm in a market sometimes dominates the supply of a particular product or service. If a firm has a near monopoly on available business, the market being sold to often appears impenetrable by other sellers. The controlled market is, in effect, one that has been sealed off by a number of powerful advantages: truly unique products, low selling prices, vast production capacity, long-term contracts, reciprocal trade arrangements, or the exclusive use of patent protection.

The telephone industry is often cited as a monopoly situation because of a single firm's apparent control of certain markets. In fact, telephone firms are usually regarded as *regulated monopolies*, due to their reliance on government approval of a variety of business activities including (rate) price changes.

Large corporations receive the greatest adverse publicity regarding their alleged monopolization of markets. The assumption, of course, is that monopolies of all types are bad for business and are in conflict with the free enterprise concept. This is not necessarily true. The ultimate goal of every marketer is to find and totally satisfy a market whose needs are not being fulfilled. In so doing, any seller naturally seeks to corner all the business of that market, to the exclusion of competitive firms. Marketers attempt to achieve this goal by developing the best possible response to market needs—quality products, good customer services, reasonable prices, and effective promotions.

Price leadership can be found in most market conditions, but it is most simply identified in markets with standardized product output. A price leader is normally the firm that controls the highest share of the market and has the technical and financial resources to withstand price wars. Such a firm is able to match the prices of any would-be competitors, even if the action requires the absorption of financial losses. The price leader holds a position of such dominance that it is able to raise or lower its prices with the assurance that other sellers will follow. Price leadership can be found in local or national markets, with manufactured goods or labor-intensive services, and at the wholesale or retail level.

Some market situations cause artificially low pricing due to the overwhelming purchasing power of only one or two major buyers. Certain government departments are the sole customer for a product. Military hardware, nuclear fuels, exotic chemicals, specialized computer equipment, and transportation equipment are only a few examples of goods for which a single government department or large industry may be the sole buyer.

Markets containing few potential customers create more difficult marketing conditions than when numerous buyers are available. The marketing firm should develop a separate comprehensive marketing plan, custom-tailored for the particular needs of each of the major potential clients. Where few potential customers exist, the marketer must take care not to offer preferential treatment to one over another. A seller who agrees to sell a certain custom product, such as disposable food dishes to one airline, may alienate other airline firms. Major buyers whose price, delivery, or other demands are unreasonable may cause one or more sellers into concessions that injure their market reputation and ultimately result in the firm's demise as a credible supply source.

PRICE CHANGE
EFFECTS ON DEMAND

Purchasers of commodity products—whether they be industrial goods such as cement, steel, coal, and chemicals, or consumer goods such as shoes, milk,

sugar, ground beef, or plastic garbage bags—sometimes react in an unorthodox fashion to price changes. Under normal circumstances, an increase in the price of a product brings a decrease in the quantity demanded. If the price is decreased, the quantity demanded is usually increased. If, for instance, the price decrease is 5 percent, and the quantity demanded increased by 10 percent, the demand would be termed *elastic*. An increase in the demanded quantity of only 3 percent against a price decrease of 5 percent would be termed *inelastic*. Small business operators can test out the demand elasticity of various products in their stores by selectively increasing and decreasing the prices of specified goods. If accurate inventory and sales records are maintained, managers can evaluate the degree of order increase or decrease over a fixed period. In so doing, small business persons learn which of the firm's goods can be increased in price to attain greater profits.

Buyers may attempt to outwit marketers by demonstrating an unusual reaction to a price change sometimes called *initial counter-price elasticity*. Usually a short-lived occurrence, the increase in the price of a product brings a growth in the quantity demanded. A seller who decreases the price on a commodity product may be met with a decline in the quantity demanded for the item. The reason is related to the purchasing psychology behind these kinds of readily available goods. An increase in the price of these products acts as a signal to the buyer of the beginning of a higher price trend. Buyers place larger orders in an effort to maintain a low average cost. Naturally, the degree to which customers stockpile depends on their usage, storage facilities, and financial capabilities. In the same respect, a decrease in the price of a commodity product may result in a significant decline in orders because of the same trend *implications*. accurate sales forecasting and an intimate understanding of client purchasing behavior helps protect the marketer from injury through misguided price changes.

PRICING OBJECTIVES
AND POLICIES

Most businesses attempt to establish some form of orderly pricing system for their goods or services. The purpose of such a system is an attempt to treat all customers in an equitable fashion. To accomplish this end, marketers must first take into consideration the nature of the product (custom or standard), the type of demand (order size and frequency), and the firm's marketing policies and objectives. Another important consideration, sometimes overlooked, is the psychological impact of product pricing. Take a look at Exhibit 5–1, which outlines some of these factors.

EXHIBIT 5–1
PSYCHOLOGICAL FACTORS IN PRICE SETTING

1. The quality of a product in some situations is interpreted by customers by the *level* of the item's price.
2. Some customer groups shy away from purchasing a product where no *printed* price schedule is available.
3. An emphasis on the *monthly* cost of purchasing an expensive item often results in greater sales than in emphasizing total selling price.
4. Most buyers expect to pay even *round-number* prices for prestigeous items and *odd* prices for commonly available goods.
5. The greater the number of meaningful *customer benefits* that the seller can convey about a given product, generally the less will be the price resistance.

A price schedule can be designed to accomplish many different goals, such as an increase in the number of clients or, in contrast, a decrease in the number of small orders received. Pricing objectives, then, are an integral part of the firm's overall marketing plan. Once the firm has established its general pricing policies, specific performance objectives and tactics can be developed to ensure their achievement.

The following general pricing aims represent operational guidelines that each member of the marketing team should attempt to follow:

- The organization will maintain the highest price possible on a product, as long as the market share is held constant or is growing.
- The organization will maintain prices at a level consistent with competitive activity and market acceptance.
- The organization will maintain prices that reflect an adequate return on investment.
- The organization will maintain prices according to prevalent market conditions except where a greater profit might be attained from a unique market opportunity.

Most organizations are naturally quite secretive about their pricing policies, and outsiders are rarely able to access such information. Four different organizations selling the same type of product to the same markets may have dissimilar pricing policies.

Many larger organizations follow a system whereby the general pricing is reviewed and documented each year at an operations review meeting of the various production, finance, and marketing managers. Revised policies are then explained to all pertinent staff, particularly the sales department, who must interpret the policy in their daily selling transactions and order processing. If a new pricing policy is not common to all participating organizations offering similar products or services, the price of a specific product may vary temporarily throughout the industry until market forces moderate the variance.

NEGOTIATING TRADE DISCOUNTS

Middleman discount privileges are determined by a variety of methods. An agreement between two parties often follows the *prescribed discount pattern* established in that particular industry. A discount is determined by the nature of the goods being distributed; for example, a slow-moving, bulky, and technical product warrants a much higher middleman profit than a fast-selling, easily stored, and nontechnical product. The nature of the market being served is also a major determinant of the middleman discount. A large number of small clients spread throughout a large geographical region will cost more to serve than fewer but larger accounts situated in a concentrated urban setting. By the same token, virgin markets, requiring a considerable development effort, represent a special cost burden to the middleman. Mature markets—those in which the product is well accepted—are more easily penetrated and may thus warrant a lower margin of middleman profit.

The functions or services provided by a distributor, retailer, or agent are significant to the establishment of a suitable discount policy. A manufacturer measures the middleman's abilities in two ways: (1) as the sum of actual services offered, or (2) as the degree to which the middleman is able to perform the functions that the producer deems essential. For example, one manufacturer with a need for a variety of sales, credit, and other services views a particular distributor as a full-service merchant middleman who would receive a 35-percent margin from list price. Another manufacturer views the same distributor primarily as a local storage warehouse, for whose services it is willing to extend only a 25-percent discount.

This example is most applicable to the multiline distributor who serves a diverse market with many different goods. A single-line middleman has a much clearer profit mandate because its homogenous product offering has an established price structure. So a carpet distributor accustomed to a 27-percent discount from several principals is unlikely to become excited about a new carpet producer's product that offers only a 20-percent margin. In general terms, stocking wholesale middlemen normally operate on a 20- to 40-percent profit margin, calculated as a discount from the product's wholesale trade price or retailer cost. An example of the various channel member discount structures is illustrated in Exhibit 5–2.

EXHIBIT 5–2
EXAMPLE OF CHANNEL SYSTEM DISCOUNTS

Product: 1 New Aluminum Tennis Racquet

Suggested Retail Price	$40.00
Retailer discount (markup)	40%
Retailer gross margin	$16.00
Retailer cost of goods sold	$24.00
Distributor gross margin—markup	25% or $6.00
Distributor cost of goods sold	$18.00
Manufacturer's agent commission	10% or $1.80
Amount netted back by manufacturer (not including federal or state taxes, transportation charges, promotional allowances or packaging costs).	$16.20

Note from this example that the manufacturer grosses only about 40 percent of the suggested retail selling price of the product. Once the costs of promotion, packaging, taxes, and transportation have been deducted, this net-back will often fall to a figure (for example, $6) representing only some 15 percent of suggested retail. The difference between the real cost of manufacturing (machine, labor, and overheads) and the net-back represents the small margin of profit available.

Products that benefit from a lower margin of distributor profit are those that are easy to sell, stock, and service. Products for which distributors demand the highest profit margins are those that require long sales negotiation periods, that are difficult to store, and that need considerable after-sale technical follow-up.

Some companies maintain a rigid policy regarding the *minimum margin of profit* that their firm is willing to accept. Yet some marketing authorities suggest that the party that holds the greatest bargaining or leverage power determines the size and extent of discounts and other trade terms. In other words, the party that needs the service or product of the other party most is somewhat at the mercy of the

supplier. The channel member able to exert the greatest influence is often referred to as the *channel captain*. Obviously, if a producer is desperate for the services of a distributor, the middleman has the advantage. Conversely, a distributor in urgent need of additional product lines is less able to influence the discount terms of the representation agreement. To a certain extent, then, negotiations between channel members to arrive at a mutually satisfactory discount policy assume all the bargaining characteristics of a hard-fought sales contract. Once an agreement is reached, the discount policy becomes a matter of record, and the two parties turn their attention towards other supply and promotion matters.

Occasionally, a manufacturer may be approached by a particularly large end-user or retail account that desires to deal on a direct basis rather than purchasing through a local wholesale distributor. The reasons for this action are many. The distributor may prompt the situation by arranging to have the client's large orders shipped straight from the factory warehouse. Sometimes the distributor is a cumbersome agent of technical information from the producer, such that the end-user feels obliged to communicate directly with the manufacturer. Or perhaps, as is occasionally the case, the end-user's consumption of product is greater than the total purchases made by the distributor for all other sales potential. A solicitation for direct dealing by an end-user to a producer is almost always accompanied by a request for increased discount consideration.

Marketers can prepare themselves for such events by providing a special volume price category in their regular schedule of discounts. Such special prices are usually placed at a point between the regular list (or retail cost) price and the middleman cost of the article, as illustrated in Exhibit 5–3. In this way, the marketing firm's authorized distributors are protected from the possible resale of the item. The volume end-user is satisfied that it has received preferential price treatment due to its large order capability. Sufficient margin is maintained between the distributor and volume price levels to permit the marketer to render a commission rebate to a wholesale middleman on each direct sale.

These policy decisions must be made by the marketing firm's managing staff in conjunction with the middleman affected. A marketer's decision-making process becomes more complex and critical when an ultimate customer makes price demands that result in a lower product cost than that paid by the firm's middleman. If any of us were threatened

---

EXHIBIT 5–3
EXAMPLE OF VOLUME PURCHASING DISCOUNT

Suggested retail price	$5.00
Normal retail cost—less 40%	$3.00

Large volume end-user price (additional 15% discount)	$2.55

Authorized distributor cost (less 30% from retail cost)	$2.10

A marketer may wish to establish a special "volume" price for large chain or department stores. Notice that the volume price is not the firm's lowest price—an even lower price is provided to protect the organization's authorized distributor.

---

with the probable loss of one-quarter or more of our sales volume from a large direct-sale account, we might feel compelled to sacrifice a middleman relationship. Such an action is usually viewed as a radical departure from normal business operating procedure and has far-reaching implications on the firm's future marketing plans. In some industries, a manufacturer that permits a customer to bypass the customary middleman and deal directly, loses considerable respect in the eyes of the marketplace. One such decision often initiates a chain reaction of price protests and less amicable client relations. Years later, the credibility of the producer's middleman agreements may still have a tarnished image. Marketers must be wary of pricing and other policies that satisfy short-term objectives but that injure channel relationships and impede the attainment of long-range distribution plans.

REDUCING CUSTOMER PRICE RESISTANCE

Any marketer should establish selling prices that reflect what the market will bear and still allow the firm sufficient volume to maximize production efficiencies and attain the maximum profit. Under ideal circumstances, a marketer should operate the production unit at capacity, turning out a single product that is sold at a high price, without competition, to a single market. This utopian model is seldom attained in either the industrial or consumer marketplace. Instead, most firms are forced to expand their product offerings to satisfy the needs of many different markets in their efforts to avoid severe price competition. Occasionally, a marketer will offer a product or service that reaps handsome profits with

little effort. But, for every profit winner, this same firm is likely to have four or five weak offerings that are under constant attack by lower-priced competitive goods or services.

One method of countering lower market prices for a particular offering is to increase customer benefits by a *product enrichment strategy.* Perhaps the product can be differentiated from the competitor's—new colors, styles, features. A more convenient package may ease handling at the client's plant. The customer's empty trucks might be used for the shipment of the product, and freight charges could thus be saved. There are just a few of the positive nonprice alternatives you have at your disposal when faced with a price decision.

A marketer should therefore interpret the term "product" *broadly.* The product or service offered should be viewed as the total customer benefit package. Any alteration to the marketing mix elements has an effect on the market acceptability of a given product. Up to this point, the discussion has involved the modification of those nonprice marketing elements that can overcome *market resistance* to a noncompetitive product price. *Product enrichment* also provides marketers with an opportunity not only to hold the selling price on an item faced with deteriorating market prices, but also to increase market share while holding a price the same.

Readers should note that the *real price* of a particular product often involves much more than the quoted unit price. It may be more advantageous for the purchaser to accept a high unit cost from a marketer and thereby gain the benefits of extra service, warranties, promotional allowances, and low interest credit plan rather than to accept a low net unit price with no extra benefits.

Any organization encountering price difficulties in the marketplace should examine its problem from two perspectives—that is, from a nonprice as well as from a price basis—before taking remedial action. Exhibit 5–4 illustrates a general model of an effective price determination procedure.

EXHIBIT 5–4
A GENERAL PRICE DETERMINATION PROCEDURE

1. Research the competitive product offerings.
2. Estimate the total market demand.
3. Calculate the available sales potential.
4. Determine your volume objective.
5. Set the company's or department's profit goal.
6. Select an appropriate price strategy.
7. Decide on the most effective distribution method.

8. Establish costs of promotion.

9. Anticipate the required discount structures.

10. Determine a specific list price.

A Systems Approach to Price Determination

This model represents a step-by-step procedure for establishing product prices. The model cannot be considered absolute because many additional situational factors—such as competitive activity, market stability, and the like—may have a significant effect on decision making. Yet the model will assist the reader interested in a clear "how-to" framework that can be a helpful guide.

RETAIL PRICING METHODS

Most retailers are accustomed to established markups on various goods. The amounts of markup enjoyed by various retail businesses have evolved over a period of years, based on the cost of goods sold, selling expenses, fixed overhead, average sale size, and inventory requirements, to name only a few factors. As a result, grocery stores become accustomed to 20- to 25-percent gross margins, appliance stores 35- to 40-percent, and gift stores 50 percent or more, as general rules of thumb. The maintenance of a sufficient average markup is a function of:

- the retailer's initial retail markup,
- the number of units sold,
- the number and size of markdowns,
- discounts and
- the extent of shrinkage as a result of theft and inventory record error.

The role of retailers is to offer a continuous flow of goods and services for sale, as long as they can recover their costs and generate a sufficient return on business investment in time and money. The more akin a retailer's product offering is to other retailers', the greater will be the price competition. Gasoline, tennis balls, cartons of milk, toilet paper, and similar goods, which have essentially the same physical properties regardless of brand, are subject to far more price comparison shopping than highly differentiated products.

Retailers must take care, then, not to develop product mixes that are totally standard in the consumer's eyes, if they seek to achieve substantial retail margins of profit. While pricing at retail is essentially based on what the market will bear, the retail merchandiser is the front-line target for consumer criticism if excessive profiteering or poor product value becomes evident. So the development of a highly differentiated product offering enables the retailer to display merchandise that has a unique design, color, or other benefits that help to justify the consumer's additional expenditure. In Exhibit 5–5, a number of retail pricing methods to achieve profit goals are illustrated.

EXHIBIT 5–5
RETAIL PRICING METHODS TO ACHIEVE PROFIT GOALS

1. *Markup formula:* The standard percentage of profit on cost or initial retail selling price; the markup size varies according to the type of goods, the type of store, and selling conditions.

2. *Odd-even pricing:* Depending on the nature of the goods and the image of the store, prices may be stated as odd ($7.97) or even ($10) figures.

3. *Price lining:* This technique is used to indicate a specific narrow price range for a group of similar goods (coats, boots, and the like), so that the consumer's price expectations can be easily channeled.

4. *Off-season pricing:* Retailers in seasonal businesses are able to pre-plan their pricing strategies according to the normal seasonal fluctuations in demand, sometimes asking for exceptionally high in-season markups, adjusting them to more normal levels as sales decline.

5. *Unit pricing:* Some products lend themselves to pricing by the ounce, liter, yard, or so on. Such pricing methods often permit the retailer to exact a significant markup while maintaining the appearance of moderation in their per-unit prices.

6. *Special-day prices:* Mother's Day, Valentines, Halloween, and other special occasions are ideal situations for the retailer to maximize markup on fast-selling merchandise.

7. *Private label pricing:* Individual stores are often able to establish their own brand of products; the store seeks to maximize its gross margin and exert some control over its market's purchases.

8. *Special merchandise prices:* The alert merchandiser seeks out special purchase opportunities to buy end-of-line, distressed goods and slightly flawed merchandise, which can often be turned over quickly at substantial gross profit.

Maintained Markup

Care must be taken not to confuse the concepts of initial retail markup and the store's *maintained markup*. The retailer may assign a proposed (initial) retail markup of 40 percent to a supply of a certain product but discover, after a period of time, that only a limited proportion of the goods have sold. Under such circumstances retailers have a number of options, including doing nothing, changing the display, allocating some special promotional funds, sending the remaining goods back to the supplier (if they can do so), or reducing the price of the surplus product according to some meaningful criteria.

This last option is the one that retailers are most often concerned with, because it addresses itself to the issue of achieving the stores *prestated profit goals*. The method is used to determine what reduced price should be charged on some remaining number of goods, after a portion of merchandise has been sold at full initial retail markup, in order to maintain a minimum amount of *planned profit* on the overall sale of the item.

For example, suppose a retailer bought one hundred pairs of shoes at $12 per pair ($1,200 total merchandise cost) and sold seventy pairs at a 40-percent initial retail markup (70 × $20 = $1,400). Thus the firm has already shown a gross profit of $200 ($1,400 − $1,200) on sales of only 70 percent of the merchandise. But assume that the retailer is really only seeking a 25-percent planned level of *maintained markup* overall. To assure a quick sale of the remaining goods, as well as the maintenance of an adequate profit, a new, lower selling price must be calculated for the leftover items. If all of the one hundred pairs of shoes had been sold at a 25-percent markup, revenues would have been $1,600 (100 × $16). Since the sale of the seventy pair has produced $1,400 at a 40-percent markup, only $200 of additional revenue needs to be generated from the sale of the thirty remaining pair of shoes. Thus if each pair *is* sold at only $6.66 each (an apparent loss of $5.34 a pair), the retailer achieves the target of a 25-percent maintained markup. Our example has been purposely exaggerated to emphasize a point. The selling price placed on any retail item is really on trial and may bear only a vague relationship to the store's maintained profit goals.

Profit Centers

Stores with several departments carrying different merchandise usually find it beneficial to adopt separate and distinct pricing policies for each department. The purpose is profit control. Separate cash registers, inventory control systems, and buying records enable management to administer the various lines as *individual profit centers*. Such a system also permits merchandising personnel the flexibility to conduct in-department price research (such as to determine the price elasticity of an item), to monitor profit flows by product, and to modify the selling price of certain goods in response to competitive pressures without disturbing price structures in other departments.

PRODUCT COST CONTROL

Companies involved in custom manufacturing, as well as those dedicated to introducing a continuous stream of new products, are less able to ascertain market prices for their goods than firms following more conventional production philosophies, for example, a firm that must determine a selling price for a custom order of telephone switch gear to serve the telephone systems of a community. Because no precedent is available, the firm relies substantially on an *accurate costing* of the development order and then adds a satisfactory amount of profit. On many contracts of this nature, especially to governments, producers are required to supply a detailed analysis of their cost calculations, along with their formal price quotations.

Marketers should establish pricing plans for new products by taking into consideration as many variables as possible. For instance, a marketer who is planning a new product introduction six months hence and who has determined the present market price for that item should establish the firm's future pricing strategies by developing a series of potential case situations of *alternative scenarios*. Each different case should reflect changes in key variables that might be in effect at the time the new product is planned for introduction. Increased competitive advertising, extended introduction time, decreased market potential, and lower market prices are key external variables that must be considered. The potential change in material, labor, transportation, and promotional costs must also be taken into consideration.

Larger firms can readily avail themselves of computer programs that can simulate possible future conditions and rapidly calculate the results. Part of the variable input are internal factors, which can alter the profitability of the new product substantially.

Small firms often determine the potential profitability of a new product simply by calculating the *fixed* and *variable* cost changes involved in satisfying various levels of market demand. Exhibits 5–6 and 5–7 illustrate the estimated differences in the profitability of marketing desk calculators at two different levels of demand. The exhibits also show the effect of *pricing elasticity* on profit margins. When the unit price of $210 in Exhibt 5–6 is reduced by 10 percent to $189 in Exhibit 5–7, higher unit sales are recorded (price elasticity).

But the firm has also increased its fixed marketing expenditures considerably, in order to improve market awareness of the calculator's technical benefits

EXHIBIT 5–6
ESTIMATED PROFITABILITY OF PRODUCING AND SELLING 1,000 UNITS MONTHLY

	Total Cost	Unit Cost
Variable Costs		
Production labor	$ 45,000	$ 45
Materials	40,000	40
Physical distribution	18,000	18
Total variable costs	$103,000	$103
Fixed Costs		
Depreciation	$ 16,000	$ 16
Maintenance	8,000	8
Administration	20,000	20
Marketing	40,000	40
Total fixed costs	$ 84,000	$ 84
TOTAL COSTS	$187,000	$187
Sales revenue at $210 per unit	$210,000	$210
Profit	$ 23,000	$ 23
Profit (as a percentage of sales revenue)	10.95%	

EXHIBIT 5–7
ESTIMATED PROFITABILITY OF PRODUCING AND SELLING 2,000 UNITS MONTHLY

	Total Cost	Unit Cost
Variable Costs		
Production labor	$ 82,000	$ 41
Materials	76,000	38
Physical distribution	40,000	20
Total variable costs	$198,000	$ 99
Fixed Costs		
Depreciation	$ 16,000	$ 8
Maintenance	8,000	4
Administration	20,000	10
Marketing	68,000	34
Total fixed costs	$112,000	$ 56
TOTAL COSTS	$310,000	$155
Sales revenue at $189 per unit	$378,000	$189
Profit	$ 68,000	$ 34
Profit (as a percentage of sales revenue)	17.99%	

keters must consider this factor carefully. Unlike consumer goods, where a price change is recorded and acted upon rapidly by customers, changes in the pricing structure of business goods must often be explained to buyers either directly by sales representatives or through trade advertising mechanisms.

Yet the successful stimulation of the market, brought about by adept manipulation of price and/or promotion variables, may place great pressure on the firm to *accelerate* the availability of supply. Small manufacturing firms in particular, often have difficulty in understanding the rationale for a move to a second or third production shift as a result of increased market penetration. The central idea behind such a move, of course, is to diffuse the effect of the firm's fixed overhead burden.

Look at the following example. A company with a yearly fixed overhead of $100,000 produces a total of 5,000 appliances from one shift of manufacturing, and it must allocate $20 of its fixed expense to each completed unit. If the same firm produced a total of 15,000 appliance units over *three* manufacutring shifts throughout a one-year period, it could amortize its fixed costs at an incremental rate of $6.66 per unit, a theoretical cost advantage of some $13.34 per appliance. Hence the importance of open, honest communication between managerial personnel in manufacturing, purchasing, finance, and marketing. Additional savings may be achievable from larger volume buying power, longer production runs, lower levels of waste, and other reductions in variable expenses.

Decisions to make large-scale increases in manufacturing capability should be made only after careful consideration of all internal and external factors. Rapid growth in productive capacity carries some considerable risk unless the organization is fully cognizant of the many dangers involved. The availability, recruitment, and training of qualified personnel are of paramount importance. Large increases in production often place severe strain on the firm's financial resources. Many firms have found themselves in the unenviable position of having to cut back on previously approved programs that may have provided higher potential payoffs. Problems in maintaining adequate quality control standards, packaging integrity, and efficient warehousing are common dysfunctions of lightning expansion efforts. Notwithstanding the need for an expeditious decision process, business executives should attempt to temper their enthusiasm for immediate cost savings, by giving due consideration to longer-term ramifications: the threat of placing a disproportionate company emphasis on a single product, the

and to reach additional sales potential. As is often the case, a simple downward adjustment of selling prices may, in itself, result in little increase in order volume, unless such a change is properly communicated to the marketplace. Commercial product mar-

inherent risks to the firm if overly *optimistic demand forecasts* fail to materialize, and the inevitable dislocations to organizational stability and control, which are characteristic of expanded operations.

Our desk calculator manufacturer illustrations (Exhibits 5–6 and 5–7) include changes in two key elements—promotion and price—that affect demand. The accompanying exhibits are intended as only one combination of changed variables and their possible effect. A product's demand may increase substantially with only a small increase in promotional expenditures. If such is the case, a reduction in selling price may only deteriorate profits. Conversely, some products may exhibit an inelastic demand when subjected to increased promotion, but they may be highly sensitive to changes in price. Our example shows a calculator manufacturer increasing net profitability from 10.95 percent to nearly 18 percent based on a doubling of productive capacity and sales. The increased volume was achieved by the firm's ability to offer a far more attractive selling price ($189 versus the original $210) and thus attract a considerably larger *market following*. The increase in the demand for desk calculators enabled the firm to expand manufacturing operations over a second shift for increased production efficiency and thereby reduce the incremental impact of fixed costs. Notice that incremental fixed costs for depreciation, maintenance, and administration originally totaled $44 per unit (Exhibit 5–6), whereas this figure is reduced by half with the increased level of production (Exhibit (Exhibit 5–7). If competitive market forces are not overly strong, the firm might be able to maintain a somewhat higher selling price and thereby increase profitability even more.

LIFE CYCLE PRICING

All products and services proceed through what is commonly referred to as a *normal life cycle*. They are introduced to the market, gradually gain acceptance, become mature when they become commonplace, and eventually decline when new substitutes are introduced as alternatives or replacements. A well ingrained organizational strategy is to preplan the pricing and other marketing mix activities according to the various anticipated stages of the product or service's development. Normally speaking, the marketer of a new item would attempt to charge the highest selling price at the time of introduction to capitalize on market interest and to offset early promotional costs.

Exhibit 5–8 illustrates one simple system whereby the marketer of desk calculators preplanned the life of a new product according to the anticipated stages of growth. This firm estimates a major decline in sales of the product once the saturation stage is reached. The company assumes that at this point the competition will be fierce and an array of technically superior products will be attracting the demand. You might question the proposed decrease in selling price to $170 at this time, since the price change would appear to contribute only further to the loss of profit. Some firms preplan their product's life cycle to allow for a significant upward movement in selling price in order to maximize unit profits, but such a decision may hasten the product's decline in sales. Possibly, however, the desk calculator marketer has previous experience showing that similar products had an even more dramatic decline than shown in Exhibit 5–8. Perhaps a further small price concession in this stage will lengthen the product's life cycle, and, while profit margins are small, the absorption of fixed overhead is beneficial.

These pricing concepts also apply to the custom manufacturer who must determine the degree of flexibility or differential (marginal) pricing to employ on orders of unequal size. In particular, many small firms that are required to submit formal tender bids on contract orders can benefit from a sound understanding of pricing strategy. Such firms require an ability to adjust selling prices to satisfy a given set of circumstances and yet be assured that profitability will be maintained.

EXHIBIT 5–8
LIFE CYCLE PRICING FORECAST

Product Life-Cycle Stage	Selling Price Level	Resulting Sales Volume		Variable Costs Per Unit	Total Fixed Cost	Average Unit Cost	Profit
		Units	Value				
Introduction	$210	1,000	$210,000	$103	$ 84,000	$187	$ 23,000
Growth	$189	2,000	$378,000	$ 99	$112,000	$155	$ 68,000
Maturity	$176	3,000	$528,000	$ 93	$141,000	$140	$108,000
Saturation	$170	2,000	$340,000	$ 99	$132,000	$165	$ 10,000

A key concept is that the so-called *real cost* of any product is not a rigid figure but one that varies with the volume of sales. As output increases, the total of the fixed costs does not change but is spread out over a larger number of units, which has the effect of reducing product cost. An important aspect of price–cost manipulation is that a market-oriented approach, rather than a purely accounting approach, must be used to determine the various *acceptable levels* of output, price, and so on. Since direction must originate from the marketplace, any price policy meetings should include representation from the marketing side of the enterprise. Without marketing input to pricing decisions, the resultant values can represent only the arbitrary bias of the producer/seller.

SPECIFIC PRICING STRATEGIES AND TACTICS

Pricing policies and strategies are commonly viewed as general plans of action to accomplish some particular objective. Rarely does a business limit itself to any single policy or strategy. One key to marketing success is the construction of an organization that is open to change and adaptable—that provides itself with a maximum *flexibility of response* to marketplace conditions. This approach is analogous to recent changes in military strategy that perceives the world at any given time in the context of a number of regional scenarios. Each situation may require the application of a different combination of unique strategies and tactics. In a like manner, marketing strategists must seek to develop a repertoire of alternative approaches to different market situations. No single pricing strategy or technique is applicable to all situations. The best or correct strategy is the one deemed most appropriate at the time, the one that achieves the firm's objectives. Let us examine a few of the basic price strategies and tactics employed by effective marketers.

Price Penetration Strategy

Once the estimated price of a product has been established, the development of a long-range pricing strategy through a preplanned examination of the product's life cycle is desirable. If a comparison of the total costs of the new product to the expected sales revenues indicates a very low profit return per unit, then immediate large volume orders will be required. The strategy for introducing a new product at a lower price than established by the market, called *price penetration*, is usually used only by companies entering a volume market late, with strong competitors in the same field. After obtaining some reasonable share of the market, company strategy will normally involve a gradual increase in the price of the product until parity with competitors' prices is reached.

Predatory Pricing

When a business adopts a price penetration philosophy as an ongoing corporate pricing policy, it may gain the reputation of a "price-cutter." This tendency is especially common in industries marketing homogeneous products—goods offering little product differentiation, such as cement, liquid chlorine, electrical cable, copper strip, or surgical cotton balls. The scope of price competition is exceptionally narrow in the sale of these types of goods.

But if the new firm continues its price-cutting behavior and threatens the security of established market suppliers, the situation may provoke *retaliatory price cuts*. A unified price challenge by established market suppliers may force the fledgling predator into insolvency. Predatory pricing is best defined as the deliberate, often unwarranted pattern of price-cutting behavior, implemented as a normal operating policy over an extended period of time, with no apparent regard for marketplace stability.

Competitive Parity

The most widely used strategy employed by companies for pricing new products is called *competitive parity*, that is, pricing new products during their introductory stage at the same price as similar goods sold by competitors. Companies sometimes fail to capitalize on the fact that their product offers unique benefits to the consumer not found in the competitor's product. Conversely, companies often enter the competitive marketplace with products that are inferior to the competition, but priced at the same level. These products never attain a measurable share of the market. The pricing strategy of competitive parity is used most frequently in the chemical and plastics industries, which supply process materials. The prices for standard-specification plastic and chemical materials are in most cases the same for a given shipment delivered to the same location. Even fuel oil for home heating generally has a stable competitive price when purchased in the same quantity in a given city.

Price Skimming

Occasionally a product not only meets all the requirements of the market, but it also possesses some unique characteristic that makes it clearly superior to another competitor's product. So a *higher-than normal* pricing strategy, called *skimming*, may be possible in the introductory stage of the product's life cycle. This is a particularly valid strategy if the new product requires considerable promotional expenditure to be successfully launched into the market. Knowledgeable marketers realize that necessity as a matter of market penetration policy, and they force prices downward at some later date. The most common rationale for selling goods above the expected or normal market price is that additional revenue is required to offset high initial development and promotional costs. As consumers, we often observe this in the 15- or 20-percent premium asked for a new toy, shampoo, or theater ticket.

Target Return—Breakeven Pricing

When marketers say they are making a 20-percent profit on an item, they really mean to acknowledge that the organization is making an average profit of 20 percent per item if sales forecasts are met. The profit margin on an item sold in volume is never fixed; instead, it depends on the amount of sales revenue generated beyond the break-even point and above the product's fixed and variable costs. A fixed cost does not change, regardless of volume of output. Variable costs on the other hand, have a direct correlation to the number of units being produced (sold). Fixed costs normally include rent payments, management salaries, and machinery payments, whereas variable costs might typically include material costs, maintenance expenses, and overtime labor.

For example, if the firm pays its sales representative a 10-percent commission on sales, the cumulative sales costs (commissions) incurred will be a direct reflection of the level of sales achieved. Using a ruler to adjust the sales revenue axis on a break-even diagram, you can visualize the anticipated effect of a price change on profitability. The marketing department of any firm would be wise to maintain a break-even analysis on all products.

Throughout this book, the importance of objective setting is emphasized. Pricing objectives are normally expressed as a *desired return on investments*. There is no preset or regular rate of return that all businesses seek to attain, although in broad terms it is fair to say that marketing management should aim at a return that is greater than the prevailing rate of bank interest, and not less than what will provide for the project's continuation. The formula for calculating the return on investment (ROI) is as follows:

$$\text{ROI} = \frac{\text{Net profit}}{\text{Investment}}$$

For example, assume that a business has invested $90,000 in a particular project and that fixed costs amount to $150,000. The firm desires to make a 10-percent return on its invested capital, or $9,000:

$$10\% \text{ ROI} = \frac{\$\ 9,000}{\$90,000}$$

Total fixed costs plus the target return amount to $159,000. If the firm's sales forecast indicates that sales will be 10,000 units, then simple division ($159,000 ÷ 10,000) yields a base fixed cost figure of $15.90 per unit. Assuming that there is a variable marketing expense of $7 per unit, the firm's lowest selling price should be $22.90 ($15.90 + $7.00) per unit.

Another point of view is that, if the sales forecast of 10,000 units is achieved, the firm will have a total sales revenue of $229,000 and will have made a $9,000 profit or 10-percent return of invested ($90,000) capital. This system focuses attention on the internal objectives of the firm and really does not concern itself with market reality, except in the sense that a forecast of unit sales is included.

Another point to note is that *a satisfactory return on invested capital may yield a less-than-satisfactory return on sales revenue*. If the sales forecast is not met—if, say, the firm sells only 8,000 units—a loss is incurred on the investment, instead of a profit. This loss shows the need for a firm to utilize more than a single price development system. For example, a target return pricing method, in conjunction with break-even and contribution analysis, is a safer, more knowledgeable approach.

Average Pricing

A simple technique, average pricing is employed by a marketer faced with a highly differentiated competitive product offering. The marketer who is uncertain about how a new item will be perceived is unable to determine a satisfactory price label with any degree of confidence. Confronted with such a dilemma, some marketers adopt a conservative price policy, one that reflects an average of the lowest and highest competitive price offerings.

One-price Policy

In this highly structured pricing approach, customers are classed by their types of operations, which correlate to fixed price offerings. Such a policy precludes any negotiation over single- or multiple-order volume or over contractual arrangements. Many steel products, industrial machine, and office furniture producers use such a fixed price policy.

Consignment Pricing

This pricing technique takes into account resellers' desire to finance goods and be assured of their ability to return unsold items. When marketers ship goods on consignment to a middleman, they retain ownership subject to the middleman's sale of the goods. If manufacturers have an opportunity to expand their sales penetration but face dubious credit risks, consignment shipments are in order. Some firms establish a special consignment price schedule reflecting the higher costs associated with the administration and "financing" of the goods placed in the reseller's facilities.

Price Lining

A method of grouping products into price categories, this technique is most effective in creating perceived differentiation in nearly identical goods. In the consumer sector, dress shops use the technique to create $10, $15, and $20 rack displays. More often than not, the retail selling price differentials are not indicative of cost–price variance. In the industrial sector, a truck tire manufacturer may wish to distinguish between tires of nearly equal quality. A significant price differential, along with dissimilar product names and guarantees, provides the desired distinction.

Uniform Delivered Pricing

In what is basically an extension of zone pricing, a seller offers a product at a price that includes transportation costs. The difficulty occurs when any number of clients distributed over a wide geographic area are paying an identical delivered price; it becomes obvious that some accounts are subsidizing others. Some government legislation prohibits delivered pricing and encourages that all prices reflect a factory door price policy. Some marketers thwart such legislation by providing special promotional allowances that in effect assist the purchaser to pay transportation costs.

Key Account Policy

In this form of discriminatory pricing, certain large or longstanding accounts are given preferential price treatment. Many industrial suppliers operate on a basis of "house" as opposed to "current" accounts. House accounts are preferred clients whose business transactions are conducted at the executive level, often between firms in similar fields. Packag-ing manufacturers, petroleum firms, and chemical companies often sell to each other in order to simplify their production mix without rationalizing their product offering. Sales personnel are prohibited from contact with key accounts. Sales representatives are rarely told about house account pricing, but they are nonetheless highly suspicious of it. Consequently, a certain amount of ill-will may be associated with a firm's implementation of a key account policy.

Price Factoring

This method determines product price levels based on competitive price activity. The system utilizes a standard factor, such as 0.95 or 1.05, which is multiplied by the competitor's current price offering to arrive at the firm's suggested selling price. If a firm establishes a policy of maintaining its selling price 8 percent below its competitors, then a factor of 0.92 would be used. Thus a competitive price of $1.82 per unit would result in the firm's establishing its selling price at $1.67 per unit ($1.82 × 0.92 = $1.6744). Similarly, if the firm desires to maintain a prestige pricing policy, a factor of 1.06 is used. If the competitors price is $1.35 per unit, the firm establishes $1.43 as the selling price.

The advantage of using a price factoring system is its standardized simplicity. A company may know that the differentiating characteristics of its products offer certain benefits or detriments to the customer. A negative (0.95) factor seeks to offset detrimental product qualities, whereas a positive factor (1.06) is applied to capitalize on an item's obvious benefits over the competitive offering.

Mixed Basket Price Policy

This unorthodox price policy is used primarily by some merchant distributors and jobbers. The method involves extending discounts to customers who place orders for a variety of the seller's goods. The technique is most commonly associated with a small middleman operation that offers a broad mixture of goods for sale.

Typically, such a firm may sell plumbing supplies as its basic endeavor, but it carries an assortment of nonrelated goods (commonly referred to as "scrambled merchandising") for which it has been able to secure a wholesale position. When clients telephone the firm to place an order for, say, pipe at a standard price, they are encouraged to purchase other items at reduced cost—sealed beam headlamps at 10 percent off list, grouting compound at a third off regular price, and so on. A customer who accepts several of the seller's "specials" is sometimes given the ultimate temptation: to purchase a specific item at the seller's "cost." So the shopper's metaphorical "basket" is filled with a mix of goods with the inducement of price savings. This type of price policy is prevalent in the textile manufacturing and wholesale trades. The objective of a mixed basket price policy is to achieve *maximum throughput* while maintaining an adequate average profit level.

Price Trading

Price trading includes the tactics of *trading up* and *trading down*, associated with a seller's desire to modify purchasing behavior towards the most profitable products in a line. The technique is employed in two ways. First is trading up. A marketer wishes to direct purchases upward to the more expensive models or styles in a line. So he or she eliminates the most inexpensive product in the line and replaces it with a product that will command the highest selling price. This change results in the seller's average product line price increasing from, say, $19.50 to $20.50 Trading down involves the reverse mechanics: The highest-priced product in the line is eliminated and a product introduced to the low price end of the line.

Artificial Pricing

This method of price trading is designed to redirect buyer attention to a more profitable model by creating a fictitious discount. For example, a distributor has two functionally identical products for sale. One of the items, product A, has the good fortune of a longstanding reputation, which is reflected in 50 percent greater unit sales than the relatively unknown product B, although their selling prices are identical. Unfortunately, product A *costs* 20 percent more than product B. The task is then to increase profitability by raising the sales of product B. One method is to increase the price of product B above product A, so that the market perceives its increased value. If, after an acceptable period of time, the market does not perceive the merits of product B as indicated by an increase in the the number of units sold, the marketer may revert to a different approach.

Loss Leader Pricing

In this method, a product is promoted at an unrealistically low selling price to attract buyers. For example, a carpet wholesaler mails a promotional flyer to dealers informing them about a "Saturday Morning Dollar-A-Yard Sale." Many dealers, sensing an opportunity to purchase some merchandise for quick turnover, appear at the sale. The wholesaler may be most willing to sell the dollar-a-yard merchandise, but the main focus is to sell regularly priced products. Loss leaders may actually be priced at less than the seller's cost, although selling exactly at cost is a more realistic approach.

Variations of loss leader pricing include tied sales and bait-and-switch tactics. A *tied sale* involves the promotion of a product (usually a loss leader) for sale, conditional on the purchase of another product at regular price. The so-called "bait and switch" tactics have been commonly associated with consumer selling and are regarded as unethical and illegal in most instances. A seller promotes and sells a client a low-cost product, and then attempts to convert the purchaser to a more luxurious model.

Resale Price Maintenance

This price tactic is under close scrutiny by those monitoring fair competition laws. The technique (sometimes referred to as "RPM") involves the enforcement of a prescribed resale price of a product by the customer. For example, a steel producer that dictates the selling price of steel rods by its wholesalers would be utilizing a resale price maintenance tactic. Manufacturers can often get away with this tactic by reason of a strong product demand and their power to control middlemen. Producers can cancel a distributor's contract, increase the cost price, short-ship orders, or refuse to provide technical service if the middleman fails to abide by the producer's resale price edict. Small retailers are sometimes intimidated by representatives of large manufacturing concerns, and they feel obliged to adhere to suggested retail prices, rather than adopt-

---

EXHIBIT 5–9
HOW TO OVERCOME
PRICING OBJECTIONS

1. Justify a higher selling price by emphasizing greater value for each dollar spent.

2. When a customer claims to have a lower quotation, ask if you can see a copy of the quote.

3. Point out the dangers of dealing with the lowest bidder; something has to be lacking.

4. Compare your product or service with that of the competition on a feature-for-feature basis.

5. Always be armed with an order alternative that permits the buyer a lower price based on some larger volume formula.

6. Provide the buyer with an extended period of time in which the product may be bought at an assured price.

ing their own pricing policies. The independent business person must assert the right to resell goods at prices they deem to be appropriate.

TACTIC 5 SUMMARY

The fifth tactic in the Marketing Tactics for Profits model focuses on the need to price goods and services to sell. Some of the major environmental influences on price include the level of market demand, competitive activity, monopolistic situations, and price elasticity. A general (systems approach) model can be followed for price determination of goods and services, but no single method of price setting is universally applicable to all product or market situations. Business people must be prepared to consider the broadest number of alternatives in their price decisions. In particular, marketers must appreicate the psychological factors that might make up part of the customer's *price expectation set*. In the setting of reasonable price objectives, several different basic orientations range from the need to satisfy internal priorities (return on investment) to those directed at the demands of the marketplace (the maintenance of market share).

Trade discounts and the other conditions create leverage for marketers and resellers. An example of a typical channel system discount structure preceded a number of retail pricing and discount methods used to achieve profit goals. In an in-depth discussion of product costing, two illustrations of profitability analysis under different price situations were examined. The key point is that *increased bottom-line profits* can often result from a decreased selling price.

As for life cycle pricing, marketers should be well aware of the inherent pressures of natural product aging on product prices. Whereas product maturity brings about increased competitive pricing, product decline stages often create new opportunities for higher prices. The brief sketches of a variety of specific pricing strategies and tactics were designed to provide you with a high degree of response flexibility under changing market conditions.

The next chapter is devoted to the sixth tactic, Advertising for Results.

HANDY BOOKS
ON PRICING METHODS

Dalrymple, D. J. and L. J. Parsons, *Marketing Management*. New York: John Wiley & Sons, Inc., 1980.

Fitzpatrick, A., *Pricing Methods of Industry*. Boulder, Col.: Pruet Press, 1969.

Harper, D. V., *Price Policy and Procedure*. New York: Harcourt Brace Jovanovich, Inc., 1966.

Lynn, R. A. *Price Policies and Marketing Management*. Homewood, Ill.: Richard D. Irwin, Inc. 1967.

Montgomery, D. B. and Glen Urban, *Management Science in Marketing*. Englewood Cliffs, N.J.: Prentice-Hall, Inc., 1969.

Rewoldt, S. H., J. D. Scott, and M. R. Warshaw, *Introduction to Marketing Management*. Homewood, Ill.: Richard D. Irwin, Inc., 1973.

SOURCES OF INFORMATION
ON ASPECTS OF PRICING

Conference Board Inc.
845 Third Avenue
New York, New York 10022

Marking Information Guide
224 Seventh Street
Garden City, New York 11530

**Institute of Advanced
Marketing Studies**
17 Lexington Avenue
New York, New York 10010

Marketing Science Institute
14 Story Street
Cambridge, Massachusetts 02138

SOME EXCELLENT ARTICLES
ON PRICING PROBLEMS

Brooks, D. G., "Cost Oriented Pricing: A Realistic Solution to a Complicated Problem," *Journal of Marketing*, April, 1975, pp. 72–74.

Deaken, M., "Pricing for Return On Investment," *Management Accounting*, December, 1975, pp. 43–44.

Gardner, D. M., "An Experimental Investigation of the Price/Quality Relationship," *Journal of Retailing*, Fall, 1970, pp. 25–41.

Lambert, Z. F., "Product Perception: An Important Variable in Pricing Strategy," *Journal of Marketing*, October, 1970, pp. 68–71.

Monroe, K. B., "Buyers' Subjective Perceptions of Price," *Journal of Marketing Research*, February, 1973, pp. 70–80.

Shapiro, B. P., "Price Reliance: Existence and Sources," *Journal of Marketing Research*, August, 1973, pp. 286–294.

Advertising for Results

The sign brings customers.

JEAN DE LA FONTAINE
1621-1695
The Fortune Tellers
Book VII Fable

Any business must maintain effective communication with three main audiences: the marketplace, its suppliers, and its own employees. The fundamental marketplace orientation of consumer product companies is directed toward groups of individual consumers having similar buying needs. In the commercial sector, marketplace communication is directed at groups of companies, institutions, or associations having similar purchasing requirements. In this section of the book, we examine marketing communications from the perspective of developing effective advertising that pays off in results.

TRANSMITTING MARKETING INFORMATION

Consumer-directed communication seeks to satisfy personal motives, while commercially directed communication seeks to satisfy the business motives of the audience. What is the difference between a personal and business motive? Personal motives are usually founded on an individual's emotional needs. Business motives are largely based on more rational need satisfaction, usually related to the economic well-being of an organization. Exhibit 6–1 illustrates several different types of audience communication in the industrial and consumer sectors.

EXHIBIT 6–1
COMPARISON OF MARKETING COMMUNICATIONS METHODS

Consumer Sector

- A movie theater communicates information on marquee to young audience regarding the all-night horror show.
- A cosmetic company communicates information via TV and radio to mature male audience regarding a new antiperspirant.
- A pharmaceutical manufacturer communicates information in the weekend newspaper supplement to elderly audience regarding a laxative product.
- A soft drink manufacturer communicates information on a contest promotion to the general public by outdoor advertising media.
- A fashion clothing producer communicates information regarding new pantyhose styles to a female audience by point-of-purchase (POP) displays.

Commercial Sector

- A steel manufacturer communicates information by direct mail bulletin to the construction industry regarding new specifications.

- An electronics firm communicates information by trade publications to appliance producers regarding the benefits of a transistorized circuit.
- A chemical producer communicates information through industry association meetings to paint manufacturers regarding a new packaging technique.
- An aircraft manufacturer communicates information to airline executives at a convention seminar regarding an economy jetliner for short trips.
- A packaging machinery producer communicates technical advances of a product to packaged goods makers at a national trade show exhibit.

The number of potential individual sales making up a consumer audience is invariably larger than that found in the industrial sector. Consumer product marketers rely on achieving volume productivity by selling each of a large number of individual buyers a single unit of their products in a given transaction. The reverse is usually true in the commercial marketplace. An industrial marketer must communicate with a numerically smaller target audience—rarely to more than a thousand potential buyers.

Marketing communications are information transfer processes whose primary purpose is to support the achievement of marketing goals. Marketing communications take the form of paid commercial information transfer activities or unpaid activities. Trade journal advertising or trade show displays are common forms of paid communication. Business letters to customers and sales reports are examples of unpaid commercial communication. Many companies design a promotional mix for each of their product markets—for good reasons. Identical marketing communications are usually interpreted entirely differently by different market groups.

Communications management pervades every aspect of an organization's marketing program. In product planning, an individual must be able to utilize a broad spectrum of communications skills: interpreting the benefits and drawbacks of competitive offerings; developing precise product specifications; translating creative ideas into practical applications; and establishing short- and long-term development programs. In sales promotion, the individual must be able to apply communications skills to contest design, trade show displays, the production of technical literature, and the organization of distributor seminars. In marketing personnel development, the training staff must be knowledgeable in all aspects of audio and visual communications. Telephone style, business letter structure, public speaking, and nonverbal behavior are all important

skills in which sales representatives should be fully conversant.

PROMOTIONAL OBJECTIVES

"Promotion" refers to any stimulus required to generate a desired purchasing response that results in an exchange of title for specific goods or services. Promotion is considered successful if it achieves the intended response from its audience. A one-minute telephone call may represent enough promotion to obtain an order for a scarce resource. But complex technical product of great value may require millions of promotional dollars and thousands of promotional hours to pursue an elusive purchase order. A firm's promotion may be as simple as a well written letter to its clients or as intractable as a three-year international multimedia advertising program.

Promotion commonly consists of five primary elements:

1. Advertising
2. Personal selling
3. Sales promotion
4. Public relations
5. Publicity

The combined use of two or more of these elements is known as the promotional mix. *Promotional objectives* are terminal goals, situations, or behavior patterns expected by a marketer from the expenditure of resources on one or more promotional activities implemented over a fixed period. *Promotional effectiveness* is the measurement of actual results from one or more promotional activities or campaigns, when compared with the desired or anticipated results stated in the firm's promotional objective.

We are all affected by promotion. All promotion has an impact on some receivers; however, a totally ineffective promotion may have an impact too imperceptible for measurement. Other factors being equal, we tend to patronize those products or services that have been communicated to us as having some unique benefits. Promotion is meant to both inform and persuade. The amount of time and money you decide to invest in promotion has a direct effect on the number of sales reached and on the amount of business attracted to your organization.

ADVERTISING MEDIA

Advertising is any paid form of nonpersonal communications that is directed at a consumer or commercial market to satisfy some individual or business need. Key nonconsumer advertising markets include government, manufacturing industries, wholesale middlemen, churches, hospitals, business offices, clubs, schools, and entertainment industries, to name only a few. Whereas consumer marketers think in terms of media groups such as broadcast, print, and outdoor, the commercial advertiser is primarily concerned with trade shows, business newspapers, industry magazines, and direct mail.

The industrial sector, in particular, has historically shunned advertising as a valuable tool in promoting sales of their products. Many firms feel that their particular business does not lend itself to the *significant brand identity* that is so prevalent in the marketing of consumer products. This reasoning has led many firms to concentrate their entire promotion budgets on personal selling, with perhaps token corporate image ads placed in business publications once or twice a year.

One of the fundamental differences between buyer motivation in the commercial and consumer sectors is that consumer purchases are largely the result of individual "wants," stimulated by media advertising. In contrast, business buyers are usually seen as having an absolute "need" to purchase, and their decision-making processes are largely rational. The performance, reliability, delivery, and price of the product are believed to be the strongest influences in the commercial purchasing process.

The Selectively Chosen Audience

The total marketing communications process— the systems approach—is based on the achievement of a meaningful dialogue with a selectively chosen audience. The dynamic character of a target audience must be interpreted to provide the marketing communications practitioner with sufficient knowledge to design a precise communication program. Communication messages have changed considerably due to the extensive use of *market segmentation* and *product differentiation strategies*. Wise advertisers design messages that point out the benefits of the unique aspects of products or services, and they direct these messages at select audiences of prime prospects.

Exhibit 6–2 illustrates a simple checklist of communications vehicles for consideration by advertising directors. The purpose of the checklist is to provide a ready framework of reference whereby a variety of alternative media might be considered for a particular marketing promotion problem. The determination of an appropriate promotional mix is

entirely contingent on the nature of the firm's objective and the situation at hand. Whereas a combination of direct mail, dealer displays and catalog inserts might satisfy one promoter's needs, another firm, under different conditions, may see the use of contests, newsletters, and technical meetings as the best mix.

Publications used for advertising should be well researched in terms of cost per subscription and

---

EXHIBIT 6–2
MEDIA VEHICLE CHECKLIST FOR PROMOTIONAL PROGRAM DEVELOPMENT

Vehicle	Yes	No
Direct Mail		
Internal distribution		
Sales presentations		
Internal display		
House organ		
Trade show		
Booklet		
Inquiry answering		
Meetings		
Publication publicity		
Annual report		
Dealer displays		
Training courses		
Publication ads		
Postcards		
Local media		
Newsletter		
Samples		
Trade show invitations		
Contest		
Announcements by salespeople		
Public showing (of film)		
Transcript of meeting		
Film slide presentation		
Plaques		
Publication article		
Presentations by dealers		
Catalog insert		
In-plant showing of film		
External showing of film		
Recruiting program		
College course		

audited readership, and they should be compared to the quality of the audience to whom the message is being directed. If a comparison of two publications reveals that one has a 10-percent higher space cost rate but a 30-percent greater readership by the specific group the firm desires to reach, the slight increase in costs is more than offset by the significant increase in market readership.

The cost per thousand (CPM) of potential audience population should never be sole media selection factor. The quality of the potential audience to be reached must be taken into careful consideration. The quality of an audience is determined by the degree of purchasing influence it holds. A company selling welding rods to heavy manufacturers should not approach the top executives of client firms, because the decision to buy such operating supplies is most often made by lower echelon supervisory personnel in the manufacturing department. Similarly, a marketer of sew-at-home clothing patterns will likely receive a poor sales response with a television commercial directed at a numerically large audience of mainly jock-type males tuned into the Game of the Week.

An advertiser can also be faced with a situation where its advertising vehicle is most readily determined by a randomly chosen opinion test administered to a given population, usually with the aid of an objective questionnaire, to measure audience readership (or viewership or listenership) recognition and recall. The design, administration, and evaluation of such tests are best handled by independent research consultants or advertising professionals. The audience to whom a message is aimed should represent a segmented market that offers maximum potential for the source.

The most significant differentiating factor between the function of consumer and industrial advertising is that most consumer advertising stimulates customers to buy as an impulse response. In a sense, then, consumer advertising has a clearer, more measurable purpose. On the other hand, industrial advertising acts in a more covert manner, as a powerful (but often subtle) reinforcement of the sales representative's persuasive selling efforts. So the commercial salesperson, not the advertising, is the critical communication link between the business seller and buyer. Commercial buyers would rarely place an order based solely on an advertisement. Compare this situation with the consumer sector, where each one of us is guided in the most minute of purchases by the impact of television, radio, and the press. Business advertising may therefore be said to fulfill a far more supportive role. Even though the underlying principles of all advertising is to provide effective information transfer, persuasion, and reinforcement, the largest share of business advertising is devoted to the simple information transfer proc-

EXHIBIT 6–3

ADVERTISING EXPENDITURES FOR SELECTED
INDUSTRIAL AND CONSUMER BUSINESSES
(AS A PERCENTAGE OF SALES)

Industrial Sector	Percentage of Sales	Consumer Sector	Percentage of Sales
Machinery	1.76	Perfume/cosmetic mfrs.	13.81
Thermostatic controls	1.35	Drugs and medicines mfrs.	10.40
Lighting equipment	1.15	Motion picture theaters	5.78
Microswitch	1.00	Real estate brokers	5.21
Plastics and chemicals	.93	Jewelry stores	4.40
Construction	.85	Furniture stores	3.31
Farm machinery	.66	Airlines	2.78
Commercial printing	.62	Department stores	2.69
Public utilities	.42	Hotels/motels	2.42
Process controls	.29	Banks/trust companies	1.31
Railway express	.07	Hardware/building materials	.85

This table illustrates some of the industry average expenditures for advertising in a variety of consumer and industrial businesses. Note that expenditures are much higher in the consumer sector, because consumer businesses must communicate with large numbers of people and attract them to their outlets. Industrial businesses do not have as large a requirement to advertise because they are able to rely on direct contact with a relatively small number of clients through their sales representatives.

ess. Seldom does a business-directed advertisement employ the sophisticated persuasive techniques associated with consumer communications.

Firms that employ product differentiation strategies should emphasize the unique benefits of their products in its advertising. As markets mature, they become not only much more price-sensitive but also, promotionally speaking, less attractive environments in which to advertise due to the *diminished profit potential*. In the absence of price competition, increased advertising is justified, but the advertisements should stress quality, benefits, and service.

In certain commodity industries, the ability of a marketer to satisfy the quantity demanded is a crucial factor in determining the allocation of advertising. A firm that is unable to keep up with existing orders is often required to adjust its advertising program to draw attention to products that are readily available. And when a marketer alters its distribution method from, for example, a direct sale to a middleman setup, an informational advertising campaign is necessary. The reasons for the change (perhaps better service) and customer benefits (reduced shipping charges or faster delivery) should be stressed. This type of advertising usually benefits both parties and the costs can often be shared.

To offset competitive promotion, some firms retain a portion of advertising funds in a contingency account as a reserve defense mechanism, to thwart promotional thrusts made by competitors. Such expenditures require the development of a specific counter-campaign to nullify the impact made by an adversary.

PROMOTIONAL STRATEGIES DEFINED

The essential purpose of most advertising and sales promotion programs is to promote the sale of an organization's goods or services. The promotional mix for a new product or service is incorporated into the preplanning of the organization's total market strategy. The marketer evaluates the allocation of advertising expenditures in light of the item's perceived sales potential and profit contribution. The old adage "no use in flogging a dead horse" is particularly appropriate when management is making advertising decisions. Distribution middlemen often apply considerable pressure on a supplier for greater advertising allowances or increased promotional activity in their trading regions. Marketers must be able to judge if such requests are legitimate or merely attempts to cover up a feeble sales force performance. A common problem is often a lack of

sales potential in the territory served by the middleman. Under such circumstances, it is customary to reduce advertising expenditures for that product in the designated area. The creation of a suitable promotion message must be tied to both the audience profile and to specific promotional objectives, such as the following:

1. Creating primary demand
2. Building selective demand
3. Stimulating buyer action
4. Transmitting vital information
5. Building corporate image
6. Supporting distribution channels

Creating Primary Demand

New products require a campaign designed to promote and to explain the use of the product, rather than to identify a particular brand. For years aluminum marketers have promoted the diversified use of aluminum in fabricating products traditionally utilizing steel or concrete. Unfortunately these companies often make the mistake of advertising the benefits of their products and processes to other metal suppliers within their own industry, rather than to prime potential users. A *pulling policy* is the marketing firm's strategic use of promotional activities to stimulate primary demand for any product that directly or indirectly results in increased unit or dollar volume for their goods or services.

Building Selective Demand

Once the primary demand is established through the general recognition and acceptance of a product by a significant base of users, marketers attempt to develop brand awareness, product preference, and the specification of their goods or services. For example, a large steel company ran a successful advertisement in consumer and business publications announcing its development of a compact built-in "babybath," a "sunken tub," a "slide-away scale," and a "recessed heating unit" for household washroom use. Plumbing fixture and appliance companies wishing to produce the items (using their steel, of course) were encouraged to obtain the specifications from the firm.

Stimulating Buyer Action

Most industrial advertising is designed to make major segments aware that the advertiser has a specific product and to solicit inquiries from potential customers. Firms marketing installation and fabricating goods are in this category more than marketers of components, accessory, and operating items. If marketers have products or services that sell under $500 and are one-time purchase items, the central objective of their advertising should be to solicit immediate orders. A *pushing policy* is the conventional use of promotional activities to persuade channel members to purchase or to sell the marketer's goods, irrespective of the existing and prospective levels of demand and competition.

Transmitting Vital Information

Although sales personnel transmit information, advertising may be used to validate and to emphasize price changes, new product features, or additional services offered by the firm. Some advertisers deliberately plan their print communication to provide an audience with specific technical, pricing, or other data that is of such great interest that a high readership is virtually guaranteed. A particularly effective tactic in this regard is to develop easily understood tables, charts, and graphs that indicate the product or material performance. A manufacturer of pipe, for example, advertises monthly to indicate the resistance of cast iron, stainless steel, and various plastics to corrosive liquids under given temperatures. Plumbing supply wholesalers, industrial engineers, and architects collect such data as a decision-making aid. Thus the advertiser gains increased recognition.

Building Corporate Image

Large national and multinational firms are extremely aware of the apprehension that the public—and in particular the youth segment—has about their size, power, function, and impersonality. One firm was under verbal attack for several years for its much publicized position of supplying warfare chemicals. The situation was somewhat paradoxical since virtually every major chemical company is involved in supplying such materials. Companies tend to emphasize such diverse attributes as their faith in youth, their equality of opportunity, the scope of their operations, their energy conservation efforts, and their contribution to the fight against pollution. Corporate image-building communication is often viewed as wasteful spending either to satisfy top management egos or to lure capital. Whatever its purpose, corporate image-building advertising rarely results in the tangible rewards attainable by similar expenditures designed to promote specific goods or services of the firm.

Supporting Distribution Channels

Marketers who depend on distributor or dealer efforts for orders will undoubtedly have an advertising and sales promotion program supporting those efforts. Some producers (and channel members) prefer this aid to take the form of cash discount allowances. Advertising allowances consist of a monetary remuneration or compensation paid to channel members in support of a cooperative advertising message or program from which both parties expect to receive benefits. Most large manufacturers avoid this scheme in favor of a mutually planned program where the costs are shared by the two parties. The cooperative program includes print media, point-of-purchase displays, customer service clinics, sales sample kits, incentive plans for the sales force and customers, trade show displays, and yearly fun events such as hayrides for clients and family.

THEMATIC APPROACHES TO ADVERTISING

The selection of a suitable advertising theme is central to the development of an effective message. An advertising theme is the primary benefit of the message subject that the encoder wishes to impress the audience. The subject of an advertisement is the product or service promoted. In the consumer sector, for example, an automobile manufacturer emphasizes that the product is available in a variety of colors and styles. Colorful, stylish automobiles are the subject; visual attractiveness is the main theme.

Advertising themes are devised by analyzing perceived customer needs and the thematic voids of competitive advertising. Marketers must ask themselves: "What are the most important benefits or attributes of this product that, if communicated effectively, will motivate prospects to purchase?" Almost every product or service has more than one quality that can be stressed. A few of the more popular themes are durability, efficiency, economics, environmental safety, portability, reliability, and convenience. Most readers will be familiar with successful consumer product advertising themes, such as "Coke Adds Life," "Crest Reduces Cavities," and "Tide Gets Clothes Cleaner." More often that not, no single theme will satisfy all a potential buyer's needs, but as a general rule no more than two themes should be used in a single advertising campaign.

An advertising theme is the common denominator that unifies all the elements of the message content. In so doing, the advertiser seeks to create a cumulative impact on the receiver's perception machinery. Visual design, color, typography, and copy language must be integrated in such a way that the seller's promotional theme is clear. Advertising themes are normally founded on the benefits of a marketer's product to a select audience. When promotional themes of a particular product become redundant or obsolete because the benefits of the item are well known to users, a shift in thematic emphasis to specific competitive advantages is in order. Themes founded on a product's performance, versatility, quality, or durability are typical of those used in the early stages of advertising campaigns. Competitive advantage themes are, as a rule, far more detailed in nature and direct themselves at the weaknesses of the competition. Such themes are represented by copy headlines that assert "30-percent faster than the competition," "once-a-year maintenance," or "five-thousand-gallon-an-hour capacity."

When a marketer is faced with developing an advertising theme for a product in which there is little or no differentiating characteristics from competitive offerings, the firm's creative ability is challenged. The single most effective method of thematic advertising under such circumstances is to seek out customer market opportunities in which the product is beneficial. Plastic resin, chemical, fiber, paper, and metal firms share this common problem. The technique is relatively simple: steel producers, for example, should utilize advertising themes that show their customers new marketing opportunities—steel in desks, flooring, patios, fencing, ashtrays, plumbing fixtures, and so on—to stimulate primary demand. Continuous audience exposure to this type of message shows the innovative image of the advertiser.

Old products can be given a new life extension by some relatively minor but novel changes in their character and image. A new quality, grade, or style can revitalize the obsolete item. To achieve renewed market interest, an extensive promotional campaign, tied to a strong message theme, is required. This approach is particularly effective in instances where the old product is given a new identity by a changed name, appearance, and package.

Lest readers interpret this type of activity as an unethical form of deception, two factors should be stressed. First, under normal circumstances some form of legitimate product change is necessary, or the market will quickly perceive that the promotion is fraudulent. Secondly, certain obsolete products are the unfortunate victims of too little or ineffective promotion in the past, thus causing their poor mar-

ket showing and leading to their ultimate demise. If such is the case, the product itself may not require any further change, only a powerful new communication program to excite interest among sales potential.

All advertising messages—whether print advertisements, direct mail, or movie theater marquees—require headlines that provide a strong appeal to the self-interest of target audiences. Perhaps the two most common errors made by advertisers in the development of headline copy are *overgeneralization* and the *use of trick devices*. Specific headline copy attracts more readers and provides a greater impact. Compare the following headlines:

- "Long life" versus "40-percent reduction in repair costs"
- "Fast shipping" versus "24-hour delivery"
- "Increased production" versus "1,000 stampings per hour"

The second error, a gimmick headline, defeats the advertiser's purpose of building increased credibility in the minds of the audience. The headline copy of an advertising message should be a reflection of the reader's need, problem, or interest.

The use of alliteration, onomatopoeia, and similar literary techniques has proved beneficial in reinforcing audience recall. A vital concern of advertising headlines is the clear interpretation of the message by the desired receivers. A common headline error is the use of "coined" terms that are perhaps used in the advertiser's industry but that the target audience does not recognize. For example, a fluorescent light tube advertiser might use the term "group relamping," a plumbing fixture advertiser the term "interceptor," or an electrical product firm the term "neutral ampacity." An overabundance of superlatives, complex technical jargon, and aloofness are also contributing factors to ineffectual message transfer and response.

In summation, the advertising headline should reflect the primary theme of a firm's communication campaign. It must attract the attention of the target audience, convey a clearly understood theme, and induce the reader to read the message in its entirety.

THE POSITIONING CONCEPT

Marketing personnel frequently view themselves as the military command in charge of strategy development and resource deployment. Sellers should effectively use the forces at their disposal to outflank, finesse, and overpower adversaries. A concept gaining increased acceptance in the marketing world is the art of *positioning*—that is, developing a unique, though often psychological, tactical posture relative to that of the competition. The positioning principle originates with the ancient Chinese master of strategy Sun Tzu, who wrote *The Art of War* in 500 B.C. Sun Tzu's thesis perceived military victory as the result of skillful strategy. As a contemporary of Confucious, he theorized that smaller military forces had the capacity to defeat larger armies by strategic positioning that *avoided head-on engagement.*

In positioning, marketers seek to discover and to take advantage of an adversary's so-called Achilles heel. In a marketing context, the competitor's weakness may reveal itself in poor delivery, ineffective selling programs, or a lethargic response to a client's problems or communication voids. Frontal attacks against larger competitors forces the smaller firm to scatter its offensive resources, resulting in a diluted effort and the relinquishment of strategic advantage.

The search for product or market position is conducted with the assistance of an activity or claims matrix. In Exhibit 6–4 the advertising programs of company A and competitors B and C is illustrated. The example illustrates the number of full-page magazine advertisements placed by company A and by competitive firms B and C. Analysis indicates two major thematic areas in which the competition appears especially vulnerable: product selection and environment protection. Upon further investigation, company A discovers that sales prospects have little interest in a broad selection of products, but they are particularly enthusiastic about environmental protection benefits.

Here is the *opportunity to gain position* on the "enemy." A coordinated marketing attack can shift the firm's position to one of industry leader in terms of environmental protection benefits. Thirty pages of advertising emphasizing the environmental-protection theme probably represents a sufficiently intense, high-frequency communication to ensure a positive imprint on audience memory. The most significant principle of this process is the creation of a new company product position in the purchaser's mind. The positioning firm establishes a powerful new image, tying its brand name to the central theme. First-strike capability is important in attaining the maximum benefit from positioning strategy; competitors that follow the market innovator are less likely to achieve the same results.

TARGETING YOUR PROMOTION

Effective market segmentation is the most essential preparatory step in developing promotional programs that bring results. The biggest mistake any marketer can make is to allocate advertising dollars to the wrong audience. All other factors being equal, promotions which are specifically designed for and directed at a select group of potential clients are the ones which generate the best response. Many small

EXHIBIT 6–4
CLAIMS MATRIX USED TO DETERMINE
THEMATIC ADVERTISING POSITION*

Themes / Firms	Low Price	High Quality	Broad Selection	Fast Delivery	Safety Features	Environment Protection	Convenient Use	Long Life
Company A	3*	5	1	7	2	4	6	2
Competitor B	4	6	2	10	5	1	6	5
Competitor C	5	8	1	14	6	2	6	8

Develop your own claims matrix by examining the major themes used by competition in relation to those you have identified as being important to the market. The idea is to find significant weaknesses or areas not addressed in the advertising of competing firms. Such voids represent marketing opportunities for your firm to stand out in customers' minds. This impact is achieved because your advertising theme appears to have a stronger, clearer direction than that of competing organizations whose messages look fragmentary and diluted.

*Cell figures indicate the number of full-page trade publication advertisements.

businesses have a history of poor cost-effectiveness in the expenditure of advertising dollars due to the following:

1. Being committed to running only the "general-awareness" type of company advertisements that have no market impact.
2. Spending a disproportionate amount of the advertising budget in areas or on products that bring in small returns.
3. Designing promotional programs with appeals that are outdated or based upon the marketer's biased misconception of the market.

Expenditures on advertising and other forms of promotion should be viewed as investments, and as such, successful marketers must be most concerned in optimizing financial returns. The small businessperson must never fall into the trap of lethargy concerning how advertising dollars are being spent. They should continuously challenge all basic assumptions being made about who their markets are and how they should best be reached.

One of the most common misconceptions made by marketers is that the ultimate consumer they are trying to reach has a lifestyle similar to their own—living in a split-level house in the suburbs, two cars, cottage at the lake, and so on. If the primary audience is female, the marketer may have a stereotyped perception of a homemaker spending hours with her neighbors and comparing the flakiness of her pastries. In reality some 40 to 60 percent of all women are fully employed in the labor force; another 15 to 20 percent hold some form of parttime work.

One can readily see that the role and needs of women have changed dramatically over the past decade. Career-oriented women are now a prime market target for a wide range of sophisticated upscale products such as luggage, travel, credit cards, business books, sports equipment, and, soon likely, residence-based computer systems. However, we must be careful once again not to develop a generalized stereotypical profile. A much closer analysis is required. Career women may be single, married, with or without children, younger or older, rural or urban, and so on. Some may be further categorized as active, affluent, family centered, or socially concerned. Although we still see television commercials depicting harried housewives pushing kitchen cleansers and virile chestbeaters urging the use of men's cologne, such stereotyping is rapidly losing favor among a more aware population. Marketers

must take care also not to assume that the identified needs of one market are common to those of another. For example, tremendous differences are known to exist between women in New York State and the Province of Ontario, even though the two areas are adjacent to each other. Canadian women have been found to be less aggressive about their careers and their use of credit. Suprisingly, American women are known to be more "outdoorsy" than their Canadian counterparts. The message is clear: Advertising messages must be custom made for different markets.

As income and education levels increase, individuals tend to watch less television but read more magazines. In turn, these factors hold a positive correlation to age—that is, the older people get, the more likely they are to be committed to reading a variety of magazines and the less likely they are to be tied to extensive TV viewing. Some researchers believe that many middle-aged people develop a "video indifference" after years of passive TV watching. As a psychological replacement, such people are thought to search out new forms of entertainment which cater to their needs. Selective topic magazines are one answer. The already broad choice of magazines available is projected to expand considerably over the decade as an older population seeks out media forms by which they can better define themselves and their lifestyle interests. (Exhibit 6–5 shows the most frequently read magazines and gives readers some basic information on the male–female orientation of these publications.) Almost all of these magazines are regarded as horizontal in nature since they cut across the broad spectrum of population. If a small marketer in, say, Illinois wishes to access one of these publications with a limited budget, this can best be achieved by committing advertising funds only to specific regional editions. Even large mass-marketing organizations like William Wrigley, Jr., Inc. (chewing gum) recognize the advantages of developing separate creative ads to appeal to the special interests of distinct groups in different markets. Organizations with large TV advertising budgets are adopting *narrowcasting tactics* whereby they target select fragments of markets holding high potential. Small marketers can adopt the same tactics through appropriate use of a few well-chosen verticle publications. Magazines which fit into this category are those which are directed to groups of people with special interests or needs, for example:

- *Travelhost*—Designed exclusively for the travel industry as a visitor's guide to theater, restaurants, entertainment. Read by one million travelers each week. Published by OMNI Industries, Inc., PO Box 31768, Dallas, Texas 75231.

- *Power*—Devoted to the transfer of information on power generation and plant energy systems. Subscribed to by equipment manufacturers, stationary engineers, and energy-purchasing management. Published by McGraw Hill, 1221 Avenue of the Americas, New York, New York 10020.
- *Coaching Review*—Directed at all people involved in sports, including coaches, trainers, sports scientists, athletes, and administrators. Provides the latest information on technical developments in sports. Worldwide circulation. Published by the Coaching Association of Canada, 333 River Road, Ottawa, Ontario, KIL8B9, Canada.
- *Money*—Designed for people involved in entrepreneurial ventures or actively seeking to further their money-making potential. Provides up-to-date information on investments, pensions, businesses operated from the home. Published by Time, Inc., 541 North Fairbanks Court, Chicago, Illinois 60611.

EXHIBIT 6–5
THE MOST FREQUENTLY READ MAGAZINES

By Males	By Females
Reader's Digest	Reader's Digest
TV Guide	Better Homes & Gardens
National Geographic	Family Circle
Newsweek	TV Guide
Time	Woman's Day
Better Homes & Gardens	Good Housekeeping
U.S. News & World Report	McCall's
Popular Science	Ladies' Home Journal
Popular Mechanics	Redbook
Field & Stream	American Home
Sports Illustrated	National Geographic
Mechanix Illustrated	Newsweek
Outdoor Life	Time
Playboy	Cosmopolitan
Esquire	True Story

Thousands of other selectively targeted magazines are available to reach particular audiences in the consumer and industrial sectors. Many large U.S. and Canadian retailers (for example, Neiman–Marcus and The Bay) have been quick to take advantage of more selective marketing practices because they represent a more clearly directed communication to which audiences are better able to relate. While advertising-to-sales ratios of budgets are remaining essentially the same, a significant trend in the eighties is to supplement traditional mass advertising (TV, radio, newspaper) with selective magazine ads augmented with booklets, pamphlets, and catalogs delivered to the client's home.

DIRECT RESPONSE MARKETING

Consumer marketers concern themselves primarily with mass readership, listening, or viewing audiences. Some marketers, however, require a more selective promotion strategy because of the numerically smaller and specialized nature of their target audiences. Occasionally, consumer goods sellers opt for a direct marketing scheme because they recognize that such a method will bring them higher returns on their promotional investment than the same expenditure applied to other selling means.

Industrial and consumer marketers should both be concerned with the applicability to their businesses of direct marketing methods. Besides the direct marketing efforts to cosmetic, food, drug, and publication subscription firms, a great potential exists for the use of highly refined direct promotion methods in the banking, insurance, education, and travel industries, to name only a few.

The Direct Mail Marketing Association sees the direct advertising process as a vehicle for transmitting an advertiser's message in permanent written, printed, or processed form, by controlled distribution direct to selected individuals. Direct advertising encompasses three distinct methods of communication:

1. *Mail order methods*, commonly using catalogs, monthly invoice mailers, letter formats, product or service promotion brochures, and nonmailed information aids, including printed handouts and display materials.
2. *Door-to-door selling*, including shop-at-home services.
3. *Electronic media*, including television, radio, telephone, and computers.

Most marketing texts differentiate these processes—the mass "shotgun" versus the selective "rifle" approach. The "rifle" promotional requirement is best fulfilled by direct marketing techniques. In fact, its importance cannot be overstressed. Given a certain fixed amount of advertising money, marketers should seek to concentrate the message on the audience that provides the greatest probability of achieving the desired payoff. Communication "overflow" is common to so-called "nuclear" mailings,

EXHIBIT 6–6
EXAMPLE OF DIRECT-MAIL RETURN CARD

Get *ahead* with The MoneyLetter

Send me **The MoneyLetter.** It arrives twice a month (24 times a year), and costs *only $65* for a full 12 months. [Regular price is $95.00 for the same full year, so you *save $30.00.*] *Bill me later.*

If, at any point, I *don't* think **The MoneyLetter** matches or exceeds my expectations or your description, I'll cancel my subscription. In return, you'll send me a full refund for unmailed copies.

Linda Martin   702
420 South Avenue
New York, New York
10012, U.S.A.

Please charge my

☐ *VISA* VISA...or

☐ Master Charge Account

_____
Account Number

_____
Expiry Date

_____
Signature

☐ Bill me later.   ☐ Payment enclosed.

"Me first" is the only sound economic idea.

GBC-162

---

where the promotion includes all sorts of nonsales potential, an obvious waste of resources. Perhaps the most excessively used term in media evaluation is "cost-per-thousand" (CPM). A comparison of most advertising media and vehicles on a CPM basis is often misleading: The audience compared is frequently too small or unequal in quality.

Advantages

Direct mail, utilizing a printed or recorded message and postal service to communicate one-to-one with sales potential, remains the most selective and most widely used of all direct marketing media methods. The major advantages of direct mail communication include:

- *Providing sales leads:* Most responses to direct mail are an invitation to expand communication between the two parties. Direct mail acts as a hidden sales force. Sales inquiries generated from direct mail have motivational value for salespersons.
- *Sales message reinforcement:* Direct mail programs are often planned to provide a continuity of the communication process between the sales

representatives' visits. If the direct mail message is essentially the same as that given by the representative, it acts as a reinforcement mechanism.

- *Obtaining direct orders:* Most direct mail promotions include sufficient product and price information to warrant inclusion of an ordering form. Mini-electronic calculators, ballpoint pens, rubber stamps, and maintenance items priced under $100 lend themselves to direct mail order orders.
- *Communicating with specific knowledge of the audience:* Advertisers select their own custom audience membership in keeping with the objective they seek to achieve. Messages are assured of reaching specific individuals.
- *Controlled response measurement:* Advertisers, knowing the type and number of the audience, can accurately measure orders, patronage, or inquiry response, thus indicating the most effective type of communication.
- *Cost flexibility:* Direct mail provides budgeting advantages to advertisers. All, none, or part of a marketer's mailing list may be used in a given month; good cost control is attained.

EXHIBIT 6–7
SAMPLE OF A RESEARCH BRIEF

MSI ──── **Marketing Science Institute**

Research Briefs

Effects of Advertising
on Retail Price

"Does advertising make the things I buy more expensive?"
This question is both of great importance to consumers and one of
the most controversial issues in the field of marketing. It is
a central point in the larger debate among marketers, public
policymakers, and consumer activists over the proper role of
advertising in society. Unfortunately, the evidence brought forth
is often indirect and taken from only a few product categories
that are not necessarily representative of all consumer products.

In an Investigation into the Impact of Advertising on the
Price of Consumer Products, Paul W. Farris and Mark S. Albion try
to evaluate this issue objectively, presenting theoretical and
empirical evidence from a variety of sources on different sides
of the issues.

From economists they derive basic models of the nature of
competition in the marketplace and the nature of the rational
consumer's search for information. To this they add the perspectives of marketers who view advertising as part of a corporate
strategy to maintain an advantage in the marketplace, support
retailers, and tell consumers about products, and of consumers,
who experience advertising in terms of costs of search for
information and psychological satisfaction.

Farris and Albion focus on two influencial and opposing
doctrines that ascribe very different roles to advertising in
our economy and society. One holds that advertising is persuasion:
it raises consumer prices by differentiating products, decreasing
consumers' price sensitivity, creating barriers to entry, and
increasing monopoly power. The other holds that advertising is
information: it lowers consumer prices by informing consumers,
increasing their price sensitivity, and reducing monopoly power.
The authors find that both theories are plausible and both have
some empirical support. However, neither one seems able to capture
all the potential effects of advertising.

The Marketing Science Institute publishes a wide variety
of working papers and reports,which are offered for sale.
The report discussed here is available for $3.50 (U.S.)
from the Publications Department, Marketing Science Institute,
14 Story Street, Cambridge, Massachusetts, 02138, U.S.A.

- *Discretionary market segmentation:* With considerable flexibility in their promotions, advertisers can divide their mailing lists into homogeneous audience groups by geography, firm size, buying potential, or business type.
- *Innovative experimentation:* In direct mail communication, advertisers can experiment with different message themes and formats for various audiences until effective communication is achieved.

Drawbacks

Some difficulties may be encountered with the use of direct mail communication. First, marketers must be involved within an industry that, by its nature, lends itself to this form of promotion. A negative example best illustrates this idea. A marketer that sells a sophisticated range of expensive production machines is among the least likely to benefit from direct mail. Such a firm has a well defined, numerically small potential with which they are intimately familiar. In addition, the purchasing decision for such products is inevitably the result of an executive committee decision, one whose objectivity is unlikely to be influenced by direct mail. Companies marketing jet aircraft, radio telescopes, atomic reactors, and ocean vessels fall into this category.

These same firms, however, are among the leading users of elaborate technical literature and visual presentations that are used in formal negotiations. A subtle exception to the rule is the open mailing policy of many house organs put out by major corporations and distributed worldwide to virtually anyone who requests to be put on their mailing lists.

A few final notes on direct mail are particularly important:

- Mail order ads positioned on right-hand magazine pages pull better than those on the left.
- Bind-in cards and coupons increase response rates dramatically
- Self-addressed, stamped envelopes (SASE) for returns *do not* show much greater return rates than unstamped.
- Contact the post office prior to the development of any direct mail program to determine which size envelope, weight of paper, and so on to get the very best postage rates. Have the post office weigh ten of your mailouts and then divide by ten to calculate the single unit weight. Do this on a dry day as humid conditions can add up to one-third to the weight of paper.

DEVELOPING MARKETING LISTS

Two main areas of difficulty are associated with the development of effective direct marketing programs. First and foremost is the *composition* of a satisfactory prospect list. Obviously, a good starting point in developing a mailing list database is the inclusion of all the firm's present and potential customers. These names can be initially coded as category 1, "primary sales potential targets." Past customers are designated as category 2, and serious inquries in category 3, and so on. The addition of numerical codes provides a simple method of identifying mail group segments by size, type of business, and geography. For example, the second digit might indicate the firm size, the third digit the firm type, and the fourth digit geographical location. Such simple coding allows the marketer to identify and direct a custom promotion towards a specialized audience. Numerical coding systems provide for computer or word processing unit storage and retrieval. For example, a 1315 mail list might indicate a compilation of present customers that produce office furniture, that have large sales potential, and that are located in the midwest.

Mailing lists can be purchased or rented from commercial mailing list producers, publishers of business publications, and certain trade associations. When a mail list is purchased, the names and addresses requested are given to the advertiser. Advertisers who prefer to rent a list are not given the

---

EXHIBIT 6–8
SAMPLE OF SELECT MAIL LISTS
AVAILABLE FROM COMMERCIAL FIRMS

• College faculty	• Nonresident property owners
• Female bowlers	• Restaurant operators
• Cable TV subscribers	• Credit card holders
• Boat owners	• Dentists and doctors
• Active tennis players	• Hairstylists
• CB radio owners	• Astrology enthusiasts

Virtually any form of market-segmented mail list can be obtained for most regions in the United States and Canada. Lists can be developed based on a variety of demographic, personal interest, and lifestyle factors. For example, if a marketer wished, a list of college-educated, female tennis players, over age 30, who own imported automobiles could be obtained. The costs of such a list would be much higher than for one of, for example, florist shops within a given region. Some of the largest mail list firms include Jami Direct Marketing (Englewood Cliffs, N.J.), R. L. Polk (Taylor, Michigan), National Demographics (Denver), B.J. Hunter Enterprises (Montreal), R. H. Donnelley (New York).

names and addresses. Such advertisers submit the materials they wish mailed to the list firm, which addresses and posts the communication to the target audience. Mail list firms offer a multitude of services including typing, labeling, packaging, premium handling, contest judging, printing, folding, and door-to-door distribution. Most commercial mailing lists are guaranteed 95-percent accurate, and some firms offer substantial cost penalties if advertisers are able to prove that a list is obsolete or inaccurate.

Another problem facing the direct mail advertiser is the maintenance of mailing lists. In a rapidly changing world the characteristics that govern the construction of an original mail list require regular modification. Data-base marketers must remain constantly aware of the so-called "deterioration index" (DI). Most mailers expect a 12 to 15 percent deterioration in the correctness of addresses on any mail list after one year. A list with a DI of only 3 to 7 percent is exceptional—look out for lists that have a DI of 30 to 50 percent since maintenance costs skyrocket. New locations of companies, new personnel, and product emphasis alterations are all factors that require monitoring by marketers who maintain their own mail lists. Commercial mail list firms send out periodic questionnaires to listed firms and make revisions to their records accordingly. Businesses interested in establishing a direct marketing program should take care to key all mail and other advertising so that sources of revenue can be tracked and analyzed. Make a careful check of post office or other regulatory body rules and standards when in the initial planning stage. A conscious effort to pretest the direct response communication in small quantities, before making a commitment to a full-scale promotion, will save many heartaches. Where possible, some effort to prequalify mail list leads according to their potential to buy, can result in significant improvement in response rate and purchase size. To qualify for a mailing list, an individual must meet the marketer's standards for the following performance criteria:

- *recency* of response or of purchase to a direct marketing solicitation
- *frequency* of response or of purchase to a direct marketing solicitation
- *volume* of response or of purchase to a direct marketing solicitation

The development of a mail list usually starts with the purchase of someone else's list that the marketer feels shares some common characteristic, for example, album purchasing or pet owners. The names on one of these lists are then correlated with the names on lists of credit card users, catalog buyers, home owners, or persons with other significant factors that may help the direct marketer arrive at a highly refined "hot" list. Generally speaking, an average response rate to a mediocre direct mail solicitation will result in a 1- to 3-percent return. A direct mail program offering a free book for a trial order of some product might typically receive 2- to 4-percent return from a cold, largely unrefined mail list. The same offer directed at a well researched, prequalified and highly specific mail list might result in an 8- to 10-percent return. Most direct marketers rate their various lists on 0 to 10 probability-to-buy scale for a variety of goods.

A very important technique used by successful direct mailers is to keep accurate records of buyers (name, address, date of purchase, type of merchandise, and the like), so that they can be made into a "hot" list of most-likely-to-buy prospects for future mailings. The use of a Micom, Burroughs, or other word processing device is particularly valuable in doing this work with ease. At the end of this chapter is a list of a number of key retail trade publications. Most such publications rent their mailing lists or provide services whereby they mail your promotional piece to a select audience.

As a general rule of thumb, most direct marketing communication results improve with the degree to which the promotion is *clear, personalized,* and *female-directed.* The success rate of female-directed direct mail advertising is thought to be the result of women being more aware of and sensitive to personally addressed communication than men. For decades, males have been the recipients of most advertising communication, resulting in a reduced level of sensitivity. Similarly, rural audiences are usually found to respond more than urban ones due to their lack of easily accessible shopping facilities.

Solo promotions of a single item of merchandise are usually far less effective in obtaining orders than direct marketing offers of a variety of goods from which the target client can choose. A winning method of accomplishing this task in direct mail is to utilize fifteen to thirty separate, 3-inch-by-7-inch full-color mailers (multimailers), one for each product or service offered. This method seems to have a particular appeal for consumers who obtain some enjoyment in shuffling through the deck of offers, eliminating those that are not of interest and saving the one or two they wish to buy. Many direct marketers claim this methodology is superior to catalog approaches. January and February are seen as the best sales months in direct marketing because of people's post-Christmas intolerance to crowds and other shopping hassles.

COOPERATIVE ADVERTISING PROGRAMS

Frequently, marketers find themselves in the position of wanting to launch a promotional campaign but discover the costs to be prohibitive. A cooperative advertising program is any campaign in which two or more parties in the distribution chain share part or all of the cost of advertising for a product or service. Retailers, distributors, and manufacturers often pool their advertising dollars to reduce the burden of the total cost to any one participant.

There are no hard-and-fast rules governing the sharing of costs. Each individual product promotion requires that the various parties negotiate a cost-sharing agreement to everyone's satisfaction. Sometimes the agreement calls for an actual cash contribution before the advertising campaign begins. Another method may permit one or more of the participants to reimburse other parties after the promotion ends. Occasionally, an agreement calls for one of the parties to contribute labor, space, designs, or mailing lists as their part of the cooperative effort.

The cost of local radio, television, and newspaper advertising ventures are often shared. Major carpet manufacturers, for example, usually have an ongoing commitment to retail dealers nationwide that they will reimburse up to 50 percent of the costs of any advertising that specifically promotes only goods of their manufacture. Sometimes an upper limit exists on the amount that the manufacturer is willing to contribute to any one campaign, dealer, or geographic locale. Such is the case with some of the major soft drink producers, who offer a limited cooperative program in conjunction with their local authorized bottlers. Billboard, Yellow Pages, and direct mail advertising is gaining increased acceptance for co-op ventures in many industries. The following factors are regarded as the most important aspects necessary for a successful cooperative advertising program:

- The campaign should have a very clear purpose, such as to attract a certain number of patrons, to sell a desired number of units, and so on. All parties should be in agreement with the objective(s).
- One member of the co-op venture should take control of the theme and design of the advertising campaign. Other members may wish to take on responsibilities concerned with sales analysis, cost control, and the like.
- Sales personnel of all the participating firms should be fully cognizant of the goals and content of the advertising campaign. In this way, they can more effectively support the promotional effort of the firms.

Cooperative advertising is most successful when a manufacturer implements a program through distributors to the retail dealer. Then the manufacturer is able to enlist the active involvement of channel members in a total national or regional campaign. From the retailer's perspective, they are able to access supplemental advertising monies, ad layouts, promotional copy, and merchandising aids of a superior quality than they would otherwise be able to afford. In addition, the association of nationally branded merchandise with a small retail store tends to improve the business image in the consumer's eyes. Individual retailers normally must pay their own advertising costs if the distributor or manufacturer supplies the prepared advertising materials. Larger retailers sometimes design their own cooperative advertising program for a variety of products, which they must then attempt to enlist financial support for by the various suppliers. In the nonprofit (NFP, not-for-profit) sector, different organizations should seek to swap ads in newsletters and magazines. Another valuable money-generating promotion method is for the nonprofit (sport, theater, social agency) organization to sell its endorsement to appropriate sales potential.

Shopping center promotions constitute another form of cooperative program that may attract the support of retailers, distributors, manufacturers, the owners of the center, and, on occasion, the local municipality. Budget allocations for such programs are usually based on the store area (square footage) and included as a percentage of amortizing costs among all the shopping center retailers on an equitable basis. Large, special promotions—those involving a rock music concert, circus entertainment, or art display, for example—may require retailers to contribute a single-time, cost-sharing fee based on the same procedure.

TACTIC 6 SUMMARY

Advertising for results means that, as an advertiser, you take the time to develop a well designed promotional message that will be communicated to an identified target audience, with the aim of achieving some very specific objective. The sixth tactic in the Marketing Tactics for Profits model helps you achieve that goal.

Many of the various types of advertising messages are common to the consumer and commercial sectors. Differences between appeals to personal (emotional) and business (rational) motives were highlighted in a comparison of marketing communications by businesses in both sectors. Promotion in its broadest sense is seen to incorporate advertising, public relations, and sales promotion, in addition to selling.

A coordinated promotional program is necessary to carry the major themes throughout the program. A media vehicle checklist will aid in the development of promotional programs. For each separate product promotion or campaign, you can quickly run down the checklist and identify those advertising mediums that are applicable. Marketers must understand the significance of simple audience exposure to a message and its ability to demonstrate recognition or recall of the communication. Hence the need for advertisers to seek objective methods of measuring the effectiveness of their promotional programs.

Advertising must be conducted under certain market conditions. Extremely price-sensitive conditions in highly competitive markets are less attractive environments for advertising than conditions in which a unique new product can be promoted without competition.

The costs of various types of promotions underscore the need to find and exploit voids in competitive promotions. The determination of a unique position, relative to the competition's strengths, is a particularly cost-effective promotional technique. Another method growing in use by business and nonprofit organizations is the use of well managed mailing list databases for direct mail (direct response) advertising. The chapter ends with information on how marketers might achieve cost savings (profits!) through cooperative promotional programs.

The final stage in the Marketing Tactics model involves the Building of an Effective Sales Organization.

GOOD READING

Bodian, N. G., *Book Marketing Handbook.* New York: John Wiley & Sons, Inc., 1980.

Crane, E., *Marketing Communications.* New York: John Wiley & Sons, Inc., 1965.

Engel, J. F., *Advertising Process and Practice.* New York: McGraw–Hill Book Company, 1980.

Engel, J. F., H. G. Wales, and M. R. Warshaw, *Promotional Strategy.* Homewood, Ill.: Richard D. Irwin, Inc., 1975.

Kleppner, O., *Advertising Procedure,* 7th ed. Englwood Cliffs, N.J.: Prentice-Hall, Inc., 1979.

ADVERTISING ASSOCIATIONS

Direct Mail Marketing Association
6 East 43rd Street
New York, New York 10017

American Business Press
205 East 42nd Street
New York, New York 10017

Magazine Publishers Association
575 Lexington Avenue
New York, New York 10022

Marketing Communications Research Center
Princeton, New Jersey 08540

National Association of Advertising Publishers
PO Box 5346
313 Price Place
Madison, Wisconsin 53705

Newspaper Advertising Bureau
485 Lexington Avenue
New York, New York 10017

Outdoor Advertising Association
625 Madison Avenue
New York, New York 10022

Point of Purchase Advertising Institute
60 East 42nd Street
New York, New York 10017

Radio Advertising Bureau
1900 Avenue of the Stars
Los Angeles, California 90067

Television Bureau of Advertising
444 North Larchmont Boulevard
Los Angeles, California 90004

Transit Advertising Association
1725 K Street, N. W.
Washington, D.C. 20006

Canadian Advertising Research Foundation
Suite 620
159 Bay Street
Toronto, Ontario

ADVERTISING PERIODICALS

Advertising Age
Crain Communications
740 Rush Street
Chicago, Illinois 60611

Journal of Advertising Research
Advertising Research
Foundation
3 East 54th Street
New York, New York 10022

Advertising World
Media Guide International
1718 Sherman Avenue
Evanston, Illinois 60201

Journal of Advertising
School of Journalism
University of Kansas
Laurence, Kansas 66045

Advertising Techniques
Advertising Trade Publications
19 West 44th Street
New York, New York 10036

Creative Magazine
37 West 39th Street
New York, New York 10018

Direct Marketing Magazine
Hoke Communications
224 Seventh Street
Garden City, Long Island, New York 11530

Direct Selling Bulletin
1730 M Street, N.W.
Washington, D.C. 20034

Mail Order Selling
Box 1047
Welch, W. Virginia 24801

Mail Order Counselor
Voice Publications
Goreville, Illinois 62939

Marketing Communications
United Business Publications
475 Park Avenue, South
New York, New York 10016

Mail Trade
Box 1302
Springfield, Illinois 62705

KEY AMERICAN AND CANADIAN RETAIL TRADE PUBLICATIONS

Appliances
Dealerscope
115 Second Avenue
Waltham, Massachusetts 02154

Home Goods Retailing
481 University Avenue
Toronto, Ontario

Automotive Products
Auto Merchandising News
1188 Main Street
Fairfield, Connecticut 06430

Canadian Automotive Trade
481 University Avenue
Toronto, Ontario

Bookstore Business
Publishers Weekly
1180 Avenue of the Americas
New York, New York 10036

Quill and Quire
59 Front Street E.
Toronto, Ontario

Children's Wear
Juvenile Merchandising
370 Lexington Ave.
New York, New York 10017

Childrens Apparel Merchandising
Suite 304
8235 Mountain Sights Avenue
Montreal, P.Q.

Curtains
Curtain, Drapery & Bedspread Magazine
1115 Clifton Avenue
Clifton, New Jersey 10017

Decor Magazine
Suite 504
The Esplanade
Toronto, Ontario

Drug Stores
Drug Topics
550 Kinderkamack Road
Oradell, New Jersey 07675

Drug Merchandising
481 University Avenue
Toronto, Ontario

Fabrics
American Fabrics and Fashions
24 E. 38th Street
New York, New York 10016

Canadian Textile Journal
Suite 307
4920 Maisonneuve Boulevard W.,
Montreal, P.Q.

Fashions
Women's Wear Daily
Fairchild Publications
7 E. 12th Street
New York, New York 10003

Style Magazine
481 University Avenue
Toronto, Ontario

Floor Covering
Floor Covering Weekly
919 Third Avenue
New York, New York 10022

Canadian Interiors
481 University Avenue
Toronto, Ontario

Florists
Florist
20900 Northwestern Highway
Southfield, Michigan 48076

Canadian Florist
Box 697
Streetsville, Ontario

Furniture
Furniture News
PO Box 1569
Charlotte, North Carolina 75205

Furniture & Furnishings Magazine
380 Wellington Street W.
Toronto, Ontario

General Merchandise
The Discount Merchandiser
641 Lexington Avenue
New York, New York 10022

Canadian Distributor and Retailer
Suite 501
1118 St. Catherine Street W.
Montreal, P.Q.

Gifts
Gifts & Decorative Accessories
Geyer-McAllister Pub. Inc.
51 Madison Avenue
New York, New York 10010

Gifts and Tableware
1450 Don Mills Road
Toronto, Ontario

Groceries
Progressive Grocer
708 Third Avenue
New York, New York 10017

Canadian Grocer
481 University Avenue
Toronto, Ontario

Hardware
Hardware Merchandiser
7300 N. Cicero Avenue
Chicago, Illinois 60646

Hardware Merchandising
481 University Avenue
Toronto, Ontario

Hosiery and Intimate Apparel
Body Fashions/Intimate Apparel
757 Third Avenue
New York, New York 10017

Ego Magazine
Suite 101
5445 De Gaspe Avenue
Montreal, P.Q.

Jewelry
Modern Jeweler
15 W. 10th Street
Kansas City, Missouri 64105

Canadian Jeweler
481 University Avenue
Toronto, Ontario

Luggage
Luggage and Travelwear
80 Lincoln Avenue
Stamford, Connecticut 06855

Luggage and Leather Goods Review
380 Wellington Street W.
Toronto, Ontario

Men's Wear
Daily News Record
7 E. 12th Street
New York, New York 10003

Menswear of Canada
481 University Avenue
Toronto, Ontario

Office Supplies
Office World News
645 Stewart Avenue
Garden City, New York 11530

Administrative Digest
1450 Don Mills Road
Toronto, Ontario

Shoes
Footwear-News
7 E. 12th Street
New York, New York 10003

Canadian Footwear Journal
1450 Don Mills Road
Toronto, Ontario

Sporting Goods
Sporting Goods Business
1515 Broadway
New York, New York 10036

Sporting Goods Canada
481 University Avenue
Toronto, Ontario

Toys
Toys, Hobbies and Crafts
757 Third Avenue
New York, New York 10017

Canadian Toy Retailing
27 Centrale
LaSalle, P.Q.

Building an Effective Sales Organization

TACTIC 7

Everyone lives by selling something.
ROBERT LOUIS STEVENSON
1850–1894
Across the Plains
IX Beggars III

The structure, function, and orientation of any marketing organization should provide for optimum sensitivity to changing market conditions. This level of sensitivity is achieved in two different ways:

1. through management's intensive efforts to heighten employee awareness of the organization's need to take direction from the marketplace, and
2. by ensuring that sufficient information channels are maintained, so that an ongoing client dialog is assured.

Marginal marketing performance is often seen to be the result of intermittent communication with customers and sales potential. Such efforts are not consistent with the attainment of optimum sensitivity to market change. The degree to which the selling firm is perceived by customers to represent an effective marketing organization is directly related to the measure of their empathy with client needs and expectations. The focus in this seventh and final component of the Marketing Tactics for Profits model is on the methods that can be used to develop an effective sales organization.

ESTABLISHING A RESPONSIVE ORGANIZATION

The nature of any firm's product is of less importance than the customer benefits it can provide. In this respect marketing organizations should attempt to develop a portrait of themselves as perceived by their major markets. Such a process may cause a dramatic shift in the self-concepts held by many organizations.

Marketing departments of larger organizations are fortunate in being able to divide the many tasks and activities among a number of employees. Although Exhibit 7–1 illustrates the six key functional elements of marketing organizations in general, such a model is by no means absolute. Each organization must examine its own individual needs in relation to customer expectations of performance.

The single-person, sole proprietorship organization may be operating at its *peak level* of capability by maintaining a satisfactory level of personal selling, client service, and market analysis with only the occasional requirement to examine transport methods, quality standards, and so on. Such situations are not at all uncommon and small business persons

EXHIBIT 7–1
FUNCTIONAL ELEMENTS OF MARKETING ORGANIZATION

Marketing Research	Product Development	Marketing Communications	Sales Management	Physical Distribution	Marketing Services
Market analysis	Feasibility studies	Media advertising	Personal selling	Product packaging	Sales statistics
Data collection	Prototype development	Sales promotion	Client service	Storage facilities	Price analysis
Concept evaluation	Quality standards	Public relations	Sales forecasting	Transport methods	Profit forecasting

Larger organizations are able to afford the allocation of specialist functions to individuals or departments. The smaller firm must attempt to achieve just as effective results by having its employees play generalist roles and by taking on more than one functional responsibility. The entrepreneur wishing to start a new business venture must often be prepared to assume the broadest activity base of all. People considering starting a new enterprise or the purchase of an existing business should consider the levels of expertise required in each of these areas.

should not feel the least bit intimidated if this is the case. By doing well what must be done, independent business persons can be secure in the knowledge that they have *total control* of the situation at hand. Conversely, spreading themselves too thin in an attempt to cover all market-related activities can only lead to frustration.

The selection of a suitable organizational posture and structure will, however, depend to a large extent, on the goals and policies of the individual marketer. Generally speaking, any organization system should seek to gain the advantages of job specialization, effective communication, and integration of effort towards common goals. When management sets up an organization structure, they also establish the means of delegating authority to the staff. Delegation is a critical element, because a structure that contains too few alternative routes for the delegation of authority creates hesitancy on the part of upper management. Conversely, an organization with too complex a structure of specialized functions creates a dilemma for upper management in the allocation of a particular authority.

Let us examine several distinct orientations from which effective organization structures can be developed. Each of these basic alignments may be regarded as organizational formats that management should adapt to satisfy its particular client–communication and organizational requirements.

PRODUCT MANAGEMENT TEAMS

Product management and brand management are often seen as similar organizational formats. Brand managers are a characteristic of consumer food and soap product organizations where an individual is given full responsibility to develop effective marketing plans and to monitor the progress of one or several brand items. This form of product specialization provides a satisfactory basis for the planning and control function, but it often results in a poorly integrated marketing effort. Product management units are frequently completed to compete with another product unit, and so sometimes a considerable *duplication* of marketing activities occurs. Product organizations are most advantageous to firms that offer a wide range of technical goods to dissimilar markets. Product-based marketing management permits everyone involved in the system to concentrate sufficient effort on the mastery of the information about specific products or services and about the specialized needs of their markets.

The product management concept demands that all facets of marketing be represented within a system. In larger organizations, each product-centered system may be capable of supporting its own sales manager, sales personnel, advertising manager, sales service department, product development section, order desk, marketing research, and so on. Obviously this process is costly in the short term, and only well established firms should experiment with its use.

There are some obvious dangers in using product management systems. The most obvious is the risk of stressing *product* management to a greater extent than *market* management. For this reason, many marketing people avoid emphasizing the use of product management teams. Whereas *the effective marketing firm possesses a broad, flexible perspective of itself,* thinking in terms of the markets that it serves or that it could serve, the nonmarketing organization maintains an introverted view of itself, emphasizing the goods it produces. Be careful not to fall into this trap.

One marketing approach to product management sees the product manager responsible for both a specific geographic market and a single-line offering. A large concern may have such a product management group for each of the major geographical markets served—for instance, one group for California, one for the New England states, another for British Columbia, and so on. Many of the large consumer product food companies that have product managers in charge of several brands could give serious consideration to the adoption of a more market-conscious approach. A company producing plastic piping, flooring, and gutters might wish to consider the use of product managers to oversee such markets as construction, building supply, hardware, and industry. Exhibit 7–2 shows the three major organizational approaches—by product, by geography, and by account classification—com-

monly used in business today. For illustrative purposes only, the author has chosen to show a variety of segmentation examples.

GEOGRAPHICAL BASIS ORGANIZATION

Companies often organize their marketing organization on a geographical basis according to the sales or market potential available to them. Every marketing organization is influenced to some degree by the geograhical location of customers, by market size, or by population. An analysis of a firm's market geography can determine a responsibility that permits the best servicing of the customer's needs. Two types of market geography exist:

1. An *atomistic universe* is the term used to describe a homogenous market condition where all customer types appear to have an approximately even distribution throughout a given geographic area. This is a relatively rare situation in the industrial marketplace, but quite common in consumer goods marketing.

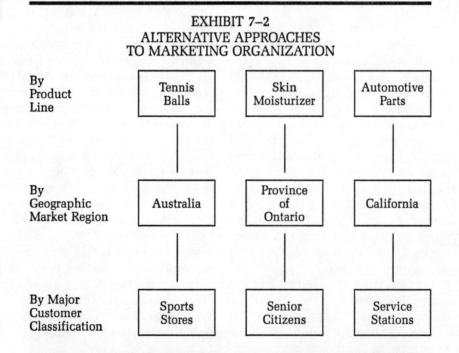

EXHIBIT 7–2
ALTERNATIVE APPROACHES
TO MARKETING ORGANIZATION

By Product Line	Tennis Balls	Skin Moisturizer	Automotive Parts
By Geographic Market Region	Australia	Province of Ontario	California
By Major Customer Classification	Sports Stores	Senior Citizens	Service Stations

New and established organizations should give serious consideration to their posture relative to the various products marketed, the areas covered, and the publics served. An inappropriate marketing organization commonly results in a reduced level of successful customer communication, increased buyer resistance, and lower rates of market penetration. Successful businesses retain sufficient flexibility to permit for necessary modification of their organizational structures to satisfy everchanging customer needs.

2. A more common market geography condition is the *clustered population,* the term applied to customers grouped together in certain areas of the marketplace.

While recognizing geographic factors in commercial goods marketing is important, it does not play as vital a part in shaping marketing policies as in the consumer sector. The development of the total marketing organization based on separate geographic marketing units is rare for most industrial corporations—primarily the result of financial considerations. The distribution of most industrial goods usually does not warrant a specific marketing organization based principally on geography.

Once a firm has decided on a geographic organization as a primary division of responsibility, a secondary system may be integrated into the structure. For example, within a firm that has first chosen a geographic posture relative to its major markets, there may be strong arguments favoring an additional organization subsystem that allocates responsibilities according to product or customer types.

ORGANIZING
BY CUSTOMER TYPE

A firm that markets many different products to a single type of customer can organize around a functional, product, or geographic basis. Customer organizations are suitable for firms that sell their products to several diverse industries. By "diverse" we mean that the end-use of the product, the purchasing motives, and the technical problems are unique to the particular type of customer business. Marketers of commercial products appear to utilize customer organization to a greater extent than in the consumer goods field. The reason is the extensive variety of end-uses for an industrial product. Plastic pipe, for example, is sold to farmers through agricultural supply outlets, to plumbers through plumbing fixture wholesalers, and to major construction firms directly.

By classifying their business accounts by type, marketers can establish a customer organization by grouping together various types of middlemen or end-user industries. Where a particular industry is served by the manufacturer through two or more alternative distribution systems, the marketer should focus its customer organization beyond the middlemen to the consuming industry. For instance, scaffolding may be sold through either building supply or through construction equipment distributors to reach ultimate markets such as the builders of high-rise buildings or bridge construction specialists. Operating on a customer-oriented organizational basis, marketing units focus their attention on the particular needs of industry firms in each of the end-user groups. Kodak is one example of a consumer-oriented organization that has reorganized its marketing operations from a product-centered structure to one based on the type of client served—retail, schools, hospitals, and so on.

Organizing on a customer basis is commonly regarded, from a structural viewpoint, as the system most in keeping with the marketing concept. On the surface at least, customer organization presents management with a method of redirecting an introverted engineering or production company ideology to the needs of the marketplace. Several considerations are necessary before a firm resolves to organize on a customer basis. A sufficient number of client groups or industries must be available to be served.

Companies that have been organized by customers may discover that their customers are diversifying into businesses that overlap other customer groups. If a marketer finds that customer markets are changing rapidly, overlapping, or becoming difficult to identify, the firm may discover a more workable organization structure founded on product or geographic criteria. As previously mentioned, a *combination of marketing organization methods* may be in order. For example, a firm producing camping tents for the consumer sector may sell industrial canvas products to trucking, government, construction, building supply, and mobile home markets. Because each product market is represented throughout the country, a primary customer organization and secondary geographical organization may serve such a firm well.

MANAGING
THE SELLING FUNCTION

The selling function of any enterprise has the responsibility of bringing revenues into the business. Ineffective selling spells doom to a company faster than any other factor. First and foremost, the sales staff of any organization must be highly effective communicators. The person in charge of any sales department carries a very heavy responsibility to be a professional in many areas of competency.

Sales managers employed by large firms usually have more clearly defined responsibilities than their counterparts in the smaller enterprise. This factor often imposes severe limitations on the small com-

---

EXHIBIT 7–3
GOAL-CENTERED APPROACHES
TO MORE EFFECTIVE MARKETING MANAGEMENT

Functional Responsibility	*Less Effective Task Approach*	*More Effective Goal-Oriented Approach*
Sales Management	Process sales reports as they are received.	Disseminate essential marketing information.
Physical Distribution	Check freight rates regularly.	Develop economical transportation modes.
Advertising	Choose media mix for advertising programs.	Measure performance of various advertising media.
Sales analysis	Prepare sales statistics each month.	Produce sales standards and measure sales performance.

As organizations become established, many jobs become preoccupied with *process* and neglect the requirement to produce meaningful end-results. This illustrates the importance of properly allocating marketing assignments and of making them goal-centered in their approach. Any business activity should have some terminal outcome capable of measurement. Marketing decision making should be pragmatic and based on well defined criteria. Marketing personnel should establish realistic objectives and practical plans for their accomplishment.

---

pany sales manager's ability to focus objectively on sales problems. Remember, there are only four distinct selling strategies with which you should be concerned:

- Selling existing products to existing clients
- Selling existing products to new clients
- Selling new products to existing clients
- Selling new products to new clients

In larger firms, pricing, scheduling, advertising, and forecasting are usually functions performed by separate marketing support departments. Yet sales managers in a small firm must often accept these functions under their jurisdiction because the young company cannot afford costly administrative burdens. Large companies are often able also to relieve their sales managers from such tedious and time-consuming tasks of recruiting and initial screening of new sales personnel. Bigger enterprises sometimes maintain their own sales training staff, thereby absolving sales management from actual involvement in the education of new personnel.

Sales objectives are more easily arrived at than profit objectives, and they are viewed as a more relevant indicator of sales force performance. Sales management can never be held solely accountable for profitability. Company profits are affected by many variables operating independently from the control of sales management, such as material and labor costs or physical distribution and product development expenses. Attempts are often made by other departments within the firm to lay the total blame for declining profits entirely on the shoulders of sales management. Sales departments are particularly vulnerable to profit criticism due to their inescapable requirement to remain responsive to marketplace demands. Sales managers are frequently required to defend selling price reductions under the critical examination of nonmarketing management personnel.

A few of the most important responsibilities of the sales manager are as follows:

- To establish measurable sales objectives that complement and support the achievement of the firm's marketing goals.
- To ensure sufficient resources are made available to enable the sales force to effectively fulfill their selling role.
- To determine appropriate incentives by which sales performance can be fairly evaluated and rewarded.

Marketing research is another activity that sometimes rests with sales management in the small firm. Sales management in smaller enterprises is made particularly difficult because of the strain placed on the individual's capacity to perform effectively in any one of a number of prescribed functions. The sales force of small firms must often take on the responsibilities of conducting marketing surveys, ensuring prompt payment of accounts, and many other ancillary duties in addition to maintaining a strong sales performance.

DEVELOPING COMPETENT SALES PERSONNEL

A company's sales force provides a communication channel between the marketplace and the selling firm. The first qualification of sales force adequacy is *quantity*, that is, the appropriate number of sales representatives required to provide adequate market coverage. The second important qualification is *quality*—the degree to which an individual sales

representative is capable of achieving sales organization goals.

The recruiting and selection of qualified sales personnel is often a rigorous and frustrating aspect of the sales management responsibility. Profiles of successful salespeople often indicate few similarities. Companies in scientific fields often regard the individual's technical training or experience as the most important factor in sales success. Nonscientific businesses usually downplay technical skills and stress human factors: personality, enthusiasm, and communicative ability. The emphasis on human or technical skills in the hiring process must be left to the individual firm to decide, and they must be based on the nature of the selling situation that requires filling.

Few people would deny that the values of society as a whole have changed dramatically in recent

EXHIBIT 7–4
CHARACTERISTICS OF THREE SALES ORGANIZATION APPROACHES

Item	Product Specialization	Geographic Specialization	Market Specialization
Primary orientation	Technical merit of product	Persuasive selling technique	Solving customer problems
Customer contacts	Many—diverse	Many—diverse	Few—selective
Client relationship	Detached	Casual	Involved
Products handled	Few—selective	Many—diverse	Many—diverse
Technology focus	Intensive	Indeterminate	Extensive
Major detriment	Limited ability to satisfy customer needs	Hit and miss approach to selling	Requires considerable planning and communication skills
Major benefit	Provides concentrated technical expertise	Provides broad market exposure	Provides concentrated selling effort

These are the three major ways by which salespeople can be organized:

- *Product specialization* is when the salesperson handles only a single product or product line to all types of potential customers.
- *Geographic specialization* is when the salesperson sells a broad variety of products to an equally diverse clientele.
- *Market specialization* is when the salesperson sells a variety of goods to only one type of potential customer

There is no one correct sales organizational approach to satisfy all business needs; the sales and cost effectiveness of each must be evaluated for the marketer's particular situation.

years. A similar transformation has taken place in the business environment. Not so many years ago, the business establishment rejected any notion of hiring individuals whose previous record of experience—socially or in business—indicated any deviation from the company's established norm. The attitudes of business have become increasingly more liberal in recent years.

Sales managers, however, have a particularly more difficult task in the formulation of an equitable hiring policy than many other department heads in the company. A company's sales force reflects the firm's image in an external environment. A sales representative whose overt behavior leads to poor relations with customers, even for a short period, causes the loss of business and permanent damage to long-term sales prospects. The effects of a poor attitude or a slovenly appearance in most other job functions within the company are far less critical to the success of the enterprise.

The Importance of Stability and Continuity

The hiring policy of some other departments of the firm permits employment on a temporary or trial basis. Such practices are untenable in the management of a sales department, which must establish the concepts of stability, consistency, and continuity in the minds of customers and prospects. A company that becomes known for its selection, appointment, and subsequent dismissal of sales personnel is unlikely to be perceived with confidence as an acceptable supplier by the marketplace.

A new sales representative should be introduced to each customer by the department sales representative. The link between the firm and the customer is maintained, and common interests are established with the customer. But if the departing representative transfers a biased opinion and adverse commentary about the customer, some caution must be recommended.

The newly hired sales representative also requires many briefings with the sales manager and with the territory's predecessor, if possible. The assigned sales territory must be described to the new representative in three ways:

1. First is its unique *economic geography*. Items in this category include area, population, weather, transportation facilities, location of accounts, areas responsible for the largest sales revenues, and strongest competitive district.
2. The second is *sales potential* data. "Who are our largest accounts?" "What is our average

order size?" "What competitive advantage do we have?" There are typical questions the sales recruit will ask.
3. Finally, the variables relating to *particular customer* requirements must be explained thoroughly. Such details as extraordinary pricing, special accounts, extended credit terms, entertainment of clients, and peculiarities of certain clients' personalities should be examined.

Selling Techniques

Sales trainers should stress persuasive selling techniques as they apply to their particular businesses. In small firms, the training function is usually performed by the owner–operators or sales managers. Larger companies have full-time employees in the sales trainer's job. Training programs must be designed according to the type of selling task—technical, developmental, maintenance, and so on. In this way, greater emphasis can be placed on skills that are demanded of the particular sales job.

Be careful to note the orientation and styles of selling of different salespeople. Some sales representatives operate best in situations where they must make formal presentations to top business executives. Others thrive on the challenges presented by having to sell to people behind the scenes, such as lab technicians, machine operators, secretaries, and so on. Failure to recognize these differences in orientation can cost the organization lost business.

The type of customer a sales representative is required to call on can also have a significant effect on selling performance. The most equitable system of establishing sales territories, especially in instances where they did not previously exist, is the allocation of a balanced workload and potential to each sales representative. Exhibit 7–5 illustrates the typical variations that often occur in sales territories. Notice the significant differences in the number of small and large accounts, the frequency of ordering, and the average value of each purchase. Sales management must take care to establish sales territories with equitable potentials, work responsibilities, and traveling requirements in order to foster optimum sales efforts.

SALES TRAINING PROGRAMS

Most sales training programs focus on the concept—that is, on the general theory or abstract process—of the selling function. Many sales training programs, for example, teach concepts related to buyer behavior, marketplace dynamics, or interpersonal rela-

EXHIBIT 7–5
DIFFERENCES IN MARKET TERRITORY CHARACTERISTICS

Item	Market Territory 1	Market Territory 2	Market Territory 3
Large accounts	20	60	30
Medium accounts	40	40	40
Small accounts	80	20	50
Average order	$120	$180	$150
Order frequency	8 days	20 days	10 days
Average monthly sales	$35,000	$60,000	$45,000

In this illustration, note the disproportionate number of small and large accounts found in market territories 1 and 2. The sales representative responsible for territory 2 is able to show greater total sales due to the higher average order value obtained from more large accounts. In contrast, the sales representative for territory 1 is faced with a much heavier workload of sales calls on small accounts. If additional differences were evident—such as differences in geographic location of accounts—you can readily visualize that gross inequities may occur.

tions. More often than not, the sales training program is designed to increase the selling effectiveness of existing sales staff or of new recruits. Most of these skills are transferable from one selling function to another. The sales trainer adapts the sales training program to the particular needs of the trainees.

A skill is a measurable unit of ability. Sales training that focuses on building skills seeks, through practice and simulated experience, to provide the individual with appropriate methods of achieving effective results in a variety of transactional situations. Formal education institutions tend to focus their teaching on the conceptual knowledge of selling. But specific training in selling skills are usually the result of programs developed "in-company" or by independent organizations that sell their training packages to concerned businesses. One of the most successful firms offering sales training programs is Xerox Learning Systems. Millions of dollars and years of research and experimentation have resulted in a series of sophisticated business training packages that include professional selling skills, managing for motivation, management discussion skills, and customer management skills. Each Xerox training program concentrates on only those measurable, demonstrable skills by which a participant can immediately increase sales performance effectiveness. The innovative nature of such training methods represents a quantum leap in practicality between the conceptual and the concrete. The following are only a few of the skill areas focused on:

Probing

How to ask questions to:

- uncover customer needs, objections, and doubts concerning company products and services;
- obtain information in order to meet customer needs, overcome objections, and relieve doubts; or
- show that the company is concerned with customer needs.

Supporting

A way of reinforcing a customer's statements that lets the service representative:

- introduce an appropriate recommendation;
- show the customer how your company's products and services can satisfy his or her needs; or
- refer the customer to other company products and services that can satisfy those needs.

Introducing a Recommendation

A way of responding to unexpressed customer needs in such a way that:

- customers don't feel they're being criticized;
- they are inclined to accept recommendations; and
- their needs are satisfied before they turn into objections.

Offering Proof

A way of handling skepticism that lets service representatives:

- clear up doubts that your product, services, and recommendations can satisfy customer needs;
- use available evidence to support what they say a product or service can do; and
- increase customers' confidence in what they say.

Handling Objections

How to use the skills of probing, supporting, and offering proof to:

- establish the real nature of objections;
- translate objections into needs or doubts; or
- handle the needs or doubts straightforwardly.

Obtaining Customer Acceptance

How to get real evidence that customers accept a service or recommendation so the service representative can:

- make sure customers are satisfied; and
- make sure that the representative has won the customer's continued acceptance of company products and services

Concluding Sales Calls

When and how to end a service call so that:

- the call ends on a positive note;
- the representative and the customer have the same understanding of what services have been performed and what services will be performed in the future;
- the customer is reassured of your company's continuing concern; and
- the customer knows he or she is appreciated.

Training in these *customer management skills* uses learning methods developed and validated by behavioral psychologists. Audio-lingual programmed instruction, structured case study role play, and sophisticated approaches to learning are brought together in the learning system, a system that provides positive, predictable results. Objectives are specified in the program overview and skill previews. Before they begin, representatives know what they'll be able to do specifically when they complete each unit and generally when they complete the program. The learning environment is designed to come as close as possible to real working conditions, particularly in the role plays. Participation is active throughout the program, whether people are completing paper-and-pencil programmed instruction lessons, responding to tapes, or playing the parts of service representatives or customers in role play. And, because they work in small groups and can be called on at any moment, participants answer questions silently even when someone else is asked to respond aloud. Skills are built a step at a time; they proceed from the previous stage, where the importance of a skill is discussed, to the role play stage, where participants actually use the skill. Skills are also reinforced throughout the program, particularly in the skill reviews.

Performance is evaluated immediately in writing, on tape, or by group members. At each step participants know whether or not they are learning correctly. Learning is transferred to the job environment during the program itself when representatives use their new skills in carefully structured, realistic sales situation role plays. Some of the most liked and disliked characteristics of salespeople are shown in Exhibit 7–6. Exhibit 7–7 presents a number of keys to successful persuasion in oral communications.

EXHIBIT 7–6
MAJOR CHARACTERISTICS OF SALESPEOPLE
LIKED AND DISLIKED BY BUYERS

Like	Dislike
• Knows the product	• Too aggressive
• Courteous	• Talks too much
• Listens well	• Doesn't know the product
• Stresses benefits	• Fails to listen
• Solves problems	• Not organized

EXHIBIT 7–7
KEYS TO SUCCESSFUL PERSUASION
IN ORAL COMMUNICATION

1. Always establish positive eye contact with the buyer.
2. Use the name of the buyer as often as possible.
3. Attempt to obtain some measure of buyer participation in the presentation.
4. Keep the essential communication simple and repeat the prime message several times for prolonged influence.
5. Express some views that you are confident will be agreed with by the buyer.
6. Emphasize benefits to the buyer rather than features of the product or service.
7. Always be explicit rather than general; present factual concrete evidence in support of your arguments.
8. The suggestion of some mild danger, threat, or loss in performance is more powerful than a strong one.

9. "Stroke" buyers by providing verbal rewards for their agreement, acquiescence, or appropriate behavior.
10. Always plan to have the last word in the communications presentation.

SALES FORCE ECONOMICS AND CONTROLS

As a company sales force grows, greater pressure is placed on sales management to justify selling expenses. The majority of sales representatives receive a base salary plus an incentive commission, the use of a company automobile, and a moderate expense account. The total cost of employing a sales representative often exceeds a figure twice the base salary.

The most significant differences between modern-day sales representatives and those of the past are the far superior capabilities of today's salespeople and their correspondingly greater costs. Increased costs have brought about a situation requiring increased accountability in the form of cost justification. Inept management is cited for compensating sales personnel purely on the basis of increased sales, when a closer investigation might reveal that a disproportionate increase in sales expenses were incurred to achieve the additional revenue. The sales department as a whole has come under closer scrutiny in recent years. The bountiful 1960s created a kind of laissez-faire psychology. Marketing management now places far greater emphasis on profit maximization, and sophisticated control devices are used to curb unnecessary expenditures.

If the actual profits generated by a sales department do not meet corporate objectives, a sales manager has two basic alternatives:

1. to reduce costs while maintaining sales revenue, or
2. to increase sales revenue while holding costs the same.

If a sales territory is in a temporary lull that is causing revenues to falter, the sales manager may be required to request reduced sales expenditures on lodging, meals, fuel, and entertainment to maintain profitability. But if cost reductions are a valid course of action, such measures should be implemented gradually. Care must be taken in the implementation of cost-saving measures because overreaction to a momentary sales declines may result in an even greater reduction in revenues. Remember that frugal marketing budgets are incongruent with high sales expectations. A classic example of short-sightedness would be to tailor hiring plans only to the immediate

state of business. This would mean, in boom times, hiring a large number of relatively mediocre people and, when a recession approaches, shunning excellent prospects who could be trained for the next growth stage. Larger organizations in particular have one great strength—their ability to absorb short-term costs for later gains. In Exhibit 7–8 some of the most common sales performance measurements are illustrated.

EXHIBIT 7–8
SOME COMMONLY USED
SALES PERFORMANCE MEASUREMENTS

1. Sales calls per day or month
2. Average order value
3. Customer order frequency
4. Percentage of the quota achieved
5. Number of different products sold
6. Profit made on sales
7. Number of accounts covered
8. Percentage of goods returned
9. Advertising costs per unit sold
10. Number of new clients

One or more of these may apply to your business situation. The best method of determining appropriate sales performance measurements is through negotiation with the sales force. Some form of reward system should always be tied to successful sales performance.

Several of the specific control mechanisms used by sales management to evaluate the cost effectiveness of selling performance are as follows:

1. Sales expense ratio
2. Average order productivity
3. Sales force activity
4. Return on sales investment

Sales Expense Ratio
This is an analytical tool used by sales management to determine the relationship between a territory's selling expenses and its generation of revenue. The formula for calculating the sales expense ratio is:

$$\text{Sales expense ratio} = \frac{\text{Selling expense}}{\text{Sales revenue}}$$

As an example, assume that a particular sales representative incurred total expenses of $1,000 and generated $10,000 of sales revenue in a given month. Using the sales expense ratio formula, the representative achieved a 10:1 sales-to-expense ratio. Obviously, larger ratios are desirable. Sales expense ratios provide management with a convenient method of comparing the sales performance of salespeople in relation to their expense investment. Such ratios must be used with caution, however, and should by no means be used as the sole criteria of selling effectiveness.

Average Order Productivity

Average order productivity is a broad topic of managerial analysis. Sales managers sometime find value in measuring the average order size recorded in the various territories under their jurisdiction. Others prefer to calculate the number of personal selling hours expended per dollar of sales revenue or per standard number of units sold. In some businesses the number of orders generated per week or per month is, in itself, an important indicator of selling performance. No single measure of order productivity is applicable to all types of selling situations due to the diversity of product values, territory sizes, and account characteristics. Sales management should take care in their selection of an order-related control device to ensure fairness in application to all concerned.

Sales Force Activity

Considered the least relevant control and measurement device by many sales managers, such activities include the number of new or established sales calls made, new contacts established, products introduced, or hours worked. Most sales managers have little interest in the daily activities of their sales force, as long as they attain their weekly or monthly profitable sales volume objectives.

But there are two sides to this coin. One school of thought maintains a simple goal orientation without regard to the quality or quantity of task performance. The other school of thought states that an implicit responsibility of sales management is to achieve the maximum level of profitable sales volume possible by ensuring the efficiency of selling activity performance. There is no absolute right or wrong; the appropriate policy for the particular selling organization is the only source of guidance. Commission-compensated representatives for a firm selling stationery to offices are unlikely to have their performance measured on the basis of calls made or hours worked. Conversely, a business machine firm employing sales/service representatives who are responsible for regular calls on a well defined client population may feel that it has a definite requirement to ensure the promised servicing, and so it may take particular care to monitor the daily activities of its sales force.

Return on Sales Investment (ROI)

The return on sales investment is a simple expression of the dollars of profit generated by salespersons in relation to the value of the operating assets or investment that they utilize. "Sales investment" is defined as the total cost attributed to the maintenance of a sales territory. Most firms classify these costs under two broad headings: operating and administrative expenses. Sales operating expenses include the sales representative's compensation, vehicle, travel, and entertainment expenditures.

EXHIBIT 7–9
SIMPLE ANALYSIS OF SALES TERRITORY
PERFORMANCE (PHARMACEUTICAL PRODUCTS)

Territory 6

January 1–June 31 (Six Months)	Drug Stores	Doctors	Dentists	Totals
Number of accounts	56	38	22	116
Number of orders	194	137	118	449
Sales calls made	164	192	140	496
Total value of sales	$61,580	$23,240	$31,500	$116,320
Average order value	$317	$169	$225	$237

This grid illustrates only one method of keeping records of sales activity. The value of such records is in the ability of management to assist sales representatives with methods to improve performance. In this example, you would question the high number of sales calls made on doctors in relation to the moderate value of sales achieved.

Sales administration expenses include the postage, telephone, office space, and typing services required to support the representative's selling effort. An outline of the major categories of marketing expenses is provided in Exhibit 7–10. Sales management normally maintains a sales budget or quota, along with a separate sales expense budget for the entire sales department and individual sales territories. Utilization of the return on sales investment ratio forces management to relate these budget elements to each other rather than treating them independently. The formula for return on investment is as follows:

$$\text{ROI} = \frac{\text{Net profit}}{\text{Direct investment}}$$
$$\text{ROI} = \frac{\$20,000}{\$60,000}$$
$$= \frac{1}{3}$$
$$= 33\frac{1}{3}\%$$

where, for a given period of time, the net profit before taxes equals $20,000 and company direct investment equals $60,000.

The resultant figure represents the percentage of profit attained by the company on its total monetary investment in the salesperson over a standard period of time, usually one year. This calculation not only provides management with a device to compare its most profitable investment among the various sales force members, but it also permits an evaluation of its return in light of alternative investment potential. For example, a sales territory that consistently returns the company only 5 or 6 percent is a poor investment.

TACTIC 7 SUMMARY

Many important factors must be considered in establishing a vital, responsive sales organization:

1. The functional setup of the departments in a modern marketing organization
2. The merits of organizing sales staff according to product, geography, or customer type
3. The importance of establishing realistic sales objectives, along with the inherent vulnerability of marketing people to profit criticism.

A number of methods for the development of competent sales personnel are available to sales managers. Some sound advice is first to identify the various styles of selling of their sales personnel in relation to the nature of their account responsibilities. Managers should also be wary of inequities in sales workloads, as well as of the importance of sales training programs that stress building skills and handling simulated selling situations.

As essential ingredients of successful sales performance, the most liked and disliked characteristics of salespeople were illustrated, along with the value of strong customer management abilities. A number of keys to making oral communications highly persuasive were also provided.

Sales managers may utilize a number of vital control mechanisms to monitor sales performance and expenses. An example of an analysis of sales territory performance was outlined and the difficulties highlighted.

Strong sales performance was shown to be con-

EXHIBIT 7–10
MAJOR CATEGORIES OF MARKETING EXPENDITURES

- Postage
- Stationery and office supplies
- Advertising production materials
- Transportation supplies
- Packing and shipping supplies
- Marketing and sales research
- Spoiled work
- Print media
- Rent for sales offices
- Wages and salaries
- Travelling expense
- Entertainment
- Telephone-teletype
- New product development

- Radio and television
- Direct mail
- Billbords and car cards
- Advertising art work
- Advertising allowance
- Contest expense
- Conventions and exhibitions
- Catalogs and circulars
- Sample distribution
- Dealer helps and displays
- Demonstrations
- Commissions
- Database management
- Consulting fees

tingent upon a host of subjective and objective factors, most of which are assumed to be under the sales manager's control. The diversity and intensity of demands placed upon the sales-management function cause it to be regarded as a role suitable only for the hardy and the competitive.

GOOD MARKETING MAGAZINES

Sales Mangement Magazine
30 Third Avenue
New York, New York 10017

Industrial Marketing
Crain Communications
740 Rush Street
Chicago, Illinois 60611

Dunsworld Marketing Management
Dun and Bradstreet
99 Church Street
New York, New York 10007

Sales and Marketing Management
Bill Communications, Inc.
633 Third Avenue
New York, New York 10017

Sales and Marketing in Canada
2175 Sheppard Avenue, East
Toronto, Ontario

Marketing Magazine
481 University Avenue
Toronto, Ontario

Marketing for Sales Executives
Research Institute of America
589 Fifth Avenue
New York, New York 10017

Customer Service Newsletter
Marketing Publications
National Press Building
Washington, D.C. 20045

MARKETERS' ASSOCIATIONS

American Management Association
135 W. 50th Street
New York, New York 10020

American Marketing Association
222 S. Riverside Plaza
Suite 606
Chicago, Illinois 60606

Industrial Marketing Association
520 Pleasant Street
St. Joseph, Michigan 49085

Manufacturers' Agents Association
2021 Business Center Drive
Box 16878
Irvine, California 92713

Tactical Planning Summary

*Assured marketing success
is best achieved by the development
of competent marketing plans.*

GERALD B. McCREADY

DEVELOPING MARKETING PLANS THAT WORK

The seven key steps in the Marketing Tactics for Profits Model described throughout this book represent the essential ingredients of a formal marketing plan. The seven steps can be used as a checklist of activities, which management must ensure are in good operating condition before proceeding. A lot of firms develop separate marketing plans, sometimes referred to as *mini-plans*, for each product or department for the coming year. This is an effective method whereby the organization can simply summarize and total all of the smaller unit plans to arrive at their larger *master marketing plan*.

Allocations for the Marketing Plan

You can readily see that the process as a whole starts and ends with the customer. The original marketing research that leads to the development of individual products for each market segment served results in the cumulative flow of want-satisfying goods and services into the customer's hands. But such a statement is a bit idealistic because most organizations are not totally free to serve all the needs and desires of their constituents.

Two important constraints are evident in the preparation of ultimate marketing plans:

1. The *organization's objectives* for the coming year may be weighted in favor of nonmarketing priorities.
2. The *resources* available to the organization to carry out the *ideal* marketing program may be insufficient.

Relating to Organization Objectives. The formulation of objectives for most organizations is usually a function of senior management's perception of the current situation in relation to some desired state of affairs. If, for example, the organization has incurred several months in which production has not been able to keep up with order demand, management naturally tends to stress the need for additional manufacturing capacity. In organizations that have a board of directors lacking in marketing experience, you can fully anticipate ready votes of confidence in favor of "safe" investments in tangible projects—new manufacturing equipment, automated accounting

123

devices, and the like, whenever the opportunity arises. Yet marketing people must take great care in communicating the importance of an ongoing organizational commitment to marketing programs.

In an ideal world, organizational objectives would be based on directions primarily signaled from the marketplace, the source of life-sustaining revenue. Yet this is rarely the case. More often than not, marketing people are forced to rationalize proposed marketing programs in light of organizational objectives stressing nonmarketing involvements. While some readers may see this as a travesty, such is the reality of many business and nonprofit organizations when they are setting objectives. The challenge for marketing personnel is to influence management decision making in such a way that the best interests of the marketplace are well served.

Dealing With Scarce Resources. The second major constraint faced by marketing people is the limited ability of the organization to allocate sufficient resources to the achievement of marketing plans. Marketing programs, like other programs within the organization, must often rely on adequate funding and staffing to be successful. Senior management may be authorized to spend only a limited amount of capital on new program developments and the employment of additional personnel. Faced with such a situation, each department must fight for its fair share of available resources. Marketing personnel hold a strong position in their quest for adequate funding, because no other function is able to show offsetting revenue potential as a result of a given expenditure.

This does not mean that marketing should have total domination of the fixed resource "pie." Indeed, all marketing programs should be justified on the basis of their contribution to the overall well-being of the organization. When a number of marketing programs have been proposed, each should be assigned a priority rating according to its urgency. Sometimes a proposed new program can be put off for a period of time without sacrificing market position or the security of the organization.

The Comprehensive Marketing Plan

Marketing plans should represent the overall strategic and tactical action program that the organization intends to implement in the coming year. Sales forecasts of existing products and markets must be modified to reflect additional revenues to be achieved with the organization's new initiatives.

Advertising plans, pricing policies, and distribution methods have to be clearly spelled out for product and customer groups. New staff requirements should be stated in terms of their function and anticipated contribution to the marketing effort. The plan should also provide detail on the firm's market position in different product markets; market shares, sales potentials, desired penetration rates, and so on should be articulated in a clear fashion.

A marketing budget must be incorporated to provide marketing personnel with firm guidelines for permissible expenditures. Some sort of *time line* must be incorporated into the marketing plan so that the document may be implemented as an action program. Deadline dates for initiation, duration, and termination of the various stages of marketing programming must be distinctly laid down.

Finally, methods of *evaluating* marketing programs and the essential criteria to be measured should be established. Once the comprehensive marketing plan is put into operation, management must then monitor operations, taking care to note variances from planned performance and initiating course alterations as necessary to assure success.

Keeping in Touch with the Marketplace

As an organization grows, the likelihood is greater that management's perception of the marketplace will become blurred. The most common terminology applied to such an occurrence is "losing sight of" or "losing touch with" the markets served. When the marketing organization is young, the markets sought are smaller, and each marketing team member plays a key role in the success of the enterprise. Marketing people must maintain that kind of high degree of intimate communication with their markets to ensure the firm's survival. The rapid growth of a company also creates a need for continuous reassessment of the organization's objectives. The loss of a single customer account represents a significant setback in the small firm's marketing plans. As the enterprise grows, so does the number and size of its customers. Many customers who were previously regarded as minor accounts may have grown faster than the supplier. As a general rule, however, most sales growth is the result of the addition of new customer accounts. To attain this strong growth rate, marketers will probably have penetrated new markets with the introduction of new products.

A number of goal-centered approaches to measuring marketing effectiveness are shown in Exhibit 8–1. The importance of focusing attention on performance outputs rather than on units of work activity cannot be overemphasized. Smaller firms in particular may be able to identify and priorize a limited number of essential directions necessary for company growth or survival. One interesting approach to goal-centered marketing management is the notion that objectives should be specific, measurable, achievable, and complimentary in nature (SMAC).

EXHIBIT 8–1
MEASURING MARKETING EFFECTIVENESS

1. How well the organization determines its direction based on ongoing research of market needs.

2. How well the organization formulates appropriate responses to prevalent customer behavior.

3. How well the organization's products and services achieve a high level of customer satisfaction.

4. How well the organization maximizes the distribution of its goods and services.

5. How well the organization provides appropriate pricing options.

6. How well the organization achieves optimum results from advertising expenditures.

7. How well the organization is able to adapt to changing market conditions and thereby to maintain or improve its competitive position.

Notice that each of these objectives relate to the seven Marketing Tactics for Profits presented in the text. Depending on the nature of the organization, you may wish to modify some of the wording used in these desired objectives.

A positive cohesiveness must also be evident in any management group for it to be effective. A spirit of cooperation and evidence of open, honest communication are seen to be essential criteria of a marketing team with a high probability of success. Persons opening their own small businesses or expanding departments of an established organization will be making a sound investment with high future returns if they place a priority on the following areas:

1. The staffing procedure of the organization should look beyond simple technical qualification and determine whether the candidate enjoys working with people and helping others to overcome problems.

2. Management should take considerable time and effort to plan and implement some thorough program of employee training, to ensure that the organization's objectives, philosophies, and work procedures are understood.

3. The maintenance of good customer relations should be stressed above all else. Each person employed in the shop or department should be acutely aware of all the likely areas of client dissatisfaction and trained to handle them.

Marketing people, much like those who aspire to vocations in personnel and social work, are most often characterized by their inherent interest in people and their problems. This is not to say that marketing persons are "soft" in their decision-making and problem-solving capacities. Indeed, the opposite is often true: The most effective marketing people tend to be highly assertive and objective pragmatists. The acid test appears to be in the individual's ability to confront the problem client or client problem, as the case may be, and to effect a rational, reasonable solution that leaves customers predisposed to continuing their relationship with the business organization.

A prevalent situation in many marketing organizations is the *negative correlation* between marketing executives' comprehension of the marketplace and their ability to make effective decisions. Sales personnel are often in the most knowledgeable position regarding the daily activities of the marketplace. Yet their ability to respond to changing customer needs is only some 20 percent as influential as the marketing director's. In contrast to the sales representative's situation, those further up the executive ladder are likely to be less informed on current market activities. Nonetheless, the amount of legitimate authority to make decisions increases as the individual proceeds upward in management rank. So a top-level marketing person may be fulfilling the planning and decision making role with less factual market knowledge than the firm's sales personnel.

The best balance of market knowledge (sensitivity) and the authority to make decisions (resolution) is commonly thought to exist in the middle-range managerial posts, such as the regional, departmental, or store management functions. Such positions provide active involvement in market activities with sufficient *authority* to effect any immediate changes necessary for adapting to a current market situation. Thus a common characteristic of effective marketing organizations is their ability to maintain a swift rate of response to changed market conditions.

Measurement of Customer Satisfaction

A small retail store is in the best position to evaluate customer satisfaction. Large manufacturing operations are usually most impersonal in their approach to the marketplace. The neighborhood jug milk outlet, ice cream place, or variety store gets to know its patrons' regular purchases and buying peculiarities. The casual chit-chat exchanged between store personnel and buyers gradually becomes more and more personal, to the point that each party could probably write a fairly accurate profile of the other's lifestyle. As a result, store managers are in a strong position to judge the relative happiness of the clientele. Any gap in the frequency of patronage of previously regular customers should alert the store manager to the possibility that some flaw in the store's service might have displeased a buyer.

Another method of evaluating customer satisfaction is by the number and nature of complaints. In a supermarket business, disgruntled customers like to confront the manager face-to-face. In the commercial sector, clients are more likely to telephone or write letters outlining their problems. Where full-time sales representatives are employed, they may be subject to the direct wrath of unhappy clients. If the nature of the business is such that customers tend to bury their true feelings from the sellers, the firm may have to introduce more formal assessment methods.

Customer attitude surveys are one positive way to measure customer satisfaction. Essentially, such a document poses a number of objectively worded questions or statements to customers for their response. Sales personnel can sometimes administer the surveys orally and simply check off the answer that best describes the customer's view toward each item. Yet the involvement of the salespeople introduces a high degree of subjectivity and personality into the process, and the business may find results to be highly colored. A better approach would be for a third party research firm to take control of administering a mailed questionnaire to all or to a sample of the firm's customers. In this way, the respondents are made to feel more anonymous and their true attitudes are more likely to be stated. The following are a number of key areas that should be evaluated in a customer satisfaction survey:

- Speed of delivery
- Quality of packaging
- Courtesy of salespeople
- Special promotions
- Warranties on goods
- Firm's selling price
- Telephone answering
- Help with problems
- Staff's product knowledge
- Help with special requests

The image that any business projects is less a function of its product than it is of its treatment of customers. All other factors being equal, people prefer to do business with organizations that show them respect, consideration, and appreciation for their purchases. The measurement of customer satisfaction should be a continuous feedback process so that the firm does not become indifferent to customer relations. Not only is this true of profit-making businesses, but it also applies to nonprofit institutions, such as schools, hospitals, and churches. A simple survey card, which allows clients to express their feelings toward the organization, might be included with a month-end billing, with a periodic newsletter, or even as part of a year-end mailing of Christmas cards. While some of these suggestions are certainly open to criticsm from a research design viewpoint, the mere opportunity for customers to express their candid view in some recordable fashion is better than none at all.

EXHIBIT 8–2
CUSTOMER ATTITUDE SURVEY

Your responses to the following questions are anonymous.

The purpose of this survey is to help the Kool Kompany give you better service.

Place a black dot (●) on each line to indicate your answer.

1. Please indicate your feelings with regard to the quality of *technical service* provided by the Kool Kompany.

0	1	2	3	4
Poor	Somewhat Poorer than Average	Average	Somewhat Better than Average	Excellent

2. Please indicate how you feel about the *speed of delivery* of your orders by the Kool Kompany.

0	1	2	3	4
Very Slow	Somewhat Slow	Average	Somewhat Fast	Very Fast

3. Please indicate how you feel about the *overall quality of the salespeople* employed by Kool Kompany.

0	1	2	3	4
Very Low Quality	Somewhat Lower Quality	Average	Somewhat Higher Quality	Very High Quality

4. Please indicate how you feel about the *effectiveness of advertising* by the Kool Kompany.

0	1	2	3	4
Not Effective	Somewhat Effective	Average	Quite Effective	Very Effective

Exhibit 8–2 provides a simple, basic questionnaire design, from which you can develop an appropriate one to satisfy your particular business needs. The scaled response questionnaire format is particularly valuable for this type of survey because a numerical score for each question allows for a detailed analysis. Businesses planning on developing a customer attitude survey program should take great care in two particular areas.

1. *Pretest* your questionnaire with sales staff, a few close customers, and friends to be absolutely certain that all the important aspects of client service in your business are covered. As a rule, questionnaires of this nature should not go beyond ten or twelve questions if a high response is desired.
2. Take great care that the wording used throughout is unquestionably clear, concise, and understandable.

Marketing organizations of all sizes and types should provide for some form of regular customer satisfaction evaluation. Once such a program is instituted, the organization is able to assess the ongoing effectiveness of its various operations from year to year. If an organization combines sound business decision making with a sensitivity to the signals from its markets for needed change, it is following effective marketing practice. The most successful marketing organizations are able not only to visualize the concept of investing in marketing assets, but also to approach business success in a longer-term context. Ultimately, the creation of assured paths to future profitability is infinitely more important than the prospects of immediate gain.

Most important, the marketing manager must be able to tie together the *seven tactics* into a comprehensive marketing plan of action for the coming year. Perhaps if these seven tactics leave you with no other lesson, they might at the very least impress you with the essential need to keep in touch with the marketplace through ongoing research and evaluations of customer satisfaction. That is, by far, the all-important heart of the marketing process.

Glossary

ADVERTISING. Any paid form of communication, made by an identified sponsor, that attempts to convey information or ideas or induces changes in behavior.

ADVISORY SERVICE. Any service that provides advice or information rather than a tangible product.

AGENT. A person or company who represents some other individual or firm for the purpose of negotiating a purchase or sale.

AIDA. A simple formula whereby a salesperson takes a buyer through the four phases of Attention, Interest, Desire, and Action.

ALLOCATION. A requirement that a business follow some equitable sharing of a limited supply of goods among its customers.

ALLOWANCES. Concessions in price, discounts, or bonus payments to a channel member for their agreement to perform some special service.

ASSUMPTION TECHNIQUE. A closing technique in which the salesperson proceeds to complete the details of the order, assuming that the prospect has decided to buy.

AUTOMATIC REORDER. The ordering of standard merchandise on an automatic, routine basis.

BACK-ORDER. A customer's order, which is being held pending the supplier's ability to supply.

BASING-POINT PRICING. A system that equalizes freight charges to those who buy from producers by charging freight from a stated common basing point regardless of the actual distance shipped.

BILL OF LADING. A receipt issued by a carrier for merchandise to be delivered to a distant point.

BILL OF SALE. A formal legal document that conveys title to specific property from a seller to a buyer.

BLANKET ORDER. A large order placed to receive a volume discount but to be delivered in partial lots over a period of time.

BOX STORE. A no-frills outlet featuring no-name generic products.

BRAND. A word, mark, or symbol that identifies a product.

BREAK-EVEN ANALYSIS. A decision-making technique based on determining the point at which the income a product brings in equals the cost of producing it, at varying prices and levels of demand.

C.I.F. PRICING. "Cost, insurance, and freight." The seller's price includes all costs involved in getting the shipment landed at a specific foreign port.

C.P.M. Cost per thousand. The cost needed to reach one thousand potential customers who would be receiving a specific form of advertising.

CALL FREQUENCY. The number of times an account is called on during a year.

CANNED PRESENTATIONS. Presentations that are memorized and used on a standardized basis throughout the company.

CANVASSING. Finding sales leads by making unrequested door-to-door solicitations or telephone calls.

CARTEL. The most organized phase of oligopoly where a few large suppliers dominate a market by centrally determining prices, market shares, and the like.

CAPITALISM. An economic system of private ownership of capital with competition in a free marketplace determining price, supply, and demand.

CASH DISCOUNT. A discount allowed by a vendor for paying an invoice within an agreed-upon time.

CENTRALIZED BUYING. The accumulation of orders by an organization from its various operations for the purpose of gaining some advantage from making single, large purchases.

CHANNEL CAPTAIN. The center of influence in a trading channel relationship.

CLOSING TECHNIQUE. A method of attempting to finalize the sale.

C.O.D. "Cash on delivery." Permits shipment to be made before payment but requires payment at the time of delivery.

COLLECTION PERIOD. The average period of time that elapses before a firm is able to collect an account receivable.

COLLUSION. Two or more persons conspiring to act to the detriment of another (such as two competing firms agreeing not to compete on price).

COMMUNICATION OVERLOAD. A result of excessive information being furnished the customer by the salesperson.

CONDITIONAL SALES CONTRACT. An agreement whereby part of the purchase price of some goods is to be paid by installments, during which time the seller retains ownership.

CONSIGNMENT PURCHASE. An agreement by which a buyer takes possession of goods for resale without taking ownership until a sale is made.

CONVENIENCE GOODS. Items that are bought from the most convenient, acceptable retail outlet.

COST-SHARING AGREEMENT. An agreement by which two or more parties agree to share the costs of advertising or some other cost.

CUMULATIVE DISCOUNT. An amount of discount off a list price, calculated as a result of the total amount purchased over a period of time.

CUSTOMER SERVICES. Activities provided by a vendor for a client that assist in the buying process and that encourage a good relationship.

DATABASE MARKETING. The maintenance of target audience mailing lists on a word processing system or computer for the purpose of solicitation.

DEALER TIE-IN. Participation by a dealer in a manufacturer's national promotional program.

DIRECT MARKETING. Any promotional thrust made by a manufacturer to a consumer without using conventional intermediary firms.

DISCOUNT. A reduction in the selling price of a product due to the volume of the item being purchased or due the special channel status of the purchaser.

DISCRETIONARY INCOME. The part of the consumer's income that remains after taxation and normal living expenses have been paid and that involves a choice of spending or saving.

DROP SHIPMENT. An order delivered to a destination other than the purchaser's normal business address.

DUMPING. The practice of selling goods to a customer in a foreign country at a price below the seller's domestic price of the commodity plus freight, insurance, and other normal selling costs.

EARLY ADOPTERS. Buyers who are among the first to purchase a new product.

ECONOMIC ORDER QUANTITY. The economic amount of an item to buy at one time to achieve the lowest costs.

ELASTICITY OF DEMAND. The ratio of the percentage change in quantity sold to the percentage change in price.

EMPATHY. The ability and desire to understand another person's feelings and the reasons for them.

END-OF-MONTH (E.O.M.) DATING. Invoice due dating that requires the customer to pay within a certain number of days from the end of the month during which the goods were shipped.

ENDLESS CHAIN METHOD. Prospecting by asking for referrals from other prospects, usually at the conclusion of the sales interview.

ENTREPRENEUR. An innovator of a business enterprise who recognizes opportunities to introduce a new product, a new production process, or an improved organization, and who raises the necessary money, assembles the factors of production, and organizes an operation to exploit the opportunity.

EQUITY THEORY. A motivational theory that assumes individuals must see a relationship between the rewards they obtain (outcomes) and the amount of work they perform (inputs).

EXCLUSIVE DEALERSHIPS. A contract that limits an intermediary from handling the products of only one manufacturer; a violation of the Clayton Act when it substantially reduces competition.

EXTENDED TERMS. Longer than the normal time given to pay a bill.

EXTENSIVE DISTRIBUTION. Flooding the market with an item to give it the broadest exposure.

FACING. A retail shelf designation that is one unit wide, extending to the top and back of the shelf in a merchandise display.

FACTORING. A process of using a third party to provide money by selling them the firm's accounts receivable at a discount, or by borrowing money from them by pledging inventory as security.

FAIR-TRADE PRICING. The practice by producers of setting a retail price that all retailers must charge. This policy, no longer legal, was earlier made legal by state fair-trade laws.

FAMILY UNIT. Any dwelling unit containing two or more related people.

F.A.S. PRICING. "Free alongside." Seller's price includes all costs in getting the goods to a point alongside the ship where the ship's cranes can do the loading.

FASHION GOODS. Products whose major appeal is a frequent change in style or design.

FIFO. "First in, first out." An inventory policy and valuation method whereby the first goods received in are the first goods shipped out.

FLOOR PLAN FINANCING. A retail method of financing goods on display that is liquidated when sales of the merchandise is made.

F.O.B. FACTORY PRICING. "Free on board." The seller's price includes an agreement to load the shipment at the factory on the carrier used by the purchaser.

FORECASTING. Planning focused on the prediction of future occurrences that may affect the organization. Forecasts can be long-range, short-range, or rolling (integrating long and short ranges).

FORWARD BUYING. Committing purchases to provide for needs during a time longer than is necessary for immediate requirements.

FORWARD DATING. The practice of billing the buyer at a later date in order to encourage present purchases rather than delayed purchases.

FRANCHISING. An agreement whereby a new business is permitted to duplicate a successful pattern of operation of another firm for a fee, as long as conditions of quality and service are maintained.

FUTURES MARKETING. An agreement to purchase or to sell some commodity at a certain price at some stipulated point in the future.

GENERIC PRODUCT. Any nonbranded item sold by its common name at the lowest cost.

GEOGRAPHIC-BASED ORGANIZATION. Refers to a sales department whose territory arrangement is based upon geogrpahic areas rather than on certain client industries or products.

GROSS MARGIN. The difference between net sales and the total cost of goods sold, from which the firm pays expenses and extracts profit.

GROUP BUYING. The process whereby a number of individuals or businesses combine their purchasing needs into a single order to achieve volume discounts.

GUARANTEE. A statement in which the seller promises to provide stipulated services to a buyer in the event that a purchased product proves defective within an agreed-upon time.

HORIZONTAL INTEGRATION. A method of expansion whereby a firm purchases other businesses in the same or related lines or with the same level of distribution.

HOUSEHOLD UNIT. Any dwelling unit containing one or more people.

IMPULSE GOODS. Items that are bought in haste with little or no thought as to the wisdom of the purchase.

INDUSTRIAL GOODS. Goods used either directly or indirectly in the production of other goods or in the day-to-day operation of a business.

INELASTIC DEMAND. A market situation where a price increase or decrease has little effect on total demand.

INITIAL RETAIL MARKUP. The original level of gross profit established by a store that incorporates allowances for pilferage, discounts, markdowns, and other reductions.

INSTALLATION GOODS. Major machinery or equipment purchases that are essential to the operation of a business.

INTENSIVE DISTRIBUTION. A distribution strategy that seeks to maximize the number of customer outlets for the sale of some product.

INVENTORY MANAGEMENT. Decision-making techniques used by managers to determine how many items the organization should keep in stock.

JOBBER. A small, usually local wholesale firm who

buys from manufacturers and importers for resale to retailers or to commercial accounts.

LIFO. "Last in, first out." An inventory control and valuation method whereby the last goods received in become the first goods shipped out.

LAYAWAY. A deferred payment purchase agreement in which an article is held for a customer until payment is made.

LEVERAGE. The degree to which an increase in sales revenue affects profits; dependent on fixed costs.

LIFESTYLES. The particular characteristics that shape a person's day-to-day quality of life and consumption behavior.

LINE OF CREDIT. An agreed-upon sum of money that a bank is willing to extend to a client over a period of time.

LIST PRICE. A price that is published by a manufacturer or retailer, such as the prices given in catalog or on price lists.

LOSS LEADER PRICING. A promotional method based upon the offering of merchandise at or below cost to attract consumers to a particular store or department.

MARKETING INFORMATION SYSTEM (MIS). Any system of marketing data collection and analysis that helps managers perform their jobs more effectively.

MANUFACTURER'S REPRESENTATIVES. Salespersons who represent producers to wholesalers and retailers on a commissioned basis.

MARGINAL REVENUE. The contribution to total revenue resulting from the sale of one additional unit of a good or service.

MARKET. A number of people or businesses that have some common purchasing characteristics. A market can also refer to a specific geographic region.

MARKET FACTOR ANALYSIS. A method of sales forecasting based on correlating sales to underlying market factors, such as economic conditions and demographics.

MARKET POTENTIAL. The total amount of available business, in units or dollars, that must be shared among all industry competitors.

MARKET SEGMENTATION. An analytical procedure whereby markets are distilled down to their purest form, all constituent parts having the closest possible commonality of needs.

MARKET SHARE. The percentage of the total available market potential that a specific firm controls.

MARKET SURVEYS. A method of sales forecasting based on surveying customers and potential customers.

MARKETING CONCEPT. A management philosophy that directs all company activities toward serving the customers' best interests.

MASS PRODUCTION. Technology in which an organization spends a great amount of money on both labor and capital equipment to produce goods in continuous volume.

MEDIA. An advertising term referring to the various forms of display, print, broadcast, and outdoor vehicles for communication.

MERCHANDISING. The planned promotion and display of appropriate merchandise at the right location, time, and price.

MIDDLEMEN. Firms that buy goods and services for the purpose of reselling them at a profit. Also known as "resellers."

NET PROFITS. The amount of money remaining from gross profits after all expenses have been paid but before taxes.

NET TERMS. An invoicing term referring to the fact that no allowance for cash discounts has been made.

NET WORTH. Another term for owners' equity, computed as the difference between total assets and total liabilities.

OBSERVATION. A marketing research technique whereby data is collected by recording visual events, actions, or behaviors.

ODD PRICING. The use of prices such as $5.95 instead of round numbers like $6.

OPEN ORDER. A purchase made without a specific price or delivery stipulation.

OPERATING SUPPLIES. Goods that are consumed in the normal operation of the enterprise.

OPTION TO BUY. An agreement whereby one person grants another the right to buy or sell certain goods at an agreed price within a stated future time.

OWNERS' EQUITY. The amount of money the owners of a business have invested in the firm.

PAYBACK PERIOD: The length of time required for the net revenues of an investment to cover its initial cost.

PHYSICAL DISTRIBUTION. The management of the physical flow of goods from producer to buyer.

PHYSICAL SERVICE. One based on performing some visible or concrete activity, such as painting or cleaning.

PRICE LINING. A pricing policy by which all products sold are grouped into two or more price lines.

PRIMARY DATA. Information collected during a market survey by observing or talking with people.

PRODUCT DIFFERENTIATION. Specific differences built into a product in order to give the item some unique edge on competitive offerings.

PRODUCT LIFE CYCLE. The various stages, birth through death, that a new product proceeds through while on the market.

PROFIT. The excess of the selling price over all costs and expenses incurred in making the sale. Also, the reward to the entrepreneur for the risks assumed in the establishment, operation, and management of a given enterprise or undertaking.

PROMOTIONAL ALLOWANCE. Concessions to middlemen in order to assist them in their promotion efforts.

PROMOTION MIX. The specific advertising, personal selling, and sales promotion activities that a firm uses in promoting the sale of its products.

PROSPECTING. The process of achieving an adequate degree of selectivity in deciding which individuals and organizations out of the total population to pursue with further sales activity.

PUBLIC RELATIONS. A planned program of activities designed to improve a firm's image among stockholders or the community at large.

QUANTITY DISCOUNT. A price concession given to a purchaser as an inducement to buy larger quantities of some product.

QUOTA. An agreed-upon goal that a salesperson is expected to achieve in a month or year.

QUOTATION. The process of developing a price for some goods or services, which is then submitted to a prospective customer in the form of a bid, with the hope of obtaining the business.

RACK JOBBER. A wholesaler who services display racks in a retail store and who receives payment only for goods sold.

RECIPROCITY. An agreement in which one party consents to purchase some item from a supplier in return for that firm's commitment to buy from them.

REFERENCE GROUP. A group of people whom a consumer identifies with and tends to follow in terms of consumptive behavior.

REORDER POINT. The specific level of inventory at which an item should be reordered in order to assure supply.

RESPONSE RATE. A measure of the number of replies obtained in relation to the number of solicitations, interviews, or contacts made.

RIFLE APPROACH. The term used to describe a firm's actions when they direct a marketing program at a highly specific target audience. (See Shotgun approach.)

RISK. The probability that a given decision may have an adverse effect. A low-risk decision is one with little potential for loss; a high-risk decision has relatively great potential for loss.

R.O.I. (RETURN ON INVESTMENT). Regarded as a key measure of performance in business.

ROUTING. The listing of the salesperson's proposed calls for a given period in an orderly and efficient manner.

SALES PENETRATION. The degree to which an organization achieves its sales potential.

SALESPERSON. An individual who represents a vendor to a market, who provides sufficient product, price, and delivery information, and who attempts to secure the client's order.

SALES POTENTIAL. The maximum ability of a firm to sell (in units or dollars), taking into consideration its product range, distribution, and productive capacities.

SEASONAL DISCOUNTS. Reductions in price by the producer to encourage purchases during a slack season.

SECONDARY DATA. Information gathered from published sources.

SELECTIVE DISTRIBUTION. A strategy whereby the marketer sells only through limited channels of distribution.

SELLING PROCESS. The identification and satisfaction of customer needs and wants through the effective use of empathetic and persuasive means.

SHOPPING GOODS. Items on which the consumer spends time, effort, and thought before making a buying decision.

SHOTGUN APPROACH. The term used to describe a firm's actions when they direct the marketing program for a new product at a large, unsegmented market. (See Rifle approach.)

SINGLE-PRICE POLICY. The practice of selling an assortment of goods at the same price regardless of each item's cost.

SOLE PROPRIETORSHIP. A type of business organization in which one individual owns the business. Legally, the owner is the business, and personal assets are typically exposed to the liabilities of the business.

SPECIALIST SELLING. A sales organization that is organized so that sales personnel focus their attention on a single client industry, such as electronics, paint, and the like.

SPECIALITY GOODS. Items about which consumers are knowledgeable, in which they have confidence, and for which they are not likely to accept a substitute.

TARGET MARKET. The specific individuals, distinguished by socioeconomic, demographic, and/or interest characteristics, who are the most likely potential customers for the goods and/or services of a business.

TERMS OF SALE. Those terms agreed upon between a seller and buyer with regard to discounts, payment, credit, and so on.

TESTIMONIALS. The paid opinion on a product or service given by an endorser, for the purpose of persuading others to buy.

TRADE DISCOUNTS. Reductions by the producer to wholesalers and retailers based on a reduction in the proposed retail price.

TRADING AREA. The geographic market region actively participated in by a seller.

TRADING UP. A substitution, attempted by the salesperson, involving a higher price line than the customer had in mind.

TRAFFIC. The number of people who enter or pass by a store or department within a store, sometimes used as a measure of potential.

TRANSIT ADVERTISING. An advertising medium typically using overhead cards on public transportation.

UNIQUE SELLING PROPOSITION (USP). The concept that any product or service should be designed to have some unique advantages or customer benefit not commonly available by competition.

UNIT PRICING. The practice of pricing an item by its component unit weight or volume on the package, to assist consumers in comparable shopping.

UNIVERSAL PRODUCT CODE (UPC). A nationally coordinated system of product identification using a ten-digit code on the package of all retail goods, such that the item can be electronically scanned, and prices and inventory levels automatically computed.

UTILITY. The capacity of a product or service to provide satisfaction.

VALIDITY. A term used to express whether the information obtained from a research effort is valid in terms of answering the research problem. Research findings are often accurate but invalid.

VALUE ANALYSIS. An attempt to analyze all aspects of a proposed purchase and choose the product that furnishes the best overall value.

VARIABLE COSTS. Operating expenses affected by changes in sales volume, such as materials and labor; for example, flour in a bakery. (See Fixed costs.)

VARIABLE PRICE POLICY. A pricing policy that allows a variance in the set price.

VENDOR. Any party who offers to sell a product or service.

VERTICAL INTEGRATION. A company's attempt to dominate a market by controlling all steps in the production process, from the extraction of raw materials through the manufacture and sale of the final product. (See Horizontal integration.)

VOLUNTARY CHAIN. A group of independent stores that agree to unite under some common banner (often sponsored by a wholesaler), for the purpose of achieving lower buying costs or increased patronage.

WARRANTY. Another way of describing a product or service guarantee.

WHOLESALER. A middleman firm who purchases from manufacturers in bulk and resells to retailers or industrial users in smaller quantities in a limited trading area.

WORKING CAPITAL. The excess of current assets over current liabilities.

ZERO DEFECTS. An inspection concept that precludes accepting any faulty or inferior quality of production.

ZONE PRICING. A system of quoting delivered prices in which the total market is divided into a number of geographic zones with the same price quoted to all purchasers in a given zone.

Index

NOW...Announcing These Other Fine Books From Spectrum

DO IT NOW: How To Stop Procrastinating, Dr. William Knaus. In DO IT NOW, the author explains how you can stop putting things off by breaking the procrastination habit. Dr. Knaus shows how to recognize and overcome the bad habits that cause you to delay and postpone. Included are simple techniques for stimulating a person into action.
$5.95 paperback (216606) $11.95 hardback (216614)

QUALITY CIRCLES MASTER GUIDE: Increasing Productivity with People Power, Sud Ingle. This book shows exactly how the productivity techniques used so effectively in Japan can be applied to Western technology to improve performance and productivity on the job. This guide explains step by step the methods used to create a harmonious feeling among workers, improve morale, produce higher quality products without increasing costs, and get started on a quality drive without having to make a large investment. A must book for managers.
$14.95 paperback (745000) $24.95 hardback (745018)

THINK ON YOUR FEET: The Art of Thinking and Speaking Under Pressure, Kenneth Wydro. For anyone who must speak in front of a large group of people, here's a book that reveals dozens of exercises, examples, and insights into the creative process of quick thinking. THINK ON YOUR FEET shows how to relax and free the creative mind instantly, how to take command of any situation, how to develop confidence, and much, much more.
$4.95 paperback (917807) $11.95 hardback (917815)